NO FOURTH RIVER

A Novel Based on a True Story

by

Christine Clayfield

www.ChristineClayfield.com
www.NoFourthRiver.com

To anyone who isn't happy with their life, I hope you can gain some inspiration from my story.

In memory of my mum and dad.

Opening Words: Living on the Other Side

What you are about to read is based on real events in my life. Some names and identifying details have been changed to protect the privacy of individuals.

My name is Christine. I don't usually share my story with others. However, sometimes when I unintentionally mention things from my past, people are intrigued. They want to know more about my life. I've often been told that I should write a book because my struggles would resonate with others and my life story could be an inspiration.

I truly believe that despite the pain of your past, you have the ability to change your future. You can make it happen if you just believe. It all starts with *you*.

Sometimes the people that we love can become cages, trapping us in a life that we don't recognize or accept. Throughout my life, I have developed strength of character—a real determination that has seen me through some dark and abysmal times. This is the purpose of telling my story—I want to help you to discover your strength. I lived on the other side for a very long time. The other side of happiness.

They say that your youngest years are also your longest; you are too new to realize the relentless pace of the world. I was trapped there in my youth, absorbing the pain of my circumstances in slow motion.

For too many years, I lived in utter misery because of my cruel dad, that evil boarding school and my slavemaster husband.

It's a strange thing living life without happiness, joy or promise. Before the age of 26, I didn't realize that was abnormal. It was as if I had my face pressed against the window of a bakery but I was never allowed inside.

Sure, I knew what the delights inside looked like but the taste, the smell, and the rapture of them were lost on me.

Happiness was something that belonged to other people. They wore it so lightly, so naturally, that it became a source of confusion for me growing up.

I learned the wrong kinds of lessons. You know, the ones that keep you trapped inside misery forever. I just didn't know any better. My normal was on the other side of living—it was coping; it was surviving. It was like being in prison.

My four brothers and I were inmates from the moment we were born. That was the luck of it. Some children are born into warmth and happiness, some are not. The tragedy of that can only be overcome by discovering the strength and happiness you had repressed all along.

That is what happened to me. During the war of my early years, when I had sustained the worst injuries, I knew I faced a terrible decision but I was on the other side. All I had to allay my fears and doubts was just an *idea* of happiness I had never known. It took faith beyond reason to jar me out of that life but I found a way to cross over.

After endless torment, I made a promise to myself: No more. It was time to build the life I desired. I made a plan to change my world.

To say that writing this book has been an emotional experience would be an understatement. I had deliberately buried any memory of my youth because it became too painful to recollect. To write this book, I had to uncover my pain and dig up those memories that were long since put to rest.

In fact, I grew so disconnected from my feelings about my past, it was as if every bad memory I had was automatically locked away in order to protect myself from random recollections.

Despite my efforts over the years to keep things buried, writing this book has uncovered these recollections and raw emotions, which now feel like fresh memories burnt into place.

Painful experiences can completely disconnect you from your feelings and the person you truly are, and worst of all, neglect your most crucial needs.

I was there. I was at rock bottom and deeply ashamed of the choices I had made. I had to try to find a way to reconnect with myself.

I want to share my story to help others who feel as I did—ashamed, alone, sad and hopeless. Join me on this journey through my life's struggles. Change comes for all of us, whether we want it to or not. Only you can control how you manage that change. Recovery comes to those who accept that change can happen in a blink of an eye, if you are prepared to face that battle head on.

As you join me in this personal memoir, a retelling of my crossing, I want you to hold a thought in mind. If life has kept you shut out of its joys and pleasures, I want to charge you with a single idea: if I could find my way through the bakery door, then you most certainly can too.

As you read my story, I hope you find your own inner strength to escape the prisons erected around you in your life.

The Lemmens Household

"When written in Chinese, the word 'crisis' is composed of two characters. One represents danger and the other represents opportunity." – John F. Kennedy

March 2016: Age 57

A phone call at four o'clock in the morning is rarely good news. A crisis is often the reason why another human being reaches out at such a time. When my phone skittered across the side table, bleating at me so loudly, I woke with such force that it took my husband several moments before he realized I was not, in fact, being attacked.

I groped around in the dark as the ringing continued echoing through our bedroom.

"What's happening?" asked my husband, bleary eyed and still in the midst of a dream.

"I've got it, I've got it, hold on…" I replied, clumsily raising the phone to my ear.

"Hello?" I croaked, my vocal cords defiantly quiet. I glanced at my alarm clock next to the bed. 4:00 flashed urgently back at me.

A disembodied voice pierced the silence, ringing in my ears.

"Christine, you need to get on the train right away. Mum's ill; she's been taken to St. Vincentius Hospital in Brussels. They say it's serious…." It was my youngest brother, Roger, and he sounded panicked.

"What? Mum's ill? What happened?" I blanched, still in the throes of a sleep-induced haze.

I swung my legs over the side of the bed, slipped into my slippers, and clicked on my bedside lamp. An immediate square shaped light hit my bedside table and the ceiling above it, casting a soft glow of warmth into my bedroom.

"Look, Christine, as far as I know, she is in an induced coma. You will have to speak to her doctors to find out exactly what is going on. They told me to get the family here…if you know what I mean," he said, trailing off.

Cold hints of panic creeped up my spine and into my extremities, or was that a chill from the open window? My mother was 90 years old and I had been dreading this call.

"Okay, okay. I'll get there as soon as I can," I told him, flopping my phone onto the bed and slipping off my nightgown.

My husband mumbled at me, hardly aware of the sudden emergency action that had to take place.

"Are you going to Belgium?" he asked, wiping sleep from his eyes.

"Yes. I have to go. My mother's in a coma, and I have to get there." As I bustled around the room in a panic, fumbling through my closet and wrenching out one of the suitcases from a recent trip to Norway, my husband tried to make sense of it all.

"You can follow later on, once you have some time to organize yourself. I don't have time to think about it right now. I just want to get on a train as soon as I can."

"Do you think you'll be back by Saturday? You have your speech to deliver at the fundraising event," he asked.

"I don't know. I hope everything's fine, my mum is more important than a speech. In the very worst case I will have to cancel," I insisted, busy with the task at hand.

I warded off thoughts of losing my mum. At such an old age, any medical concern was urgent, and a coma was no small thing. My husband shuffled out from the nest of blankets, slipping on his dressing gown.

"I'll make you a coffee." He disappeared from the room. I packed with purpose and renewed haste as Roger's voice hung in my mind like a terrible fog.

I took the essentials from my wardrobe and crammed them into the bag, then hurried off to the bathroom to get ready. After that, I randomly added my toiletries, a brush, and whatever other items I could remember to grab while in a flat spin.

By the time I got into the kitchen, my husband had made me coffee and some quick toast to go.

"Thanks, darling, just have to check when the next train is leaving and make sure I am on it," I said aloud, heaping myself onto a chair and snapping open my laptop. I could see my husband was concerned but my heart was with my mother now. I had to do all I could to get to her in what could be the final hours of her life.

I was a seasoned traveler, so the Eurotunnel page was already bookmarked. I navigated there and booked the 5 a.m. train from Folkestone, in the UK, to Calais, in France. I quickly worked it out in my mind: after 5 hours travelling, at approximately 9 a.m. local time (Belgium is one hour ahead of the UK), I would be with my mother but I had to leave home within 10 minutes to catch the 5 a.m. train.

"Christine, I know this is going to be difficult. I'll join you as soon as I wrap some things up and shuffle things around here. Everything is going to be okay. I love you…just stay calm and take whatever comes as it does." He kept gazing lovingly into my eyes. I kissed my husband goodbye. He pulled me into a warm hug. My heart fluttered. There was always something fortifying about his embrace.

"Keep in touch," he called to me, blowing me several more kisses as I snaked my way across our driveway like a human train with my bag-on-wheels in tow. I waved without looking one final time.

The Eurotunnel journey was predictable and I had time to close my eyes for about thirty minutes. I arrived in Brussels and decided to leave my car in a huge car park outside the city center. It was 8:30 a.m. and the traffic in Brussels would be a nightmare. Furthermore, I wasn't used to driving in Brussels so I took a taxi to the hospital.

"Where to?" the driver asked me in Flemish. Flemish is a dialect of Dutch and is the same as Dutch when written but pronounced completely differently.

Belgium has three parts: French, Flemish and German. I was born in Flanders, a Flemish part of Belgium.

"St. Vincentius Hospital. please," I responded, keeping it short. "Quick as you can…thanks."

I could have taken a detour and dropped my things at mum's house but I decided against it, fueled by my need to be by mum's side; I did not want any delays. Better to make a beeline directly for the hospital so that I could find out what was going on. I was her only daughter and I would regret it forever if I was not there by her side if the worst should happen.

It was a 15-minute drive to the hospital but I had been so lost in thought that it felt like five minutes. I paid the taxi driver and lifted my bag out of the back and onto the curb. Pausing briefly, I sent a text to Roger to let him know that I had arrived and fired off another to my husband to let him know I was all right. I walked through the rather grand-looking doors of the hospital and met a nurse at reception.

"Starla Lemmens, please." I blinked away the harsh fluorescent lights of the hospital. The nurse tattered away on the computer before giving me a private room number on the third floor.

The lift clattered to a halt on the third floor. I stepped out of it prepared to see my mum in a hospital bed. Hospitals always scared my mother. She didn't like the smell of anti-bacterial cleaning liquid or the stark way everything was decorated in whites.

As I lingered on that anxious thought, I ran into Roger. He is two years younger than me, balding, with kind eyes and a slim figure.

"Christine, good to see you." We fell in step together en route to the private room where my mum was waiting for me.

"Any more news?"

"From what I can gather, she has pneumonia and a urinary tract infection. She's very weak." The weight of his words clung to his brow. We crossed a threshold into a new room and there she was. My oldest brother, Oliver, eight years older than me, stood to greet me. We half-hugged awkwardly as my bag dropped off my shoulder. I stood my luggage upright at the foot of mum's bed and looked at my brother.

He had aged a lot since the last time I saw him. He was almost completely bald and his skin was starting to show his age.

My mum was so quiet and as white as the sheets around her. Her grey hair curled in wisps around her face. Her eyes were closed.

A gentle beeping emanated from a machine nearby and tubes led to her arms and into her nose. My heart shuddered briefly before settling into my stomach, where a mild nausea began to rise. I skirted the bed and sat down on it, taking her cold hand into my own. Her skin was thin with age but still flawless in many ways.

"Oh, mum…" I said to her, then looking over at Oliver. "Roger said it's pneumonia. And she has yet another urine infection too?"

"Sandy brought her in last night. She collapsed whilst going to the toilet. Dr. Veldman says that it's common at her age. Her immune system is struggling, it might be her natural time to go," Oliver responded, looking worried. Sandy was the carer we paid to look after mum, a carer who was skilled at her job.

Five years ago, after a routine check-up, the doctor concluded that mum's irregular heartbeat was more frequent compared to the last ten years and she needed to start new medication. Mum was given an injection into her stomach before she could start the medication. The injection caused a huge hematoma; a collection of blood outside of the blood vessels.

The blood coagulated after a few days and that triggered her dementia because of lack of oxygen to her brain. There were no warning signs at all. All of a sudden mum had dementia; it was devastating news! Now she drifted in and out of focus, remembering us one day and forgetting us the next. She probably couldn't remember to tell Sandy how ill she felt and this was the result: an emergency hospital visit.

Oliver spoke for a while longer about the tests they had run and about how an infection could make her so ill that she needed to be admitted to hospital.

At 90, after all she had weathered, would it be an infection that took her from us? I pushed the thought away again.

"All we can do is wait and see," Oliver finished. "The doctors have done all they can for her."

The late morning leapt ahead to the late afternoon; once I had tired myself out talking to my mother's doctors, I told my brothers I would stay with her as they went to find something better to eat than hospital food.

Roger had been there nearly all night and was hankering for a proper meal that did not come from a vending machine. I settled next to my mother in silence as the rhythmical beep of her machines comforted me and stretched endlessly onward. The room was nice, spacious and clean—everything you would expect from a hospital of this caliber.

Two large, broad windows took up most of the space across from her bed, though the blinds were slanted to keep the sun out and keep the room at a steady, predictable warmth.

Being back in Belgium brought back a lot of memories and it was hard not to dwell on them as I sat there alone with mum. One by one they rose to the surface, reminding me of a life I had long since left behind. I flashed back to the life I had with my parents and brothers as a small child.

1964, Belgium, Age 5

Life in the Lemmens's household still haunted me. Most days I would not think about it, determined to forget what once was the only reality I had ever known.

I have always loved my mother dearly despite the many mistakes she made. She was a social butterfly, an attractive woman, with short, light-brown hair and a little plump.

She met my father when she was 20 years old. My mother played handball at that time—a game she was very skilled at— with her friend Rosie.

One day, after one of their games, they walked over to Rosie's husband who was having his car looked at by his friend.

That friend, a car mechanic, was my father. He was rather short and broad-shouldered with a square face and black hair.

He and mum started chatting right away and went for a drink together. Then he asked mum if she'd fancy accompanying him to the local fair held two weeks later and that was it; they fell in love. At least, I assume they did. Some form of love or another. The kind that is defiantly brief and aggressively short-lived.

I am sure back then she had no idea she was playing with dark matter. That loving such a destructive, complete and all-encompassing force could do such long-term damage in her life. She was a kind woman but not a smart one by anyone's estimate.

I imagine she had no idea that when she was walking down the aisle to marry my father, she was actually manacling herself to a life of fear, oppression and constant pain.

My father was born into a poor family and was one of eleven children. He only attended school until the age of 14 and had no skills or qualifications whatsoever.

He would regularly help his dad, who was a builder, but my father's real passion, at the time, was cars. At the age of 16, he went back to school to become a car mechanic and achieved his diploma. After a while, however, he had a change of heart.

Diamond polishing became popular in "De Kempen" (a rural region in Flanders), at that time, so my father became a polisher.

He soon realized how profitable the diamond trade was; and after a few years polishing, he became a diamond manufacturer.

Thanks to my father's ambition and involvement in the diamond trade, we quickly became the richest family in our small town. Being a "De Beers" sightholder was a prestigious thing. A marvel really for someone like my father, who worked his way up from nothing.

De Beers, owner of several mines, mainly in South Africa, controlled the world's supply of rough diamonds in those days. They appointed just over 100 diamond companies worldwide who could buy diamonds from them. These companies were called sightholders, of which my father's company was one.

He bought rough diamonds from De Beers and he ran several factories with the purpose of manufacturing the rough diamonds to become polished diamonds, which he then sold.

Antwerp, approximately 30 kilometers from where we lived, was the diamond center of the world, and my father would drive to Antwerp almost daily to sell his polished diamonds.

I remember moving into a grand three-story house when the money started to flow. Locals called our house "The Castle." My father had made sure that he purchased the biggest house in the village, just in case anyone doubted his position and importance.

To a young child, the three-story house was a towering mansion with expansive rooms and fine living areas. Its size turned out to be both a blessing and a curse, in that while it was our prison in those years, it also hosted many natural hiding and punishment places.

One of my earliest memories is of a specific Sunday when we sat around the bright white breakfast table listening to one of my father's long and self-indulgent lectures on life before it was time to nip off to church.

Mum was busy serving several expertly-cooked dishes, first to my father, who always picked what he wanted before anyone else, then to us; whatever was left, she took for herself.

Our kitchen extended into a broad dining room with olive green finishes; everything had its place—and the children were no exception.

Even when you are born into them, regimens and rules can feel unnatural for a child when they are taken as seriously as my father took them. He demanded obedience, perfection and compliance, and God help us if we didn't meet his expectations.

"...As I was saying, if I can transition from being a car mechanic to being a key figure in the diamond trade, then I expect you can finish your bacon."

He pointed at Oliver, then a young boy of 13. Oliver gazed back at my father blankly, torn between fear and a strong dislike for the bacon on his plate.

"I don't want it!" he pleaded with mother.

Christine Clayfield

"You see that, Starla?" My father jabbed his food-smeared fork at her. "The boy thinks wasting food is fine. Is this the kind of child who will do well in the world? No!"

He slammed his fists down on the table, giving everyone a fright. When he spoke, we listened. That was the rule. My mother simply smiled slightly and shook her head.

"Your brother has eaten all of his bacon," my father declared, gesturing to Kane, his favorite son. Kane was only six, one year older than I was, but he worked very hard to be exactly like my father, which of course pleased him.

"Eat it," Kane said to a stricken Oliver. None of us would ever have dared emulate my father. None but Kane.

"I'm not asking you, Oliver. I'm telling you. Eat it. After church you can cut the grass outside with a potato knife." Father chuckled.

Oliver's face twisted and fell but he ate his bacon. He had no choice. Violence would be unleashed with another word. Facing a long afternoon outside snipping at the vast grass with a blunt knife would leave him aching and exhausted.

This became a favorite punishment of my father's; all of us, except Kane, at one point or another had to cut the grass or trim the hedges with a potato knife or another ridiculously inadequate tool.

With the exception of Kane, the rest of us—my mother, Oliver, Lucas, Roger and I—stayed as still as possible. That is what it was like in my home: my father was the hunter and we were his defenseless prey.

All we could do was comply and hope that his fury would subside. I thought everyone's father was this way—a regimental tyrant with a penchant for punishment. Fear was the first emotion any of us ever learned. As a result, love was not a big priority in our house.

My mother didn't really support his cruelty but couldn't do anything to change it, as she was getting her own fair share of it as well. My father didn't reserve his "lessons and lectures" just for his children.

He intimidated and humiliated her in much the same way as he treated us. That was why none of us were ever close.

The feeling of isolation was what my father used to maintain his control. Because my brother Kane was similar to him and seemingly immune to the harshest of the punishments and torments, we were resentful of him as well.

"Get up. In 20 minutes, we're going to church," he announced after flopping a napkin down on top of his dirty plate. He retired into the parlor to smoke one of his large cigars. For as long as I could remember, he was always surrounded by smoke, like some kind of mythical beast breathing fire on us all.

As a young girl living under such tyranny, my instincts were to appear as small and unimportant as possible, to work hard to comply, and to accept my punishments when they came as graciously as I could. I may have been five years old but I understood one thing perfectly. He ruled. The rest of us, we were nothing but an imposition to him.

To further exacerbate my isolation, I was the only girl, the middle child between four boys. I would have loved a sister to play dress up and paint nails with. Instead, rough housing was the norm. I was largely left to my own devices, my only role model my mother, who, as I got older, did not give me the answers I needed to understand why we were raised so harshly.

I had dark brown hair and usually had high bunches or a ponytail and a fringe, covering my round face and hanging just above my black eyebrows and green eyes. I was thin, smartly dressed and of normal height for my age.

In the tiny village of Keldonk, my father was the king. He always held his face forward in a steady gaze to carry his air of authority wherever he went.

In our home, he was the tyrant who oppressed us, training us to embrace a life of misery and servitude. So, from my first steps to my first rebellious thoughts, I believed I was worth very little because he deemed it so, and constantly reinforced this. To the world, we were privileged but alone, together in that mansion of a house, we all knew better. Something was terribly, terribly wrong.

Growing Up, Down

"Once in a while it really hits people that they don't have to experience life in the way they have been told to." – Anonymous

We were all survivors, programmed from the very start of life to tiptoe around the pillar of fury that was my father. My mother used to tell me that before he became successful in the diamond industry, he didn't touch alcohol. Alcohol did not excuse who my father was to me and to his family.

He was the kind of man who would strip his children of all self-esteem, then blame us when we could not perform. He delighted in mental harassment and physical beatings.

He was a chain-smoking, whisky-swilling king of the diamond trade. A tyrant to his children.

My brothers and I learned all about the dark, solitary places of our house. At five, I remember hearing noises from behind the cellar door one morning, so I investigated, only to find my brother Oliver huddled in the corner on the cold stone floor, throwing rocks at the wall. My father had sent him there the night before, without supper.

"Oliver, you okay?" I screeched, taking note of his wide, round eyes. They were full of fear and something else…shame.

It was dirty in the cellar and the stone was so cold that the air coming up from the bottom felt like a wave of freezing mist.

He was trapped down there, alone in a frozen ocean of stone, framed by the light coming from my open door.

"Shh, dad might hear," he called up to me.

"He's not home." I sniffled at the weakness and helplessness of my words. I wanted to help him but I couldn't. It was against the rules.

"What happened?" At least I could give him some company.

"I'm not allowed to grow my hair. Dad told me to cut it, and I told him I wanted to keep it long." A slight hint of anger lined his voice.

I would not understand that feeling until I was much older.

"Oh. You look cold."

"I am cold."

"Should I bring you a blanket?" I noticed there wasn't so much as a towel on the floor where he sat.

"Better not. I'll be fine. You go upstairs and play." He turned his face into the darkness of the cellar. I obeyed and gently shut the door on my brother and walked to the lounge, where my other brothers were. Oliver was not allowed out of the cellar for four days over a long weekend.

Mum brought him a plate of food, once a day. There was no washroom, and he would do his nature calls in a plastic pot with a lid on that mum had to clean every day.

Oliver seemed resolutely quiet, as if his isolation was something to be taken seriously or a vital lesson might be missed. I was very sad about Oliver being in the cellar and didn't quite know what to do with my feelings.

There were long periods of time when I had no one to talk to. That's when Lucy showed up in my life. I imagined her into existence, a little girl my age with a wild and free spirit. I loved her.

We would spend long hours chatting together, playing the most extraordinary games in the house. She was my shield against the chaos. Sometimes even Lucy was not exempt from the climate in our home.

I remember one day very well; my brothers and I were watching television, except for Oliver, who was still in the cellar.

We heard my father's car pull into the driveway. I will never forget that noise or that sense of panic.

"He's home!" Lucas, my brother, one year younger than me, shouted, his voice quivering with fear. Even my mother would immediately begin to double check that everything was ready for dinner.

Every night was a game, a lucky dip of punishments and hell my father might inflict on one of us next.

He blundered into the hallway, red-faced and surrounded by his usual cloud of smoke, puffing hard on the stump of a cigar.

He dropped his briefcase and staggered drunkenly into the lounge, where we were all now doing something constructive. We pretended to be engrossed in educational children's books. We switched the television off the second we heard his car pull up, as we were not allowed to watch TV.

Only a few weeks before, my father came home quietly, nobody heard him, and he found us watching the TV. He smashed the TV into pieces.

He called the TV "the box" and absolutely hated it when we watched it. He didn't like the idea of us relaxing in a comfy chair while watching TV. He felt that we always needed to be doing something and we didn't need or deserve downtime.

My mother was in the kitchen.

"Get me a drink," he roared at mum without greeting her or checking in on the kitchen. He knew she was in there because that is where he told her to be.

He knew she feared him and he enjoyed her fear. He went to sit down then thought better of it, rising again to wobble off to the cellar door. He swung it open haphazardly.

"Boy, get out of there!"

Oliver emerged from the cellar, ashen-faced and meek, ducking under my father's arms as he obeyed the command.

"Go wash up for dinner. You're getting that damn haircut tomorrow." With another puff of his cigar, he returned to his chair, where a fresh whisky in a short tumbler glass was waiting for him, courtesy of my mother.

I didn't understand why my father did that to Oliver. When I tried to ask my mother, she hushed me, and I wouldn't dare question my father or risk being put in the cellar myself. Why couldn't Oliver continue to grow his hair? It wasn't very long.

That night at dinner, Kane had a peculiar grin on his face, as if he reveled in Oliver's discomfort.

My father droned on as usual, drilling his life lessons into us while we all sat quietly and listened as good children did. "…and you, boy, you've learned a valuable lesson, haven't you?" wolfing down his steak while addressing Oliver. Oliver nodded his head neatly but his face was blank and subdued.

"Good! It's your own fault you were in there." He spat and pushed around his peas and carrots. "It's time you grew up. All of you need to grow up. I'm sick and tired of the constant disobedience in this family. It's an embarrassment!"

Seeing that he was riling himself up, my mother got to her feet and offered him more mash and meat, which he took.

Kane looked from Oliver to me to my father, his mind working hard at something. Once my mother had seated herself again, he spoke.

"Christine kept visiting Oliver in the cellar. I saw her." Kane shoved out his chest. My father froze and considered it for a moment.

"Ah, you can't blame the girl." Dad waved dismissively, forking another load of mash into his mouth. Kane was not happy. His story did not get the rise he had been hoping for from my father.

In many ways, I believe that he craved our father's attention and approval in a manner far beyond what any of us did.

His survival strategy was clear from a very young age—be our father's go-to. It made him different from the rest of us, and he was always a threat.

"What about Lucy then?" Kane said to our father.

"Lucy? Who is Lucy?" he replied, looking from Kane to me. It felt like a nest of wasps had buzzed to life in my tiny stomach.

"Christine's new friend. Her *imaginary* friend! She talks to her all the time, like she's real!" He threw up his hands for dramatic effect.

"Is that true?" My father flicked his red eyes from me to my mother, who had gone silent.

"It's just harmless pretending," she eventually said when no words would come out of my mouth.

My other brothers sat with their eyes cast downwards while Kane smugly watched the scene unfold. I was afraid, to say the least. My heart hammered in my ears, and I felt lightheaded. I couldn't get enough air into my lungs, and my feet just hung there off the chair, useless, even though I wanted to run away and find a place to hide.

"Stop that, Christine, do you understand?" my father boomed, bits of meat dropping to his plate. "We can't have people thinking that you're not right in the head."

My mother started to explain in earnest.

"She's so young; it's normal…"

"It's not normal enough!"

He balled his fists.

"I don't want to hear about this again, young lady. I forbid you to talk to Lucy again!" The threat was imminent but it never bloomed.

Kane sunk back into his chair, and we finished dinner as my father launched into a story about how good children work hard and not enough hard work is done at home.

Roger and Lucas sat as still as statues, though they were only three and four years old. My mother helped them with their food as she always did, and dinner mercifully ended without incident.

Oliver, at 13 years old, harbored a lot of resentment towards our father—something we all came to understand as we aged.

Even Kane, in his adult years, realized how much psychological duress our father placed us under. Though he constantly curried favor, it was no assurance that he would not be subject to some of the abuse.

Still, throughout his childhood, he kept trying and clung to the belief that if only he could be good enough, he could avoid the beatings and humiliating punishments.

The moment dinner was over, after hours of preaching, it was off to bed for all of us. This was my least favorite part of the night, when we had to line up and kiss my father goodnight.

I could never quite wrap my mind around this. My father certainly did not seem to love us openly, so why should we kiss him goodnight?

He settled like a great smoky walrus into his evening chair in the lounge, and after another drink, we were called for the goodnight kiss routine. We arranged ourselves into order from youngest to oldest—me in the center and my tiny brothers standing behind me. We all hated doing this.

My father stank like booze and cigars, and there was never any affection behind the act. Roger was first.

"May God bless you, may God save you," father said to Roger, reaching out to trace a small cross on his forehead, and then leaning in to kiss him on the cheek.

Roger accepted the kiss and then traced a cross of his own onto father's forehead without saying anything, as he was only three years old.

Next was Lucas, he started the blessing and mumbled: "Maygoble, maygosavyo," (an extremely short version of "May God bless you, may God save you"), he rambled and traced a cross, gave a peck on the cheek before he, too, received the blessing, was shooed away and sent upstairs to be confined to his room.

The blessing meant nothing to us because it lacked affection and love, which is why we never tried to say it properly. It was my turn next. Every time I kissed my father, I looked for that affection that every young child craves.

It was always absent. He barely moved and was always disinterested and on edge—like the act was a learned behavior from his own dysfunctional childhood. Perhaps he was taught that to be a good father, all he needed was that one nonsensical ritual.

"Maygoble, maygosavyo," I recited. I put my little thumb on his hot forehead and traced the cross.

The kiss and returned blessing were over quickly, and off I dashed to my bedroom, wiping my mouth and face, once I was out of sight.

We were forced to say goodnight to him this way every evening, and if we refused, there was always a horrible punishment—maybe the worst of the punishments waiting for us. That is why we hated it.

That night I lay in my bed, dreaming about better things. I imagined Lucy and how free she was and how trapped I felt in that room. I thought we had all escaped that evening without punishment but I was wrong. In the lounge below, we heard the clattering of furniture and my father's raised voice.

It was my mother who was getting it tonight. For whatever threadbare reason, she must have provoked him, and the result was a glass object smashed against the wall, and what sounded like slaps and then a larger crash against the wall. The night was dark, and all around me fear filtered in from the noises outside, like mist coming under my door.

I wasn't allowed to talk to Lucy; she could not make me feel better. There was so much that I couldn't understand that didn't make sense. My blankets felt like restraints, my mattress like a chopping block. I was quickly learning to internalize all of my anxiety and fear. My father did not approve of crying.

The next morning I woke from a restless sleep, with wetness all around me from wetting the bed again. I had been wetting my bed for a few months. In retrospect, it was a reaction to the constant fear but at the time, it felt like daily humiliation and evidence that my father was right about my general worthlessness.

I called my mum, and she stripped the bed. I don't remember ever being told that it would be okay to wet the bed. My father was disgusted at the sight of my sheets and I felt a deep sense of shame that never really went away.

Morning time meant re-entry into rigorous routines and rituals dictated by my father. Everything had a place, a time, a function, a use. One of his favorite things was to tell us that we were lazy and useless.

We all lived in a desert of darkness, wandering blindly from one command to the next, waiting for that devilish quicksand to take whatever life was left in us. There was always more to take.

At the same time, I was developing a strong kinship with music. I started to listen to a lot of children's songs, as well as other music. It was soothing to drown out the sounds of the house and imagine a life past what I knew.

Later, when I neared my teenage years, music would be instrumental in my life. There were even moments, mid-song, when I thought I felt the warmth of what real happiness might feel like, but of course the moment the song ended it was just me again, alone and confused.

It was difficult coming to terms with my father's temperament and actions. Inside, where the light of your soul lives, you can always feel when something is wrong. With someone like my father, the wrongness compounds over time, until everything about him becomes a series of traits you are forced to openly reject in everyone else—and in yourself.

Number 49

"The greater part of our happiness or misery depends on our dispositions and not on our circumstances. We carry the seeds of the one or the other about with us in our minds wherever we go." – Martha Washington

2016, St. Vincentius Hospital, Age 57

The nurse came in and asked me to leave the room. Coffee, I thought to myself, glad for something to do. Oliver and Roger were not back yet. Getting a coffee would give me a break from watching my mother breathe what may be her last breath. I rose, trailed my bag into my mother's bedside wardrobe, locked it with the key provided, and left the room.

I asked the first nurse that passed me where the vending machines were. She directed me, and I set off with purpose down the long cream-white hall. Halfway around the corner, I nearly stepped on someone—Lucas, my brother sandwiched between Roger and myself.

He looked as harassed as I did when I first arrived.

"Christine. Is mum still…?" he asked, an apprehensive look creeping onto his face.

"Yes, she's fine for now, in an induced coma. Her room is just around there…I'm off to get some coffee," I responded, gesturing towards my mother's private room around the bend.

Without a second glance, Lucas set off towards our mother's room—he was just as anxious to see her for himself as I had been. Now though, some hours later, I felt like I needed to surface to find brighter air.

I must have been at the coffee vending machine for three minutes, scratching around in my bag for change, when Lucas caught up with me again.

"That was quick," I said, slotting some coins into the machine to obtain a coffee. Lucas jingled around in his jeans pocket and decided on a pineapple juice from the other machine. The springs whirred and cranked out the drink, dropping it from the topmost shelf into the slot below, making an obscene amount of noise in the solemnly quiet hospital.

Lucas is of average height and weight, grey hair, neat looks and a good personality. We sat together on some fuzzy red chairs a few feet away in an ordained sitting area.

"I've never been a fan of hospitals." He kept fidgeting in his chair. "Couldn't stay in that room on my own, you know? Mum looks so frail. Do you think she'll make it?"

"I hope so," I said cautiously, afraid to make him any promises my mother could not keep. "Pineapple?" I asked, pointing to his drink.

"Oh yeah, haven't had one in years. Just felt like it today." His voice found a steady footing now.

"I know what you mean."

I knew exactly why he chose a pineapple drink out of that vending machine—he was dwelling on our childhood too. When we were younger, my father gave Lucas the task of cutting a pineapple for my mother as she was cooking. He cut the pineapple badly; it was uneven and chunky.

Any normal parent would have been thrilled that he had made it all the way to the end but my father was not any normal man. He was furious at Lucas for not taking care to cut the thing as straight as he wanted it. As punishment, Lucas had to sit in front of the pineapple for three hours and think about his shoddy work. He was not allowed to take his eyes off it.

Since then, Lucas has had a strange relationship with pineapple—craving it subconsciously when things are bad and he feels helpless to make them better, almost like my father trained it into him.

I felt sad for my brother, and we fell into a chat about those years.

"Remember when you got so sunburnt that you couldn't move?" he reminisced, smiling.

I nodded. "We all looked like little red dumplings after that day in the sun."

"Mum never did watch out for us much, did she?" Lucas said, sipping his drink.

"She did in her own way," I insisted, although as I cast my mind around, I could not help but agree with him. My mum was never the most attentive, caring or responsible sort.

Lucas said he was going to get some fresh air and I walked back to mum's room and sat on the chair next to her. The nurse had left the room.

The blinding fluorescent lights of the room pressed on my eyes, and I closed them momentarily to orientate myself. I generally avoided revisiting my early years because despite how long it had been, those memories still cut into my psyche with a searing pain but today—with my mother lying in a coma in front of me—it seemed impossible to shut out the emotions of that time. They all came flooding back, like water pushing against a dam so violently that it burst into pieces.

1964, Belgium, Age 5

Mum could never do anything right in my father's eyes. She was, just like the rest of us, constantly told that she was useless. Mum never got involved in any decision about our education. She could never say anything that was acceptable to him.

Her opinions were always considered useless. She grew, in her later life, to be a person with low self-esteem because of this. I have never blamed my mum for anything that ever happened to me or any of my brothers. I saw her as a fellow victim of our father.

She did the best she could in the situation. She lived with my father all her adult life, so she had plenty of misery with him. We only had to endure everything when we were at home, but she was home most of the time, therefore she suffered much more than we did. She was exposed to mental torture just like the rest of us.

She would regularly let things happen to us, preferring a distant style of parenting that led to a lot of wounds, scars, and burns.

We were like a pack of raving penguins, and she left us to it. Mum had four children in four years; that is not easy for any mum. I think she couldn't cope. A low level of education, coupled with a lack of experience with children resulted in a more permissive style of parenting, causing all five of us to have some sort of accident before the age of six.

Oliver fell down our stairs and ended up with horrible bruises. Kane fell off a table and injured his arm. Lucas ended up with stitches in his head whilst playing with stones during a holiday, and Roger got stitches in his arm after falling out of a tree. As for me, I fell out of a swing and broke my arm, and another time fell off a chair and ended up with stitches in my chin.

However, the scar that haunted me for most of my life happened when I was just 18 months old. Mum was not watching me. Oliver went into the cellar to grab some potatoes for mum, I followed him and I fell into the cellar on top of a glass jar of mayonnaise. The impact crushed the glass, which splintered, partly into my eye. I was rushed to hospital, blood everywhere.

Back then, doctors were a hair's breadth away from being butchers. They pulled great big stitches through my cheek, ensuring that I would forever be marked as a young woman. I almost lost my left eye. The scar healed well but it was also the most prominent feature on my face.

Bright red and uninviting, it stretched from the top of my left eye to the bottom of my nose, five centimeters long. It was a big and bold straight line, and on both sides of the line were bright red marks from all the stitches. A total of 18 thick, round dots.

Some of the happiest times I enjoyed with my family were when we headed out to the beachfront together. My father usually didn't join us, so each visit to the beach was a mini holiday away from his control and influence.

My mother was the best version of herself when we were there, and she loved to lie in the sun. Her friends would often join us with their kids, and we would set up a huge corral of beach umbrellas, deck chairs, and cooler boxes brimming with ice-cold things to drink and delicious snacks to eat. I loved the colors, the sounds of laughter, and how everyone was always in such a good mood when we had a day at the beach.

One evening, my father came home and found us all in serious pain because of yet another case of sunburn. They were so bad that our young skin was scorched blood red. Mum used to rub vinegar on our red backs, and it felt as if she'd set us on fire. My father said that vinegar would heal the burning fast. Did he actually believe that, or was it another excuse to inflict more pain on us? I will never know.

One Saturday, we were giggling too much for his liking at dinner, and he boomed at us, "You are all going to boarding school. The nuns will give you a good education, and you will learn discipline there!"

Panic rippled through my young body. I did not want to go to boarding school and leave my home and my family.

"We will get better," I told him, as I watched him stalk around the room. "You don't need to send us away."

"It's the best thing, Christine. You need it."

My world was imploding, swirling around me as if a bomb had hit the house. I was terrified of my father but more terrified of being sent away to some strange place, mainly because of my bedwetting and my ugly scar.

"Please, we will be good. I do not want to go to boarding school!" I cried; fresh tears blossoming from my eyes as the nerves set in. My tears only provoked anger in my father.

"I am not interested in what you want, girl. You will do as you are told, and I am telling you that you and your brothers need a strong hand. The nuns will make sure that you are put in your place." There was a sharpness to his tone as he teetered on the edge of shouting.

"Please no," I begged again, not thinking.

"I will not have my children acting like this!" His fist crashed down on the table, shaking the dishes.

"I don't want to hear another word from you. You *will* go and you *will* make our family proud there."

Soon after that Saturday, I found myself packed and shipped off to boarding school at the tender age of five. I took my harsh upbringing, my suitcase and my bedwetting problems with me.

Mum was sad to see us go and missed us terribly but maybe she was happy that she had more time for socializing and shopping now that there was less stress for her during the week. We would leave for two weeks at a time, Sunday evening to Saturday afternoon, coming home on alternate weekends. At first, when I realized I *had* to go, I told myself it might be an adventure leaving home behind. I soon discovered, however, that the nuns had other plans for a girl like me.

My brothers had gone, all together, to a different school, a boys' school, so as the only daughter, I was left alone to adjust to my new surroundings. I walked through the large iron doors of the school, all alone with the ugly, long scar on my left cheek. A big scar like that only does one thing at a boarding school—it sets you apart.

I hated the thought of a boarding school and I tried to go with high spirits, as I didn't have a choice, but when I arrived at the school, my spirits were soon stamped out by the establishment.

I was jostled around by two large, imposing women in black and white habits, with square heads and robed bodies. Each of them wore a wooden rosary with a crucifix around their necks.

I was given a uniform to wear and told to change into it. It smelled so strange in the school, like chalk and linen detergent. I felt like my own family cast me aside and sent me to a school where everybody was a stranger. I felt abandoned and I felt that I wasn't loved at all. I thought my parents didn't want me at home.

The emotional impact of being separated from my family at the age of five was shocking and I didn't quite know what to do with my feelings.

Being "dumped" in a boarding school ended up defining me, and my ability to cope with it.

A nun took me to a huge room with 50 other beds in it lined up against the walls with a wardrobe next to each bed and a trunk at the end of each bed. My cold, metal bed was the second to last one in the line, number 49. I was introduced to the nun in charge of my dormitory, Sister Henrietta. Her round glasses perched on the tip of her nose, too close to her perpetually scowling mouth.

Sister Henrietta loved her rules. The moment I met her she began firing them off at me, one after the other, warning me at the same time that I had better remember each one for my own good or there will be punishments.

"This is your bed. Bed 49. You will make your bed at 5:25 sharp every morning before church. If your bed is not made correctly, you will be punished."

I wasn't allowed to talk to Lucy but I still thought about her. I imagined myself as Lucy hearing all of these commands and orders. If I had been her, I would have been intimidated but as far as I could tell, the rules at school were similar to those at home. As long as I stuck to them, I would be okay. Even at age five, I was pretty good at toeing the line, courtesy of my father.

My scar seemed to offend Sister Henrietta and she was never particularly nice to me. As she continued to lecture me, other girls stopped and stared at me. I could see from their faces that they delighted in my scar. Perhaps it was because with a feature like that, attention would be diverted from their fallibilities. I was an easy target.

My scar, noticeable as it was, was not the only thing I brought with me from my home in Keldonk. I also brought my bedwetting with me. The nuns were even more disgusted by it than my father was; and now, I didn't have my mum there to help. That is when I knew the next few years were going to be hell on earth for me.

I remember the first night in the dorm, surrounded by strange girls.

I sat on my own for dinner—a simple meal of meat and potatoes—then retired in a queue to my appointed bed, where I would have to face the long night alone.

Several girls had already asked me what was wrong with my face. I don't think they wanted an answer because they didn't listen as I tried to tell them. They were simply pointing out that I was different and laughed at me.

Boarding schools with strict authoritarian leaders, as these nuns were, tend to breed cruelty. The children—of all ages—that were already at the school were quick to exclude, taunt, mock and humiliate the new girl.

All of the girls in my dormitory were the same age as me and many of them were cruel. This, I realized, was due to the environment. Name-calling and harassment were openly praised and encouraged. I thought my little heart would be all right as long as I kept my head down. I was wrong.

They called me "Number 49," they took away my clothes as I had to wear a uniform, and they also cut my fringe. I was robbed of my own identity. It's rather difficult at such a young age to cope with that.

I slid myself into the rough cotton covers that first night and hoped for a better day in the morning. Instead, I woke up at 5 a.m. with a familiar problem, one I had been facing for quite a while.

My bed was wet, again. Only this time, there were 49 other girls around me—and I was struck with the terror of them finding out. I snuck out of the room and found Sister Henrietta's office, which was just off the main floor.

I knocked on her door. A nun shouted "Enter" and I opened the door. Sister Henrietta was already dressed and engaged in Morning Prayer with two other nuns.

"Sister, I wet my bed. Can you help me please?"

The nuns looked at me quizzically.

"You have what?" she sneered.

"Please, Sister, I have wet my bed." I hoped that one of them would help me remove the sheets so that none of the other girls would see it.

I assumed that the nuns knew about my bedwetting but from the way they reacted, I had the impression they didn't know.

"You dirty little girl," the nun to the left of Sister Henrietta hissed.

"March back in there, strip your bed, and take the sheets to the laundry. No one is going to do it for you, you are a disgusting child!"

"Sister Henrietta, go with this child and make sure that it's done correctly. Out with you now," she finished.

Horrified, I followed Sister Henrietta back to my bed amidst many eyes that had woken up, and were now tracking us back to where my bed was located.

Some girls were up now and making their bed; others were getting dressed by their bedsides.

"Strip it, all of it," Sister Henrietta demanded. The bed was large and broad to my five-year-old eyes. At home, my mum stripped the bed every day; I wasn't used to doing it myself.

I struggled with the stiff mattress and the bulky bedding, aware of the growing number of eyes on me. Those several minutes felt like hours. Then when I had bundled my wet sheets into my arms, a giant boulder of soaked embarrassment, Sister Henrietta announced it to the room.

"The girl from bed 49 has wet her bed. This is what happens when spoilt little girls move away from home." Her voice boomed into the room. Now the other girls stared openly.

Sister Henrietta marched me through the room of 49 girls and through four more rooms just like it. Each of the adjoining rooms had 50 beds in them, and each was for a different age group. In total, I had to walk past 249 girls, who were laughing and shouting horrible names at me.

The loudspeaker came on by the time I entered the second bedroom. It was the nun from earlier.

"Attention. The girl in bed 49, has wet her bed. Make way for the bed-wetter."

I didn't think that I could ever feel worse than I did at home but I was wrong again.

As I marched through each room, girls were spitting at me and hurling their hurtful comments at me. "Ewww! Gross!" and "Disgusting girl! Dirty! Sick!" I felt something break in my soul.

It was difficult carrying those bundled up sheets. I was so small, and they were so big. I passed a sea of faces smiling gleefully at my misfortune as they pointed and shook their heads in disappointment. I felt it all. There is such a thing as embarrassment, and then there is total humiliation. The difference is in how it feels.

Walking past those girls, I knew that the nuns were intentionally humiliating me. It burnt in my chest, causing my face to flush and my ears to prickle. I cried silently but the hurt was beyond tears as I stepped forward into louder waves of laughter and judgement.

I felt closer to death then, than I ever had before. Every breath was a betrayal, and I wanted it to end so that the nuns and the girls at school would be satisfied with my reaction.

I could barely stand to exist in my own body during that walk. The voices converged on me, a cruel hatred like none I had ever known from my family. At home, six of us suffered equally under one tyrant. Here, I was alone with 249 bullies *plus* the nuns.

That night I had to fetch my clean sheets from the laundry, and I was made to walk that same gauntlet back through 249 girls to dress my bed for the night ahead. Well, you could imagine Sister Henrietta's disappointment when the next morning, I had wet my bed again and the morning after that.

Every morning I was forced to strip my bed, carry my wet sheets through those five bedrooms to the laundry, and then back every evening. They stripped me of my identity *and* my chance at a happy childhood. I became "Number 49, the bed-wetter" and "Number 49, the one with the ugly scar on her face."

I wasn't even a person. Just a number!

No one wanted to be friends with a bed-wetting number with a big and ugly scar on her face.

Already quiet, shy and socially awkward, I entered a bustling community of expert bullies, a hierarchy of them starting with the most fair-tempered child leading all the way up to the most outrageously cruel nun. Everyone was above me in rank and I had no allies.

Behind Locked Doors

*"I've learned that regardless of your relationship with your
parents, you'll miss them when they're gone from your life."*
– Maya Angelou

1965-1967, Belgium, Age 6 to 8

For the first few years in boarding school, I cried every day,
begging the nuns to send me home. "I want my mummy! I want
my daddy!" I cried, heaped against the wall at break time while
the other kids played and enjoyed the sun.

"Your mum and dad don't want you at home, child. That's
why you are here. Cry all you want; no one is coming to get
you." the nuns would tell me. It didn't stop the tears for a very
long time.

Crying became the only way I could function through my
early studies. There was so much trapped pain and misery that it
had to go somewhere. I kept asking to be sent home during
classes but I always got the same reply.

"No one wants you at home. You are ugly with that scar on
your face, and you wet the bed! You are disgusting! When are
you going to stop wetting the bed?"

Shame is a funny thing. It stretches across your heart and
keeps you from the experiences that might reignite the spark to
make you happy again. I wanted to make friends, I wanted to
have a normal school experience—but I had no control over my
bedwetting. I didn't know why it was happening or how to make
it stop. I just wanted it to stop.

During meal times, I queued up for my food, faces staring at
me, girls pointing at me and giggling. On many occasions, I
walked with my tray to tables asking if a seat was free only to be
told:

"No, not here, you smell of wee; I don't want you at my table!"

The weekend came, and I was sent home. I don't think I had ever been happier to be home, away from those god-awful nuns and the bullies. One kind of abuse does not remove the pain of another, especially when you are plunged back into it like a seedling drowned in water.

We started a new family routine—going out for dinner on Sundays. After late morning church, we would pile into my father's Mercedes and head to the best restaurant in town, where we had a table reserved. My father would order the best food; he loved seeing other people envy what he had.

It might have even been a good time, if it wasn't for other people. They seemed to inspire my father to be even harder on us and the restaurant became a breeding ground for horrible punishments if we dared to misbehave when we were out as a family. Oliver received a severe beating one evening after getting up from the table before my father did.

The restaurant was warm and inviting and the staff were incredibly helpful, despite the fact that we all sat like statues, caught in the net of my father's ever-enduring ego.

"I have heard from your teachers, Christine, that you are not doing so well in class," he sprang on me that afternoon between slices of fillet steak.

"Are you working hard?" he asked me, a loaded question.

My mother silently chewed her food with a fake smile on her face.

"Yes, Father," I assured him, feeling the danger rise around me.

"Not hard enough I imagine. You cannot be so lazy, because then you are nothing but useless to yourself and to the world…" he began. I hoped it was nothing more than a lecture.

"You have to work hard like me to get ahead. I will not tolerate hearing from the good women at your school that you are having trouble. You must do as they say. You will do well there. Understand?" He glared at me.

I nodded enthusiastically, snapping my head up and down, my eyes wide and fearful. In truth, I could not focus in class in the slightest. My work was poor because my self-esteem was poor.

I had no encouragement, only threats. My father never did explain why I needed to listen to the nuns at school or why I had to do well there. He never gave a reason why he wanted things done, and we all knew better than to ask.

From my perspective, the people at school were terrible people and did not deserve my time or effort.

"What is it with this family, always letting me down…?" My father launched into one of his rants. He reviewed the crueler punishments he'd inflicted on us like the time that he had made Oliver stay in the cellar for several days in a row simply because he argued about having his hair cut. It was Oliver's defiance more than the actual hair that enraged my father.

Another time he had beaten Oliver for the same thing. He rehashed these tales like other fathers retold funny stories. It was for his own enjoyment as much as it was to remind my brothers of what he was capable of doing to them. I could see the pain of each punishment flash across their faces.

Oliver was the most affected because he was the oldest and acted out more often. I could barely eat as he recalled past punishments and listed our failings.

"It's your fault, Starla," my father said to my mother, "for coddling this one because she is a girl. She needs to learn discipline and respect or she is going to be worthless forever. You like being worthless, Christine? Because that's what you are."

The words rolled around me like my father's smoke did around him. I could not help but feel happy despite his threats and coming punishments. I was at a restaurant where no one knew that I wet my bed, and the best part was there wasn't a single nun in sight.

Though I hated those Sunday outings, I came to value them anyway. I was able to drown out my father's voice but I could never stop hearing the laughter from those 249 girls.

It waited for me every Sunday evening and every day thereafter—another prison I was locked inside and could not escape.

As it was a Bank Holiday the next day, I didn't have to go to school that evening. Bed time routine was predictable that night and I lay in the dark, thinking.

I always wondered what the nuns told him about me and if my father knew about my daily humiliation. I wanted to tell my parents about the way the nuns treated me in school but thought they wouldn't care at all. After all, they dumped me in that school because I wasn't wanted at home; the nuns told me so, on many occasions. On top of that, my father instructed me to listen to the nuns and do as I was told, no questions asked.

So, I spoke to my friend Lucy. My father did not want me talking to her but I decided not to listen to him. I may not have been able to control what was happening to my family but I couldn't stop thinking that my father was wrong. It was wrong of him to put Oliver in the cellar, it was wrong of him to shout at my mum and to beat his children.

Maybe he was wrong about Lucy as well. I had missed her since the night Kane had exposed her to my father but I didn't have to miss her anymore. As long as I only spoke to her when no one was around, my father could not punish me for it.

Knowing this brought me immense comfort at a time when everything else felt uncertain and foreign to me. I was grateful for the time I spent with Lucy, although she wasn't real. During those very young years, she was the only source of light I had in a very bleak situation.

Lucy would often tell me that everything was going to be okay and that she had a plan to have fun. With her, I did not have to hide any part of myself, which felt good.

Having an imaginary friend at that age is not only normal but it inspires creative thinking and provides a child with something that is lacking. For me, there was such a total absence of love in my life that I didn't know what to do with the feelings in my heart.

Lucy never judged me; she never punished me or made me do anything I didn't want to do. I had no other relationship like hers in my life. As the days wore on, I developed a special made-up language that only Lucy and I understood. For every Flemish word, I invented a new word. I was careful never to use it around my brothers again, which made it all the more special.

Later in life, I realized how important Lucy had been for the language development part of my brain. They say that you need to access this part of the brain when you are very young so that it grows and develops as you age. That way, learning languages becomes much easier.

As a child, I was not stimulated enough in conversation. My brothers were always playing "boys games" and were too busy for me, and my mother was very much into her social circles. "Normal" conversations were extremely rare in our house; it was always my father preaching about something.

I was lucky that Lucy came along to challenge me. Although she vanished as I got older, she made a lasting impression on my language knowledge that made me who I am today. I will never forget her.

In boarding school, we had to get up at 5 a.m., get washed and dressed, do our chores, then go to church, to be followed by breakfast before classes would start.

Once a week, we had to go to confession. We had to sit in a big box, opposite the priest and tell him what we had done wrong that week, confess our sins.

In my little mind, I never did anything wrong so I used to say to the priest, "I didn't do anything wrong." I always thought the nuns were the sinners because of the way they treated us.

The priest told the nuns that I said the same thing for 4 consecutive weeks and I was punished. Instead of joining the other children on the playground, for one week, I had to stay in class, on my own, to think about my sins. I had to write lines for fifteen minutes: I will not wet the bed again. I will not wet the bed again. I will not wet the bed again, etc.

From then on, when I went to confession, I made up some sins and said things like, "I didn't listen in class," or "I didn't eat all my food," or "I have wet my bed" as, clearly the latter was a sin in that place, so I started to look at it as a sin.

The nuns had spoken to my father about my bedwetting and told him that they were sick and tired of it. He was very angry with me for tarnishing our family name at school and yelled at me forcibly; telling me it had to stop. I couldn't stop crying, as I didn't know how to stop it.

It never got any better. In boarding school, every year the oldest pupils finished and a fresh load arrived. Each year I had a new bunch of girls to laugh at me. Yes, I was older than they were but while they might have been intimidated by the older girls, they immediately saw my scar and delighted in finding someone they could laugh at. On the playground, it was a casually brutal environment.

One girl, Marlena, really disliked me and regularly called me names, in front of the other kids: "Ugly, weirdo, horrible." The bullying didn't stop at the verbal taunts either. On several occasions, I was pinched so hard on my arms that they bruised.

One time, Marlena pushed my chest so hard that I fell right over. Lying on the ground, I could hear all the other girls laughing hysterically. I felt so embarrassed that I just wanted to crawl under a blanket and hide away from them all.

All of this abuse started to take a toll on me and I began to think very badly of myself. I grew up thinking I was weird and ugly because that's what the children and the nuns constantly told me, and useless, as that's what my father drummed into me. This caused me to become highly sensitive.

Wetting the bed was considered a horrible crime. It was one of the worst things you could do. Sometimes, I wasn't made to do the walk of shame past all the other children but the nuns came up with new ways to punish me.

On one occasion, the nuns dragged me into a bathtub, forced me to undress completely, while they proceeded to pour four buckets of ice-cold water over my head.

They made me sit in the tub for twenty minutes, totally naked and shivering of cold. During those twenty minutes, I had to repeat: "I am sorry; I won't wet my bed again. I am sorry, I won't wet my bed again, I am sorry, I won't wet my bed again."

One Monday morning, Sister Henrietta came to my bed at 5 a.m. and said "You don't have to walk with your sheets to the laundry today, just leave the sheets on the bed." I thought I misunderstood and asked her to repeat it.

She slapped my head so hard that I nearly fell over. "You don't have to walk with your sheets to the laundry today, just leave the sheets on the bed." I didn't mind the slap at all and forgot about it in an instant.

I was so relieved at the thought that perhaps the nuns realized that I wouldn't stop wetting the bed, and whatever punishments they gave me wouldn't change that.

The day progressed with the normal boring routine: wash, chores, church, breakfast and classes. At 10 a.m., it was time for morning break and all children appeared on the playground.

Sister Henrietta came to me, and I felt sheepish at the look on her angry face and the sound of her ominous steps she took towards me. I knew right away that I was about to experience something horrible. She dragged me by my ear, all the way through the corridors to my bed.

"Now pick up your wet sheets and come with me!"

We marched all the way back to the middle of the playground, where she slapped my head and yelled in a very angry voice,

"You dirty child, I've had enough of you. You *have to* stop wetting the bed!"

I started to cry, as I realized it wasn't the end of my punishments for bedwetting at all.

"You will stand here for 30 minutes, with the soaking linen on your head so that everybody can see you," she commanded.

Immediately all the children gathered around me and began laughing and spitting at me, calling me dirty names. The nuns encouraged the children to do so.

That was the worst 30 minutes I had endured in that rotten place. Thirty minutes of my life that I will never forget, as long as I live. My hair was wet and dirty, I smelled of urine all day, and I wasn't allowed to shower. Consequently, all the girls avoided even walking close to me and purposely took big side steps away from me, even when entering the classroom.

The next day, the same punishment was repeated and the day after too. After one week, it finally stopped and my usual walk of shame continued.

Humiliation was the norm in that place, as was physical abuse. The nuns often used the belts they wore around their waist or their horrible sandals to hit us. We would be subject to beatings for just about anything: forgetting the words of a hymn, talking in church, being late in class or accidentally dropping a pencil.

We were punished merely for being children. While I endured my fair share of beatings at the hands of the nuns, it was the mental abuse that stayed with me to this day. No wonder I was withdrawn and silent as a child. How does a child cope with psychological abuse like this? None of the children understood why the regime was so cruel and cold or why their families had put them there in the first place.

However, Sister Henrietta took a special interest in me and adopted me as her pet hate. I was therefore always first in the line of fire and experienced a disproportionate amount of abuse.

Leading a normal child's life became impossible because of the psychological distress I endured both at home and at boarding school.

The years I suffered in that boarding school have left me deeply wounded and scarred. I lived for far too many years in a constant atmosphere of fear, hate, humiliation and worthlessness. I suffered alone, in silence.

Being referred to as a number rather than a person is just one example of the complete absence of any shred of love or compassion in that place. It was utter agony behind locked doors.

The Core of the Problem

"The most confused you will ever get is when you try to convince your heart and spirit of something your mind knows is a lie." – Shannon L. Alder

1968, Belgium, Age 9

My early years were peppered with confusing ideas, questions that had no answers and a life that seemed impossible to escape. I adapted, as children do.

Too young to realize that escape was only a conversation away, the fear I harbored of my father and the hatred I nurtured for the nuns at my boarding school kept me locked in place.

My father was a big talker.

"Get to the core of the problem and analyze things," he would tell us over and over again when we approached him about something. Talking to him about anything was like tiptoeing through a minefield laden with so many punishments and lecture-traps that eventually we stopped approaching him altogether.

It was just easier to deal with things alone. I tried hard to make him love me but it never worked as I never felt a grain of love from his side. No matter how hard we tried, no matter what our answer was to any given question, any conversation with him ended with feeling humiliated.

He changed the accepted answer each time as well—he could repeat a question to each of us and then declare that every answer was wrong, just like that.

The core of my problem, as a nine-year-old girl, I hated being at home and I hated being at boarding school, with no real friends there. The daily routine with the nuns was a perpetual reminder of my failure to fit in with everyone else.

I only realized many years later that what made me different was an asset, not something to be ashamed of. I did what I could to maintain some semblance of normality amidst the morning and evening gauntlet run of laughter and soul-prickling mockery.

I breathed in and out, I went to class, I did the work I was told to do, and I followed the rules—for a while. Aside from my differences, I tried to be the model student—but no one could see it. No one cared.

Many a night I spent crying myself to sleep in the dormitory. I wished I was someplace else. I constantly tried to hide my grief and I tried my best to be strong but was often overcome by the wave of emotions resulting in a stream of salty tears, releasing my sadness and sorrow. The crying seemed to ease some pain but there was no end in sight.

One day I just couldn't stand it any longer in that cruel regime so, together with three other children, we managed to break a door, in an attempt to escape. Of course, what we didn't understand at the time was there was nowhere to escape to, as the gates were always closed. Inevitably, we were caught and all forced to kneel down, kiss the floor and whilst our mouth was on the floor, say ten times aloud "I am sorry, I will not run away again."

I started to realize that I had to hide my feelings to avoid ridicule from both the nuns and the bullies. Not knowing any other way to cope, I decided to bury my feelings and pretend not to care. I hid my true emotions by wearing a mask of coping.

So, as the years went by, rebellion began to swell inside me as I rejected the people who had consistently rejected me. I spent all week wishing for my home weekend off to arrive and all weekend wishing for school to start again. It was a seesaw of emotions, taking me from one state of intoxicating despair to the next.

Emotional confusion and pain became old friends that weighed on my shoulders from these years of neglect. I still recall a particular weekend home when we were allowed to leave school in the morning, instead of lunch time.

Mum had picked me up in our brand new black Mercedes and we trundled away from boarding school, arriving home in time for a late breakfast. The weather had turned icy and snowy and throughout the house, there was a lingering chill chased away by hot pockets created by my mother's crackling fires.

Mum informed the babysitter she could go home. My father was at an early meeting in town. My brothers, my mother and I sat around the dining room table eating bread rolls and cheese with genuine enjoyment.

Those times when my father was not around were special. We got to experience what life might be like without his autocracy and heavy-handed parenting style. We could talk about anything, eat anything, and smile as much as we wanted. My father's presence was felt most when he was absent, an unfortunate by-product of his personality.

It was, as I remember it, a wonderful morning. After breakfast, we all went into the lounge. Oliver and the boys were roughhousing and teasing each other and my mother watched the silliness of it as she clicked her needles together, knitting a winter scarf for one of us.

During the evenings, when no social or business events were organized and my father wasn't home, mum was home alone a lot. That's when she started to do crosswords, puzzles and knitting. She joined a knitting society and had weekly meetings with them to show each other what they had been knitting. Mum became very good at knitting, sewing and crotchet. She enjoyed it very much.

I felt apprehensive and nervous about my father's return. The previous day, we were given our report cards by the nuns and were instructed to deliver them directly into the hands of our parents.

"We want these signed and returned by Monday, 9 a.m., or we will have to call your parents and discuss why you did not show them your grades for this school term," Sister Henrietta told us.

A threat like that was particularly disturbing for me. I had watched as my father punished Oliver and Lucas for getting bad school results in the past, and I knew that my marks were not going to be acceptable to him. He had already instructed me to do well, and not doing so was going against an expressed command.

Every creak and noise outside drew my attention. As the boys played and my mother knitted, I grew increasingly apprehensive, and dread settled on me like a sack of flour pressing down on my chest. I was close to the lounge fire but the heat I felt was quite unrelated to the snapping and spitting of the wooden stack in front of me.

I was the first to hear the screeching of the tires outside, the herald that announced my father's arrival back home. I sprang up and peered between the lacy curtains. The drowned-out light filtered through the mist outside, casting a gentle glow on my worried face.

"Dad's home! He's here!" I announced to a room of already scrabbling people.

Oliver pulled out his study books from behind the couch pillow, and Lucas produced a wad of handwritten notes from a bag nearby. Kane thumbed through a book he was reading. Roger skidded to a halt next to Oliver and grabbed one of his books. My mother sat up, looked around, then settled back down again—content that all was in order and ready for him to enter.

The door opened, letting in some of the freezing wind outside. There he was, in a sharp suit and a great, heavy black coat shaking off his umbrella and hanging it up on the stand at the front door.

"Morning, morning!" he said in jovial spirits. A moment later and a cigar was perched in his mouth, a spurt of flame from a match sending spirals of smoke into the air. I had forgotten to move from the window seat and was petrified in place—a pair of wide eyes fixed on the large black figure moving into the lounge.

The rich, smoky trail of scent wafted in with him.

He sat down next to Kane, taking off his dark leather gloves, finger by finger, as he scanned the room.

"Good meeting. Looks like we have the deal we need to extend the factory," he started telling my mother. "What are you doing there, girl?" he asked, spotting me instantly.

"I was just watching you come in, Father," I said, trying desperately to look innocent. Stowed away in my trunk upstairs was my report card.

"What have you got to show me, then?" he persisted, seeing through my thinly veiled efforts to keep something as important as my report card from him.

"What has she been up to now?" he demanded from my mother, who just shrugged and continued to knit.

"Out with it, girl," he redirected to me. I could see no way around it. I had to present him with my report card and accept my punishment. There was no other way.

"I have my report card upstairs for you," I told him sheepishly.

"Well, go and get it…don't dawdle! We'll see how hard you have been working." At those words, I unfroze and scampered up the stairs to my room, where I withdrew the card that was my school report. I already read it at school, and was well aware of what was in store for me. Except for languages, my marks were 30%, 40%, and 50% for most subjects, barely passing or not passing at all.

My heart starting to pick up in my chest, I carried the card down the stairs and over to my father, who stared at me the whole way down. I knew that he knew it wasn't good news. On presenting it to him, he snatched it from me, tearing open the envelope I had resealed. Kane leaned in and read it with him; he sniggered.

"Yes. These are very disappointing grades! You are shaping up to be just as lazy and as incompetent as your brothers." His voice matched those cold eyes.

"Have you seen this?" He grunted over to my mum, who rose and took it from him to read.

I watched her scan the card as my father's gaze burnt my face red.

"She just needs a little help. Perhaps extra classes?"

My father exploded. "She's lazy! Uncooperative! I am wasting that tuition money sending her to such a good school!"

He stood suddenly, grabbed me by my ear, and yanked me over to his office, my ear crackling like the fire. Everyone stopped to watch the scene unfold. Two large, double-glazed doors separated the lounge from his office, completely transparent, from one side only, so that he could always see what we were up to.

"I know exactly what a disobedient little girl like you needs—discipline! You *will* learn it!"

He forced me to my knees on the hard wooden floor in front of his office doors, pausing only to stride back across the room to snatch my report card back from my mother. He shoved it into my hands roughly and lifted my arms above my head.

"Now sit there, and hold your report card high until I tell you to stop. Do you understand me? I will teach you what discipline means, and maybe you won't grow up to be nothing! At this rate, I doubt it!"

I knelt on the floor, my knees digging into the surface, pain crumbling around my lower legs as he cast his office door wide and disappeared inside. I stared at him, the weight of my arms and the report card already becoming too much to tolerate.

He pointed his finger at me. "I told you to work hard, Christine. I told you to be better."

After the first twenty minutes, my arms wilted from fatigue. My elbows kept dropping and shards of pain trickled down my shoulders and back. Each time my father noticed my elbows dropping, he shouted,

"Arms up! Arms up, I said!" It was impossible. I concentrated hard on keeping my arms above my head. I was not close enough to the wall to lean on it and my father was in my direct line of vision.

He would not let me lower my arms, and if I did, the punishment would be far more than what I was currently enduring. I steeled myself and fought against the pain. My arms became a chewing gum extension of my body, weak and uncooperative, trembling and searing.

I cast around the lounge for some help but no one dared interrupt my father. I was alone and in hell. I swayed my body from side to side to try to relieve some of the ache building in my muscles and joints. The acid that settled in each arm stung and throbbed with the effort of it.

As I sat there, I did everything I could to distract myself from the pain. I thought of Lucy and of the morning I had enjoyed with my brothers and mother.

More than once, I recklessly thought about dropping my arms in defiance when the pain threatened to overwhelm me. Each time it did, I pretended to be a statue and swallowed the ache back down.

Somehow, I managed to make it for three hours, sitting there on my numb, tender knees. My whole body was sore now, so much so that I believed if I dropped my arms I would surely pass out. When my father did eventually get out of his office, he snatched the card from my aching hands.

"Go to your room. Think about the lesson you have just learned. I will not tolerate sloth and idleness in my house. Your grades will improve, or you will get very used to sitting outside my office with your arms above your head." He wrenched me up off the floor and flung me towards the stairs.

I struggled to walk normally. Blood rushed to my arms, which hung limply by my side as my weakened knees tried to battle their way up the stairs. I burst into my room, teary-eyed and grieving for the punishment I was made to endure. I collapsed onto my bed, new life being born into my body from the support.

My mother brought me a small plate of food as I was not allowed to come out of my room—which I far preferred anyway. I fell asleep that night exhausted.

That was the first of many times my father used the office door punishment on me. On more than one occasion, even as a teenager, I was made to sit there on my knees while his business colleagues visited him in his office.

They all saw me there and I was humiliated each time. To this day, it strikes me that not one of them ever remarked on this cruel treatment; they were all too frightened of my father or too worried about their own business pursuits to spare a thought for a young girl. Maybe some of them even agreed with the punishment because my father was always quick to tell them how lazy and disobedient I was, how little I cared about my education, and how worthless I was turning out to be.

Living with my father was very tough, I cried a lot. Crying seemed to ease the pain, to blur the meanness and unkindness that he dished out to us.

When I was younger, family used to visit now and then. A few years later, they soon got the message that they were not welcome and that too many problems existed in our household. Eventually, they all gave up. This did not stop the consistent flow of business people from my father's diamond factory 300 yards away. They would visit us day and night with business for my father to attend to.

My father had become a very influential businessman in the diamond trade. He was elected chairman of several Belgian diamond organizations. We were invited one Saturday to attend the wedding of another prominent diamond merchant in the area. On occasions like this, mum always looked very glamorous, and put on her best jewelry, with the most expensive diamonds. It was always a competition between the diamond dealers' wives as to who wore the biggest and the most diamonds.

I don't remember much from the wedding itself. I do remember the drive home very well. It was a defining moment for me in my life, when I started to realize that the things my father did were unacceptable and very wrong.

Back then, he had a large Mercedes, the latest model you could buy. It was black and had an all-leather interior, which was a creamy color.

People would stop and stare at the car because it was one of the most expensive on the market. We all piled in—Oliver, Kane, Lucas and myself, with Roger on my lap and my mother in the front seat.

As we were getting into the car, we already knew something was coming. My father had enjoyed one too many drinks at the wedding, and my mother wanted to drive us home.

"There is nothing wrong with me or how I drive," he insisted, slurring his words as they poured out of his mouth too quickly.

My mother tried to stand her ground but one violent look from my father and she backed down, getting into the car with visible fear etched on her face. He flumped down in the driver's seat, muttering and laughing to himself.

He started the car and rolled down the window, and we slowly pulled away from the hall where the wedding party was.

The tension in the car was as thick as pudding. I was not sure what was happening. I knew it was bad. The car shuddered a few times and my father swore aloud.

"Please…" my mother started, eyes wide in fright.

"Enough from you! Get out! If you have such a problem with my driving, you can walk. I mean it, Starla. Get out, or I will throw you out. You don't tell me what to do. If I say I am driving, I *will* drive!"

It was late at night, and my father had just exited the parking lot onto a long stretch of dark road for the five-kilometer journey home. My mother, in her beautiful evening gown and high heels, opened the car door without my father fully stopping the car and skittered onto the pavement.

I could hear my own heart pounding wildly as I squeezed Roger, and we all leaned over to watch my mum regain her composure.

"Well, walk! Walk and see how much better it is for you!"

She walked, and walked, and walked.

My father drove the car slowly beside her, berating her and throwing nasty comments out the window and into the night. It was cold, and my mother had no shawl.

She did all she could to keep a steady pace, and when she slowed, he beat at the car horn and revved the engine, threatening to leave her out there alone.

I will never forget how my mum still smiled at us to calm us in the back of the car. Oliver tried to protest but it was clear that my mother didn't want him to. Thinking of that night always astounds me. The cruelty of it. The inhumanity of subjecting your wife to such humiliation and grief while her young children watched from the back seat!

Five kilometers is endless when your mother is suffering at your father's hand a mere meter from you. To her, it must have felt like an eternity. The tarred road stretched ahead into the never-ending darkness, and all you could hear was my father's taunts and my mother's heels. We barely dared to breathe. When we reached the last kilometer, my father took off with us in the car.

I watched my mother's face as the glow from the taillights faded the further away she got. I imagine she felt helpless then, with my father drunk and driving all five of her children home like that. I will never forget what her face looked like or her icy breath as it dissipated into the air around her. We could not help her. When we arrived home, we were all worried about mum but none of us dared speak of her. My father grumbled and shouted as he opened drawers in search of his cigars.

About half an hour later my mum walked inside with her elegant shoes in her hands. Her feet were bleeding and swollen. She did not say a word. Quietly, she slipped into the kitchen to tend to her wounds. When my father demanded another drink, she brought it to him. Even now, I cannot imagine the pain that she had to live with as his wife.

We kissed my father goodnight, parading ourselves in front of him for our evening blessing ritual and were all sent off to bed. It was very late and we had church in the morning. No amount of incident or complaining would allow us to miss it.

I creaked up the stairs and opened my bedroom door, letting myself into my room. Another night of confusion, of fear…of not knowing whether mum or any of us were safe.

Dysfunctional Love

"If a country is to be corruption free and become a nation of beautiful minds, I strongly feel there are three key societal members who can make a difference. They are the father, the mother and the teacher." – A. P. J. Abdul Kalam

2016, St. Vincentius Hospital, Age 57

There lies my mum, a consummate survivor; I thought as I briefly pushed down the memories that snapped like a piranha in my mind. I could not keep them down. As I watched mum in that hospital bed, my childhood unfurled in front of me.

1970, Belgium, Age 11

At 9 years old, I began wondering if life was nothing but pain and torture, and by 11, I felt sure that it was. I had a sense that it didn't have to be that way. I couldn't understand why things were as they were. More and more I began lashing out internally at my father, hating his punishments and the way he treated his family.

He was the blazing sun to our planetary rotations. It all revolved around him. I remember feeling grief for the person I wanted to be but couldn't be because of him, and despair over the punishments I received when I couldn't be the person he wanted me to be.

We were all extremely scared of our father, especially when he was drunk—so much so, that on several occasions mum called the local priest to our home to speak to him to calm him down.

Strangely, my father and the priest seemed to be friends. Much later in life I learned that my father often made huge donations to the church, so I guess the priest formed some sort of relationship with him and tolerated his idiosyncrasies.

On the Saturdays that we didn't sit with my father around the table for hours, listening to him preach, my mother often took me shopping for clothes, which was nice. She always bought me the most expensive items in the shop, flashing our money to assert our position in the town. In Keldonk, we were the Kennedys, practically royalty. This might have been an advantage for a happier girl but for me, it only meant one more obstacle to friendship.

The other girls in my town avoided me, despising me because of my family's wealth and position. They lived in simple, modest houses and lived on small salaries. If only they knew that I would have given anything to find a friend among them. Money never meant a thing to me because it could never buy me what I so desperately wanted: a real friend and love.

Around this time, we were introduced to some new staff members in my home. My brothers also suffered from nightly bedwetting and my mother had found herself overwhelmed with these problems at home. When we tried new remedies to stop our bedwetting, mum had to get out of bed every two hours, to wake all five us to go to the toilet. This went on for 2 months during the summer holidays. In Belgium, the summer holidays are always 2 whole months—July and August.

Managing a house with five children who all wet the bed, doing all the washing, ironing, cleaning, cooking and household management would leave her exhausted.

Those days, adult nappies didn't exist, so the bed sheets needed washing every day. My mother always placed a large slab of plastic material on top of the mattress, as well as a large absorptive sheet. Even still, this did not prevent the bedsheets from getting wet. The time came when mum could no longer handle it, so, we got a housekeeper to do the cleaning and washing for us.

This left my mum with the time she needed to engage in her social activities, which seemed to make her happier. We were also introduced to a gardener. We had enormous and magnificent gardens and there was always work to be done. Taking on staff meant that my father showed everyone what he could afford and what an important figure he was.

Each year, I was so excited to be free of the nuns during the summer holidays. At least at home, I didn't have to strip the bed and die of humiliation or I didn't need to be concerned about washing the sheets, as the housekeeper took care of it. However, often, this was also the time when new things were introduced or implemented by my father.

At eleven and on the cusp of puberty, things can seem long and tiresome. I had tried so many things in the past to stop my bedwetting, such as not drinking anything after 6 p.m., various types of medications, and setting the alarm and waking myself every two hours to go to the toilet. But alas, nothing seemed to work. Nevertheless, this year on the first day of the summer holiday, my father told me to try something "new."

This time I had to eat 25 extra salty TUC biscuits (a salted savory cracker) each day at 6 p.m., and I wasn't allowed to drink anything for the rest of the day, no matter how thirsty I was. I had to do this for two months. One specialist believed that my bedwetting could be caused by the salt levels in my body. This new method was a test to see if extra salt would stop me from bedwetting. I ate the first biscuit, the second one, the third one and up to the tenth biscuit. I couldn't eat any more.

"I am not eating another biscuit!" I told mum.

"Please, Christine, just eat them; it's for your own good," mum replied.

"No way!" My father heard me shouting and stormed into the kitchen asking what was going on.

"Please, dad, I can't eat any more biscuits. Can I please stop eating them?"

"You *will* eat them all. Do you want to keep wetting the bed for the rest of your life? Eat them now!" he roared, glaring at me.

I ate another five biscuits and gagged. I couldn't possibly eat another ten! I pleaded with him for a sip of water. He refused to give it to me. I looked at mum but she just looked away.

"Christine! Eat them all," he growled at me. "I'm telling you, if you don't eat another ten in the next few minutes, I will give you an extra ten." I just couldn't do it. I needed a drink and begged again to get one.

"I told you to eat them! Now sit here and eat an extra 10 biscuits, on top of the 25!" he ordered with cold fury.

I had no choice; if I could not eat them, my father would make me eat even more! It took me until 8 p.m. to finish all 35 biscuits, and I was then sent to bed. He shouted, "Nobody is allowed to give Christine a drink."

He followed me upstairs and inspected my room to make sure I had no drinks hidden anywhere. I never felt so thirsty in my life. I cried myself to sleep. The next morning, I woke up in my wet sheets and ran downstairs, where I must have drunk a whole liter of water.

For the next two months, every evening I was made to eat 25 TUC biscuits, and I wasn't allowed to have even a sip of water. My father never had to interfere again, as I ate those 25 biscuits as quickly as I could in fear of being made to eat 35 again. To date, when I see TUC biscuits anywhere, I get flashbacks and I could throw up!

After the two months, it was concluded that the new method didn't work, as I had wet the bed every single day during the TUC-method trial.

Unfortunately, the summer holidays also came with a report card, which invoked the office punishment for me once again. I started to expect this now and complied automatically when my father unleashed the verbal storm upon me.

I had built up the courage to tell my father about my report card a smidge too late, and there were repercussions for my actions. Around 9 p.m. one Friday, on a cold summer evening, my father was in a reasonably good mood after a productive business meeting.

I felt that it was the right time to break the news about my report card, hoping beyond reason that he would not send me to his office doors. I showed him the report card at what I thought was the right moment.

I was wrong. My father was angrier than ever. He marched me out of the house, and I was forced to sit on my knees with my report card above my head, outside, on the concrete ground this time. For four hours, I sat there shaking in the cold while he watched me through the window.

My father had stayed awake to make sure that the message was driven into my mind, loud and clear. At 1 a.m. he allowed me back inside and I dragged myself up the stairs to my bedroom in agony.

I don't remember climbing under the covers. I just hit my pillow and fell asleep, exhausted from the punishment. The morning light drifted into my room like the slow-moving mist outside had propelled it forward.

It was a bone-tingling, ragged kind of tired that a child can only experience after a day of holidays and a night of punishment. I did not realize that my alarm clock had gone off hours earlier or that I had missed breakfast.

I woke—plunged into an icy lake of cold water—as my father stood over me holding a bucket. My bed had been wet already from my bedwetting problem. Now I was drenched from head to foot.

It had been a very large, very full bucket of ice-cold water that my father threw over me. We were never allowed to sleep late, not even during the holidays.

I sat upright gasping but my father forced me to lie back down. "This is what you want to be, girl?" He switched his cigar from the left to the right side of his mouth as the bucket hovered over me. "People who sleep late don't succeed in life. I am tired of your behavior—it stops today!"

He had opened the window. The cold air from outside rolled over me and I felt my body shiver with exposure.

"I'm sorry, father. I didn't mean to sleep in...the punishment was so late," I started explaining to him.

It was no use. He leered at me, with disgust and judgement etched on his face.

"It's easy to blame other people for your laziness, isn't it? Worthless!" he spat. He moved towards the door, the bucket bouncing off each of his steps. I lay there, afraid to move.

"Please, Dad, it's cold…may I go clean up?" I begged him, my head melting into a wet pillow.

"No, you may not. You will lie there until I say you can get up. Your mother and brothers have gone grocery shopping. I will be in my office."

His voice trailed off as I begged him to hear me.

"Please, dad! It's cold…I can't lie here like this. Dad? Please, it's freezing!" My mother and brothers were out; I could not ask anyone for help.

I dared not move, just in case my father was standing outside the door, looking for another excuse to punish me. I lay there, pleading with no one for some time. Eventually the shivering was all I could manage. It was a cold summer's day. A few days before that it had been positively sweltering but not on the day my father decided to douse me with ice water.

It was two hours later when my father made his way back upstairs to check on me. I was still there, frozen in the wetness of my bed.

"Have you learned anything yet?" he asked me as he paused briefly by the door.

"Yes…y-y-y-yessss…I will never sleep late again" I said as steadily as I could, my voice vibrating out of my throat. "P-p-p-p-p-please can I g-g-get up now?" I begged him. I was colder than I had been in my entire life.

Perhaps he took note of this; perhaps he didn't. When I started to rise, however, out of sheer need to get into a hot shower, it provoked him again.

"Sit up then but you will not move from this bed. Your punishment is not over. You will sit on the wet sheets." A flick of his jacket and he was gone. I was left to sit there for another two hours in my wet nightdress on my soaked blankets.

No one was home, only my father and me. I remember the fear of it, of having no one to protect me, if things would get out of hand. The thought of what might happen chilled me more than the freezing clothes I was wearing. I sat there patiently until the punishment hours were over.

I caught a cold from the exposure that day. The next Sunday morning, I was coughing, sniffling and feeling dreadful and asked if I could stay home instead of going to church.

"Church is more important than your cold. Go and get ready. We both know why you have become ill, and you must ask for forgiveness for your sins."

My father was not attending church that day but he would be there to question us about it afterwards. The service was slow and deeply boring, as it always was but we listened raptly, preparing for the test that would inevitably come from our father later.

Throughout the entire service, I clung to my coat, although it was warm outside. I wished for my warm, dry bed back home, returned to its original glory by our housekeeper by now. Soon after church, we would head to my father's favorite restaurant for Sunday lunch. After grabbing our coats and piling into my father's Mercedes, we were offered our usual table—the best seats in the house. My father ordered for all of us, and soon after, the test began. "What did you learn at church today, Christine?" a wall of smoke obscuring his face.

"We learned about kindness and giving."

"Good. What about it?"

"How it's important to be nice to people and to help them when they need it," I parroted, as rehearsed on our car trip home from the service.

Kane interjected, "It was a lesson teaching us to be generous givers, dad, based on the book of Mark." My father smiled slightly at Kane then returned to leering at me.

"You should learn to remember details like your brother, girl. Empty-headedness is not an asset you need to nurture. Now—and don't you answer this Kane—what was the story used to teach this lesson?"

I knew the answer but I still hated reciting it for him. "The generous giver and the sacrificial giver," I finished. My father was placated—for now. He moved around the table, asking my brothers and mother various questions about the service.

Lucas couldn't remember the Bible passage and was sent to the car without food, to wait there alone for us to finish our meals. I managed to sneak out a small piece of cake for him when I pretended to leave the table to go to the toilet.

At the table, Roger blew his nose with a handkerchief that had a bright red design on it. My father was convinced the handkerchief had blood on in and he became furious with Roger.

"Leave the restaurant immediately, and sit in the car, you disgusting child. Blowing your nose with a bloody handkerchief is rude and disgusting."

"But dad…" Roger said.

"Now!" he replied. Roger didn't even get the chance to explain there was no blood on the handkerchief. No one was permitted to question our father's judgement.

The entire drive back, my father ranted about Lucas's indiscretion and how none of us could ever get anything right. "No one is going to employ you if you can't even remember basic things. You are all stupid and useless," he raged, knocking on the dashboard. It didn't matter; soon I could disappear up to my room. Soon I had to face the laughter again.

Not only did I face cruelty at home—and usually for nothing at all—but I faced the same and worse treatment at school as well. I had no one that I could tell these things to, no friends, and there was no sympathy from anyone. At home, my mother and my brothers were subjected to the same treatment, and at school, the nuns believed I deserved everything that I was getting and more.

No matter where I went, I was being given the same message: I could not do anything right. I was useless.

I did not matter at all.

A Sweet Woman

"Mothers of daughters are daughters of mothers and have remained so, in circles joined in circles, since time began."
– Signe Hammer

1971, Belgium, Age 12

As I approached puberty, I started to see my parents' relationship differently. When I was younger, I had no idea that marriage was supposed to be this wonderful two-way street—quite the contrary.

My earliest idea of love and marriage came from my parents, and that meant I thought of the whole thing as something of a misery—an enslavement of sorts.

It was only after getting out into the world that I realized my parents' relationship was not the definition of anything. For many years of my childhood, I made sense of the world through the autocracy of my father's abuse and the complacency of my mother's acceptance.

She was very much as we were—confused and hopeful, terrorized and compliant. I often wondered if it was because she was a hostage, trapped by my father's wrath and the relentless fear he managed to create in his family. This was not the case, or was it?

My mother was a sweet woman, simple and loyal, dutiful and social—if a little distracted. She worried for us often and for herself too. I know she loved my father at one point but sustaining that kind of sentiment for such a cruel personality is impossible over time.

I remember my mother telling me once, in later life, that she stayed in the relationship because of my father's money.

It gave her the life she wanted and guaranteed us opportunities she never had as a young child, coming from a poor family herself. It was the best she could do for us. In a way, I admire mum for admitting that she stayed with our father for no other reason than the money.

It is easy to look at a woman like my mother and see the mistakes she made. She did the best with what she was given, and she worked hard to never be a burden to anyone. In many ways, I admired this about her, although it kept us all locked into the daily dance around my father and his many creative punishments.

For a woman like my mother, it was better to be a somebody and deal with the abuse, than to be a nobody with nothing. It was a hard choice but one she made willingly. Mum regularly got the worst of my father, and she never seemed to be able to please him for long, although she never gave up trying.

One warm summer weekend, all the kids were home from our various boarding schools. My father had decided to work from home that day, preparing a business meeting with De Beers. My mother had convinced him to join us after breakfast for a family game of Tell Me, a popular quiz board game that we brought home the last time we all went shopping together.

Quiz games of any kind were not my mum's strength. My father rarely tolerated inaccuracy of any kind, believing it to be a weakness or a deep-seated character flaw.

We placed the green and yellow spinning top on the coffee table in the lounge, and Roger lined up the blue, yellow and pink cards.

My father sat on the brown leather sofa next to Kane. Roger and I kneeled on the floor at the coffee table. My mum sat in her luxurious designer chair next to the sofa, and Oliver and Lucas were perched on the sofa opposite mum.

Underneath the glass coffee table was an intricate Persian carpet of beige, green and brown tones to tie the room décor together. My father was the first to spin the wheel. He drew a card, "language."

"Okay. Tell me a language spoken in South America," he declared, squinting at his blue card.

Kane went first, with ease. "Portuguese." Next was my mother's turn. A sinking feeling squirmed around in my stomach. I doubted my mother knew any languages from South America.

She thought about it for a few seconds and then said, "English? I don't know." Five heads snapped from my mother to my father—we knew what was coming.

"English? Is that your answer?" my father said, already shaking his head. "This is why I can't play with you. I ask you for a language in South America, and you say English? That is the only other language you know, so you say it? You are plain stupid."

He puffed on his cigar, and three small smoke rings expanded over the coffee table.

"I don't know then…pass," my mum said, trying to smile.

"Yes, pass. Saying pass is less embarrassing than an answer like that. Kane got it right, and he's 13 years old."

I could see color rising in my mum's cheeks.

"I'm sorry. I'm sure I will get the next one."

"The next one? Only if it's about our next-door neighbor or what happened at your ladies group last weekend. You don't know anything. Nothing—I wonder what would happen to you if you didn't have me around."

We never did get into the swing of the game that morning. Every time one of us got something wrong or could not answer, my father criticized us harshly—but none so severely as my mother.

He took it very personally that his wife was not clever enough to name a language in South America or a river in France.

He put a stop to the game after just 10 minutes.

"I can't play with you, Starla. You set a bad example for our kids. You never get anything right. Why are you playing at all? It's better if you keep your ignorance to yourself rather than share it with us."

The only person in good spirits was Kane, who was amused by the confrontation with my mother.

After that, my father sat back and lit another cigar, pulling out a newspaper from the stack of them that stood next to the sofa, neatly folded and filed between cast iron pillars.

My mother took that to mean the game was over. I could see she was close to tears and flustered but she never broke down in front of us. She smiled through it and cleared away the cards and wheel.

"I'd like to take Christine into town today to get her a few things for school, and I have to drop off the new crochet patterns at Nancy's house for the meeting next Thursday." She didn't glance at my father while stowing the board game in the fireplace ottoman. The boys disbanded; Oliver, Lucas and Roger ran off outside and Kane returned to his bedroom.

I sat motionless at the coffee table, listening for the permission we needed. Going shopping with my mother was one of the few pleasures I sometimes enjoyed, without any sort of harassment.

"Yes, you can go, I expect you back by 4 p.m. Not a second later." He didn't glance up from the paper.

My mum looked over at me and winked, and we immediately bustled off to the front door, my mother pulling on a light summer coat as I stood waiting to leave.

"There are pies in the fridge if the boys want some food. I'll see you later." Her voice trailed behind in the smoky lounge corridor.

It was a gorgeous day, bright and clear like the world was vibrating with energy and promise. I followed my mother to the car and got inside, smiling.

"I need you on your best behavior." She grinned as she started the engine. "Nancy, Mariette, and Francine will be joining us in town."

My face fell; I knew what that meant. Out of the need to minimize my father's control, she regularly misinformed him about where she was going and what she would really be doing there.

Instead, she would give him a good reason—enlisting one of her society responsibilities—so that she could get out and away from home for a while.

My father accepted these without question, which I believe was the point. In any event, it gave my mother the freedom she needed to move around town and enjoy her time there with friends and the money she was given from my father.

Truly, she may have been bad at quizzes but my mother was a force of nature when it came to shopping.

Mum was never short of money. My father had a drawer in his office with lots of cash. Mum knew where the key was hidden and she could open the drawer whenever she wanted and took all the cash she needed. No questions asked.

We arrived at a beautiful coffee shop in town, where her three friends were already waiting for her. They were the cream of Keldonk society, all of their husbands involved in one way or another with the diamond trade. Each had a small fortune behind them, and so they were the elite of the town and knew everybody's private business.

Though my father hated gossip of all forms, my mother was especially gifted at navigating the dangers and delights of upper-echelon society life. Her personality shone beyond others—not because of my father's wealth but because of my mother's tact and kindness; she was widely respected for these characteristics.

She bought me an ice cream and sent me off to play in the park. I chose a swing and settled down for the long haul—her coffee meetings often took hours before we got to any actual shopping.

I was alone again. The swing set was useful; it kept me from having to talk too much to the other children there. I did try to make friends in our village but soon realized that I could never sustain the friendship with my father's rules in place.

He and his draconian rules made it hard to make friends; and my deep insecurity due to my scar and my bedwetting didn't help either. I rarely got to socialize with other little girls when I was home because he disapproved of everyone.

He wanted my brothers and me only to be seen with other children from rich families. Because of this, even when I enjoyed someone's company, I was always on the outside.

Curiously, I enjoyed the moments in the park without anyone expecting anything from me. I ate my ice cream in peace and watched the other kids roar around the playground.

Society life was very important to my mother and in many ways, to my father as well. I think he enjoyed my mother's prominence among the other women because it enhanced our family's status and position. That was why whenever my mother mentioned one of her duties to her associations or organizations, my father was quick to agree. Though not ideal by any means, it worked for them both, as they ruled the small town of Keldonk together.

After a while, mum took me to a few of her favorite boutiques along the main road with Nancy, one of her society friends. I preferred shopping alone with mum, which made it more fun for me.

Today, I was largely left to my own devices, trailing after them quietly as they picked up item after item, discussing if it would look good on me or not. It was always strange being spoken about while being completely ignored.

"This one would look darling on her, they would need to take up the hem a little here," Nancy said, holding an elegant grey coat.

"Is it the right color though? And it's a bit thick for summer, isn't it?" my mum asked, thumbing the material as I looked around the room at her side.

"Yes," Nancy replied, "but winter comes quickly, and these are in right now." As they picked apart the very plain-looking grey coat, I entertained myself by looking through some of the rails myself. The shop assistant was very nice to me because she knew who we were.

Knowing better than to interrupt my mother's intense shopping discussion, she would hover around me, watching for the opportunity to suggest an expensive item.

Even though the assistant was only talking to me because she wanted to make commission on the sale, I still felt good about being there. It was a rare and beautiful thing when people would treat me with reverence and respect, almost like they knew something about me that I didn't understand yet.

Of course, at twelve years old, I had not fully realized the power that comes along with money and so I accepted their kindness and played into it.

My mother and Nancy had made their way to the shoe section. I wandered over to them to show my mother a pale blue dress that I liked. I strode up the aisle and turned the corner to reach her.

"Mum," I said, standing just behind her.

Nancy stepped forward to look at the dress while my mother's eyebrows huddled together on her face, arranged in a gentle pitying formation.

"My goodness, my dear, absolutely not. Look at it! It must be three seasons old." She looked up from me and ushered the shop assistant over, who was mortified at my selection. I had genuinely liked the dress and had plucked it off a passing rail myself.

"Is this the kind of thing you want my daughter to wear?" my mother asked the horrified assistant.

"No, Mrs. Lemmens, not at all. Not at all," she stammered.

"Please only show her the latest styles in the store," my mother commanded abruptly, "and nothing from the sale rails," she added as a zinging finish.

Eventually the novelty of looking wore off and I slumped onto a soft chair—the shop assistant immediately handing me a tall glass of water while showing me a leather designer school bag.

I wasn't even allowed to wear the clothes that I liked. I sat on the chair, all feelings of self-importance eviscerated by my mother's superior knowledge of fashion.

I imagined how well she would do in a quiz if the questions were all based around fashion, gossip, and shopping.

"What is the best material to wear in April?" I imagined my father saying—to which my mother would reply, "Cotton."

In my mind, this would bring great joy to the whole experience of playing a game together as a family and as I lost myself in daydreams, my mother and Nancy approached the payment counter, two shop assistants in their wake laden with items from the store. It was a general practice of my mother's to buy whatever she liked, even if she was not sure it would look great. Keeping up her social status meant spending a lot of money.

It had been a long afternoon of ignoring the neighborhood children, waiting, shopping, moving from store to store, and being as invisible as possible. In many ways, I enjoyed it, being out and about. Unlike many other children, we were never confined by the limitations of lack of money so we always went to the best places and had the best things around. However, although my father had the money, he never gave us any luxuries. It was always mum who indulged us with expensive items.

We arrived home to my father scribbling away in his office and speaking loudly on the phone with one of his diamond clients.

"You're late," he barked to us as we moved from the lounge into the kitchen to wash up.

"That's my fault, dear. A lot of traffic coming back and Nancy would not stop talking about making our meetings mandatory for all members," my mother said like a well-rehearsed pro.

"Well, don't get comfortable. There are a lot of stones that need counting and Bill wants to meet for dinner tonight, so we're taking the family. We're leaving in two hours. Tell everybody to come down and help counting stones."

He disappeared up the grand staircase leading to our upstairs landing. "I am going to get ready and will come to my office where I expect you all to be counting."

Mum told us all to come downstairs and in no time, we were all counting diamonds.

That's the way it often was: when my father had lots of work, we all had to help him count money or stones. Sometimes he would have a huge pile of money and we all had to count it and put the money in elastics, in bundles of 100 notes. This time we needed to count diamonds and put them in small packets of 1000 stones each.

Sometimes diamonds would end up on the floor by accident. I remember very well that when the cleaning woman had done the hoovering she would shout, "Who wants to find some diamonds?" When we heard that, we all ran as fast as we could, as we all wanted to be the first to find a diamond in the hoover bag. We would cut open the hoover bag and dig in all the dirt to find diamonds. That is actually a good memory. All found diamonds had to be returned to our father, of course.

When all diamonds were counted, mum carefully unpacked the items she had bought from the store, handed me a new green dress and shoes, and unwrapped a black number for herself.

"Now we have an occasion to wear these to. Just as well we went shopping today," mum whispered. She raced up the stairs. I did as I was told and retired to my room, quickly pulling off my comfortable trousers and jumper and dressing at top speed. I brushed my hair and slipped on my new shoes—they were hard and tight—and met my family downstairs.

One last inspection from my father and we were whisked away to The Marnix, a five-star, fine dining establishment close to where my mother and I had just come from earlier that day.

Oliver wasn't home as he had a girlfriend and went to her house, where he often was.

The boys were restless after an entire day under my father's supervision, and we were given a table behind my parents, who sat down with another couple, a man we knew to be an important business contact of my father's.

Invigorated by being given our own table, the boys and I chatted politely to the couple's two children—and soon the shenanigans started.

My father and mother's backs were turned so they could not see us, which to us was a golden opportunity.

If only we had known at that age how to keep things contained—but we did not.

The first time my father turned around, it was because Lucas had lost control of the volume of his laughter. The second time was when the other man's son dropped the saltshaker on the floor and it smashed to bits. My father only caught the end of it: my brother Roger picking up the pieces off the floor.

One look and we knew we had better behave ourselves. The rest of the meal passed in relative silence and some very quiet polite chatter. The food was excellent. The march outside to the car might as well have been a walk to the execution chamber. My brothers hung their heads and exchanged knowing looks at each other as the safety of the other family was left behind along with the restaurant staff.

For a few seconds I thought we had escaped punishment. My mother, the boys, and I got into the car with my father, who was very quiet, and we pulled out of the parking lot.

He had been drinking a lot during the meal, as he always did, each time we went out to a restaurant. Roger smiled and then Lucas. Kane never did. Perhaps he was the only one of us who truly understood our father. Another corner and the car came to a shuddering halt.

"Give me your bag, Starla," my father demanded, his voice low and steady. My mother, confused by my father's orders, handed him her designer bag on cue.

She had been charming, the perfect dinner guest. "Take off your shoes, all of you." He glared at us through the front windshield. We did as he ordered, fear rising in the car like a flash flood.

"Now you will all enjoy walking home together. Maybe then, you will remember to be polite and uphold your family name at a restaurant. Get out!"

His voice was so calm and refined that three doors flung open at the prompt, and we all slid out into the night, collecting on the tarred pavement. Then he sped off, leaving us all barefooted on the side of the road in town.

My mother was visibly upset. She hated being kicked out of the car.

"Are we supposed to walk back with bare feet?" Lucas asked my mum.

"Why am I here? I didn't do anything," grumbled Roger. The irony was that while we knew my father had reacted badly, we all still felt ashamed for causing such a reaction.

"I didn't even drop the salt. It was Braden's fault—he threw it at me!" Roger said. His blood was boiling.

"I hate this family," he muttered into the dark.

My mother had no intention of forcing us to walk home barefoot and in the dark. She may have been a simple woman but she found ways around my father as the years wore on.

As a precaution, she always kept a small bit of money tucked away in her pocket for just such occasions, a lesson learned after having to walk home in an evening gown and high heels. Father had driven slowly beside her that night, taunting and teasing her and worst of all, making his children witness his cruel treatment of their mother.

"Let's get something to drink," she announced wearily, walking awkwardly towards the nearest sidewalk café.

The waiters didn't dare mention our bare feet. They all knew who we were and how our father treated us; the whole village knew, and so did the surrounding villages.

After two hours, my mother had the café call a taxi, which dropped us off 100 meters away from our house. We all feigned the pain of having walked home that night and disappeared into our various rooms, my father satisfied at our miserable, tired faces. He never knew that we had been sipping on tea, getting the one-up on one of his punishments.

The following morning we were awoken early by the sound of the builders. For the past two months, builders had been at our house, as our father decided to give the whole ground floor a makeover.

Today was a big day for him; he invited business people, the press, architects and magazine reporters to the house as the new interior underwent finishing touches with ridiculously expensive designer furniture, intricately placed for maximum impact.

Knowing that mum spent a lot of time in the kitchen, she said to my father, before the building work started, that there was one thing that she really would like: a sliding glass door in the kitchen that would lead to the garden.

She never got her sliding door, and she mentioned this countless times later in life. She was deeply hurt by the fact that my father totally ignored her wish. Mum never asked anything of my father but the one thing she asked for, she never got.

My father was the first person in the village to own a dishwasher and he extended the invitation to others so they could not only see that he owned one, but to iterate that it was something "only the rich" could afford.

As he showed off his dishwasher that was built into a luxurious kitchen with a landscaped garden view, he continued to walk with his guests through the entrance hall with a grand staircase, to the dining area where a magnificent massive marble table with eight stunning designer chairs and a four-meter-long aquarium could be seen.

I vividly recall driving to the aquarium shop almost every weekend to buy more expensive fish, as the fish in the aquarium kept eating each other or just died for no apparent reason.

Less than a week later, our father showed us all the articles in magazines featuring his house. It was the talk of the town for quite a while.

People in the village, family, and mum's social circles came to see the dishwasher and the new interior when our father wasn't home, as they were all too afraid to face him. Everybody knew how horrible he could be.

Around this time in my life, Maddie and I started to write letters to each other. She lived next door to us and had a strict father too. Maddie's mum was our cleaner for several years, so by default, we used to see each other very regularly. From all the people I knew, she was the person I enjoyed being with most.

Maddie, a bright, self-confident, slim individual with very long black hair was someone I looked up to, although I didn't see her often during the week as she attended a different school. I remember that I always felt good in her presence.

Maddie's school and my school had a program, where we were able to write to each other. I finally had something to look forward to, as it was always a happy moment when I received another letter from Maddie. We used to write silly things, making each other laugh with what we had been up to in the weekends, laughing at our teachers, etc.

The happy moments never lasted long though. After the makeover of the ground floor, architects were visiting us to discuss landscaping the back garden to incorporate a swimming pool or a tennis court.

"Please Dad, can we have a swimming pool?" I begged, as I loved swimming. My brothers, except for Roger, preferred playing tennis so they all preferred a tennis court. However, Lucas and Roger also loved swimming.

My father grunted. "If you want a swimming pool so much, dig it! Prove to me that you want it and dig it yourself. In life, when you want something bad, you have to work for it, just like I worked hard to build my diamond empire. When you have dug it, I will consider building a proper swimming pool. I will hold off on landscaping the rest of the back garden."

Over the next months, my brothers and I manually dug a massive hole in our back garden, with spades. We worked on it every spare second we had. During the holidays, we started early morning and finished late evening.

When the hole was large and deep enough, my father purchased a massive plastic under sheet, we filled the hole with water and our swimming pool was finished. It was approximately 10 meters long, 5 meters wide, and 2 meters deep. We spent hours and hours playing in that pool. After a while, the water became filthy and needed replacing.

"Dad, can I have a real pool now please?"

"I can see you really wanted a pool as you have put in the work with your brothers," he replied.

He continued by saying, "the problem is that three of your brothers would prefer a tennis court, so I have decided to build a tennis court instead. It will also require less maintenance than a swimming pool."

"Dad, but you said you would…," I said with tears in my eyes.

He interrupted me and replied angrily, "I never said I would, I said I would consider it. I have considered it and the answer is no. Your pool will be destroyed. End of conversation."

There was nothing I could do about it and for as long as I lived at home, I could see my brothers and their friends enjoying their tennis court.

I guess a tennis court was more of a status symbol, and therefore more important to my father than making me happy anyway.

Coping with a Hostile Environment

"If the structures of the human mind remain unchanged, we will always end up re-creating the same world, the same evils, the same dysfunction." – Eckhart Tolle

2016, St. Vincentius Hospital, Age 57

Lucas went outside to catch some fresh air and a while later, I decided to join him. We exchanged a memory or two; awkward recollections of a shared childhood that was best left in the past but refused to stay there. The things we had in common, the reality of our childhood, was too much. We decided to head back to our mother's hospital room together.

I settled into the chair directly across from my mum, who was still hooked to machines and breathing lightly, her chest rising and falling as she slept.

The stark reality of the room closed in on me, and I could see it was affecting Lucas too—he chose to sit in a seat closer to the door and cabinet, at the foot of my mother's bed.

Reflexively, I pulled out my phone and checked for messages: a note from Oliver saying that he and Roger would see me later at mum's house—they were not returning as planned. I had one missed call from my husband.

I called him and he said he arrived at the train station and would be at the hospital in five minutes. I told Lucas I was going down to the hospital entrance to fetch him and left him with a look of displeasure on his face. "I'll be back in a moment," I told him, trying to ease the situation I had put him in.

It was clear that he did not want to be in the room with mum on his own. I sped away at a walk-jog pace, eager for the comfort of my husband.

When I saw him, my spirits lifted and shone: my loving husband, who looked appropriately rushed. When he wrapped his arms around me, tears sprouted from my eyes, suppressed emotions from the panic and pain of seeing my mum in such distress. I did not want to leave mum for too long, so we set off at a lively trot.

"How is she? Have you heard anything more?" my husband asked as we made our way up to the room. Lucas was hovering around outside the room with a fresh cup of coffee in his hands.

"Nothing new, the doctors are hopeful," I said. We spoke for a few moments about her condition, and a doctor joined us to check her vitals and update us on her progress.

"We have every faith that she will recover," he explained to us. "But because of her age, we cannot be sure if this will happen. If the pneumonia gets worse, the infection might take her. It's best to prepare for that." He left, leaving behind a more somber mood than before. Lucas excused himself, unable to sit in the room any longer.

"I'll see you back at the house. We can talk about all of this later on," he said, buttoning up his jacket. As mum was still in a coma and all I could do was wait, I sat in her room and started to think about my youth again.

1972, Belgium, Age 13

At 13, I was beginning to battle with the onslaught of hormones regularly gushing through me. I noticed boys but still kept mostly to myself, my childhood scar an active reminder that I was not like other girls my age.

We still drove to the coast regularly. I loved watching my mum and her friends nattering away at the beach but her constant distraction nearly always resulted in sunburn for all of her kids.

She would have the best intentions on arrival, instructing us to put on suntan lotion. The protecting factor was never high enough and it washed off in the sea.

That, combined with the cool ocean currents, made it appear as though our suntan lotion was working—until it was painfully apparent that it did not.

I remember one day well, we had been to the coast for the day. By the time we returned to the car, it was my mother and her four beetroot children. Oliver didn't come with us, that day. Roger cried all the way home; he was burnt so badly and in pain, while the rest of us tolerated it.

I didn't understand why we kept getting burnt when other people did not seem to be as prone to it as we were. I guess my mum never took the time to properly understand the sun or why it continued to burn her children. We arrived home that day to a very aggravated father. He was on the phone in his office, pacing up and down and shouting at someone on the other end.

"Don't tell me you can't make it happen, Klaus!" His voice boomed in frustration. "I did not hire you to give me excuses. I hired you to do what you are told! This merchant is important to me. You don't force him to reschedule a meeting, then cancel on him! It's disrespectful—and now? Now he is negotiating a deal with another diamond dealer! Fix it, or you're fired!"

He slammed the phone down hard, leaning his arms on his desk and puffing with fury. If there was one thing my father hated, it was losing a deal to one of his competitors.

He always blamed his employees and would go on long tirades about their incompetence and how they were losing him money.

My mother had disappeared upstairs, leaving us to our own devices. We were little stinging beetroots wandering around the house, trying to keep our distance from our father, who might have been looking for someone to take his frustrations out on.

I think my mother must have realized this because she came back down into the lounge a few minutes later wearing a pretty summer dress and smelling like coconut oil.

Roger, at age 11, was still teary-eyed from the pain of his sunburn. He sat on our brown leather couch just outside my father's office, the cool leather providing some semblance of relief for his pain.

My father strode out of his office, sweat trickling down his face from the heat of the day or the frustration of the phone call—perhaps a little of both.

He locked in on Roger like a scud missile just as my mother swept past, greeting him.

"Look at this. Again, Starla? He's burnt!" He fumed until something better caught his attention.

He cut his eyes at Roger. "Stop crying, boy. Stop that immediately. Men don't cry. You take the pain and you live with it, you never cry—you hear me?"

Kane pulled out the kitchen chair and settled down with a book. Lucas hovered around the doorway connecting the kitchen with the pantry. I stood next to him, watching the scene unfold. My mother spun on her heels and sat down next to Roger, comforting him.

"You should know better by now, Starla!" my father shouted. I felt the energy in the room ignite. We all felt it. My father was upset, frustrated, and drunk—a lethal combination. Oliver had gone to fetch some vinegar and started to put it on Roger's back.

Roger started to cry again and his cry incensed my father, a direct violation of his command to stop crying. He reared up to strike Roger, when my brother Oliver collided with him, tackling him to the ground. Oliver was no stranger to my father's temperament. As he got older, he tolerated it less and less.

Oliver had never openly attacked my father before, not like this. Sure, he had fought back during beatings when he was younger—but that was like a chicken trying to fend off an ostrich that already had him pinned down.

The two of them clattered to the floor, knocking a side table over as a vase with flowers in it smashed into tiny pieces.

My mother leaped up and put herself between them, the shouting climbing so high that it almost drowned out Roger's heaving sobs and wild screams. Lucas and I watched as our mum was jostled between our father and Oliver.

I thought for a second that my mother managed to calm the situation down but it was just the eye of the storm.

My father reached around my mother to grab at Oliver, his face red with effort, the ecstasy of fury raging in his eyes. She was knocked sideways onto the broken shards of vase and the scattered flowers that now littered the floor.

Oliver was a strong young man but still significantly smaller than my father, who had weight, years, and the benefit of violent experience on his side. Fists started to fly in every direction, Oliver doing what he could to keep them away from where Roger was sitting frozen in place, screaming.

There was a point where my mother had to move or risk being caught in the fight again, so she pulled herself up, blood leaking from the glass stuck in her arms. She limped around and in front of the couch, grabbing Roger and heaving him out of the way. A second later, the couch skidded across the floor, slamming into its twin on the other side, shooting the coffee table into the fireplace.

Two bodies crashed down to the floor again, one clearly in the dominant position. It was not Oliver. He had been knocked down and his head slammed into the wooden floor. My father climbed on top of him and began punching his face and body.

I did not know a lot about fighting back then but I had been on the receiving end of a beating from my father more than once. I knew that with every punch, it felt like Oliver's teeth threatened to crack loose and choke him. I knew that swell of pain that lingered after every blow was worse than the blow itself.

My mother was shouting now as Roger cried next to her. She stood just ahead of us, shielding the children she still could.

It was a savage beating—the worst of Oliver's life and the last. My father beat him, not until he believed Oliver had suffered enough but until he had sated the violence in his own heart. There was no sense to it, no love, no caution. Our father started beating Oliver that day, and why? Because our father was who he was.

He did not need a good reason to lash out at his family, and things always became worse when things were not going right, down at the office.

Oliver spent a week at home recovering from his injuries and soon after moved out of the house.

None of us were safe from our father's rages and violence. My turn came soon after Oliver's beating. I had begged for two weeks to be allowed to go to a party, together with Maddie.

I had gotten ready and asked my father what time I was expected home. The top I was wearing was white with just a small hint of cleavage. When my father saw what I was wearing, he was outraged and said, "Christine, the clothes you're wearing are completely unacceptable. You are to change! Right now!"

I tried explaining to him, saying, "But dad, my top is similar to what others would be wearing."

He screamed at me and replied, "If I say you need to change that top, then you need to change that top, right now! Nobody in my family will be seen dressed like that!"

He then seized me by the shoulders and shook me so hard my head flopped back and forth like someone getting whiplash in a car crash.

"You are totally useless!" he roared. "What sort of child are you? You will never make anything good of your life dressing like this! Prostitutes dress like that. You are representing my family, my name and you want to dress like a prostitute?"

He knocked me to the ground then kicked me until every bone in my body was sore. He kicked me with his feet and punched me with his fists. It seemed to go on forever and I felt his anger through every punch and kick that came down on me.

It was brutal, a beating that I will never forget and by far the worst that I ever got from him. I suffered agonizing, chronic headaches for the next 5 days.

I did not go to the party that day. Even if I wanted to, how could I go out covered in bruises? I spent the rest of the day in my room crying. I have never been able to wear anything with even a hint of cleavage and to this day, when I see a woman with a low-cut neckline, I shudder with the memories of that savage beating.

Dr. Kitzel

*"Loving people live in a loving world. Hostile people live in
a hostile world. Same world." – Wayne Dyer*

2016, St. Vincentius Hospital, Age 57

My husband and I sat in the hospital room. I was lost in thought
again. Each time my eyes settled on my mother, I was
overwhelmed by memories I had tried for so long to forget. She
was so quiet and pale. I worried that at any time the machines
would grow louder and take her from me.

"Are you all right, sweetheart?" my husband asked me as a
distinct chill rippled over me.

"Fine," I replied.

"It's just all of this, you know? Bringing back some tough
memories."

"Yes, it would do that," he agreed, concern spreading from
his eyes to his mouth.

My mum had always been a flawed woman but a gracious
one. We got along as well as anyone until puberty raised the
flames of anarchy inside me.

Staring at her took me back to my early teenage years, when
the hormone cascades would jar me out of a passive state.
Something new was growing in me, new feelings beyond my
childlike sadness.

1973, Belgium, Age 14

I often wondered how I could come from such a dysfunctional
place. Instead of love, my childhood was steeped in fear. My
father loved no one; he only loved control and power.

It left an uncomfortable pressure on my heart when I was young—this idea that love was such a powerful, wonderful thing.

I knew we loved each other—my mother, my brothers, and I—but I did not know how. It was never freely expressed, willingly given, or openly spoken about.

My mother and brothers had demonstrated their love many times by putting themselves between me and my father and his rage. Unfortunately for me, I could not recognize this at a young age, too traumatized by fear and too unable to fight my own battles. When my father decided that I needed a punishment or a beating, all I could do was make myself as small as I could be.

My beatings never lasted as long as my brother's; they were attacked with far more precision and a lot more brutality. Nevertheless, I grew into my teen years believing that all love came with a sense of violence, having only ever experienced my parents' relationship and the challenges that my mother faced loving a man like my father.

Puberty made me aware that one day I would meet a man who would love me. I suppose I expected it to be similar to what I had always known. Children can rarely imagine a different life when all they have known is isolation and rejection.

The seventies brought a culture of defiance, freedom, hippies, free love, color and community. I began venturing out more often, drinking in the village like I never had before. My brothers would take me to the local bars and give me beer, which I quickly delighted in. I was a newborn dove finding my wings in the world and I wanted it all.

The rocky truth, however, was that I could not escape the home I was living in. Still an outcast and increasingly so, I suffered with debilitating moments of anger and was stricken with the injustice of my bedwetting. Boarding school was predictably cruel, and I knew I would never find any *real* friends there.

I had so-called friends I used to hang around with but somehow they never felt like good friends.

In my home village of Keldonk there was opportunity to meet new people and make new friends, in the pubs. I had survived a childhood with few people to talk to and had decided early on that I would not allow that to continue into my teenage years.

At age 14, I walked around with a deep-seated anger in my heart, swathed in helpless abandonment, which primed me for drinking.

I loved how it felt to be drunk and free of anxious thoughts, how it removed my fear and replaced my heart with something stronger. A few glasses of beer could wash away the massive scar on my face. I could even forget my bedwetting and the weekday horror of my life at boarding school. With alcohol, I could be anyone and do anything.

Then one day, I drunkenly fell asleep on the brown leather designer couch in the lounge while my parents were out at an important dinner in town. When they returned, they found me lying there, my trousers soaked dark with urine and so was the couch. I was sent up to bed with a promise from my father that he would get my bedwetting under control.

One by one, as my brothers had aged, each of them had stopped…but not me. I wet the bed night after night, powerless to stop it.

Soon after the couch incident, I found myself, with my mother, in a urologist's office, who combined urology with psychiatry. Nancy had recommended the man, a tall, skinny, gaunt fellow with bony fingers and a brisk, hard countenance about him. I sank into a yellow chair in his office as my mother sat beside me in one emblazoned with large blue flowers.

Dr. Kitzel sat across from me looking like a lanky piece of driftwood that had developed an insatiable hunger for young girls.

He eyed me with a sly smile, and my stomach lurched. I didn't like him, and I didn't like being there. The air was stiffer than he was, and I felt persecuted for a fault I could not control.

"How long has she been wetting the bed?" he drawled at my mother, treating me with a blatant insignificance that kept me statue still.

"Since she was five, doctor," my mother said. "She was dry at night when she was five but a few months later started bedwetting again, and since then she has wet the bed every day."

"Have you tried any remedies before?" he asked, looking up at me while frowning deeply and scribbling on his mini notepad.

"Yes, yes, we have…one doctor recommended that she eat a whole packet of extra salty TUC biscuits every night for two months to control the salt content in her body. However thirsty she was from the salt, she wasn't allowed to drink anything. He believed lack of salt in her body could have been causing the incidents," my mother finished, looking hopefully at the man.

"Anything else?" Dr. Kitzel asked.

My mother paused and then took a list from her bag. Scanning it, she recited,

"We tried not giving her anything to drink after 6 p.m. for five months, though this has not proved effective.

We have also tried waking her up every two hours for a period of five months to use the bathroom; uhh, the TUC biscuits I've mentioned.

She has been on four different medications. All of them had horrible side effects.

We have tried a chart-based rewards system for every dry night; unfortunately, nothing ever appeared on the chart.

She has visited several psychiatrists without any success.

We tried several machines that sound an alarm each time she wets the bed…nothing has worked so far.

Several doctors have done various tests, x-rays, scans and ultrasounds to rule out any physical causes and they have concluded it is all in Christine's mind. Four different psychiatrists have confirmed this but none have been able to help," she concluded.

The doctor put his pen and notepad aside abruptly and addressed my mother directly.

"Madam, it is not unusual for none of these remedies to work in severe cases. I would say that your daughter is a severe case, an unusual case."

I was used to being a number in boarding school. Now I was also "a case." My heart sank into my new pair of leather boots. I had a severe case of something and that was never a good sign with doctors.

Every time we saw a new doctor about my bedwetting, I reached a new level of shame. I was further convinced that I would never be acceptable to the world.

Then he cracked an unnatural, strained smile that looked more like a scowl.

"The good news is that it is treatable. Very treatable. Now, the treatment is not a pleasant one but it is effective."

"Oh, that's wonderful news!" My mother reached over to grab my hand, hers still inside of her white gloves.

"Yes. There is immediate treatment that you should consider. I will speak to you about that in private," he added.

I was made to leave the room shortly after that and I was almost glad because the doctor's office was unbearable with its strange instruments and his leering gaze. My mother emerged sometime later looking paler but resolute. The hospital had several consultation rooms and no one in the waiting room looked happy to be there. I wondered how that could be if they were meant to improve people's problems.

I thought the doctor was being kind and walking us out of the building. I was wrong. Instead, we were herded towards a room at the far side of the practice with a large machine in it and a single bed...with straps running across it. I may have only been 14 but it looked like a torture chamber to me.

"What's going on, Mum? What's happening?"

"It's going to be okay. Dr. Kitzel says this is the latest and most effective treatment. I have already called your father, and he says to go ahead with it. It will be over in 15 minutes."

Afraid but hopeful, I allowed the doctor to seat me on the bed as he powered up the machine next to me. It whirred to life, crackling and spitting with static.

He roughly took each of my arms and strapped them down. Then he removed my boots, my trousers and underwear, pulled my legs open and strapped them down. I was very cold.

The room was cold, clinical and bare—nothing but the machine could survive in there. As the machine grew louder, I became more panicked.

"Please tell me what this is. What are you doing?" I pleaded with the doctor.

"Calm down, I will explain it as I go, all right?"

I nodded to him, sweat breaking out on my forehead. He lifted up a large, long device and attached it to a long cord that snaked its way back into the large machine.

"I am going to insert this device into your vagina." He moved to the foot of the bed, where the straps held my legs open. "It's going to execute a brief electric shock protocol for about 15 minutes, in pulses. It will only hurt a little bit. We have had some great results with severe bedwetting cases like yours with this treatment."

"What? No, Mum, I don't want to do this!" I called out to her. She rose off the chair by the door and stood beside me. It didn't matter what I wanted; the doctor had already inserted the device into me. It was cold and hard. The first shock felt like my insides had been suddenly submerged in ice. It radiated through my legs and lower body, causing my muscles to tense.

The pain was not severe to start with but it grew with each pulse. They came in five-second increments and held me tight in that freezing cold room.

It got steadily worse. By the second minute, I was crying. The pulses kept coming and increasing in intensity. With every pulse, the electric shock was higher and I was in more pain.

The room and everything in it was reduced to slow motion. My toes curled and my legs shuddered, jolting me with pain for thirteen more minutes.

"This hurts!" I shouted to the doctor. "You said it would only hurt a little bit. This hurts *a lot*! Make it stop! Mummy, help me. Please make it stop! Mummy, Mummy, I'm sorry. I won't wet the bed again! Please help!"

Nobody cared, my shouting didn't change anything and the pain became worse and worse.

I pressed my head hard against the pillow, trying to cope with the pain. I wanted to pull the horrible thing out of me but my arms were strapped down. The pain was ripping through my guts, muscles and bones. I clenched my fists, crunched my teeth over my lips, trying to cope. The sobbing, when the pain wave came, was broken apart by short pauses of recovering breaths.

By the end of the session, I was an emotional wreck, which Dr. Kitzel was kind enough to explain to my mother was a "common side effect." It took me several more minutes to gain the courage to walk once the device was removed. I felt desecrated and deeply confused. How could something so unforgiving happen in the presence of a doctor and my mother?

It had to work. That was the only thing that would make it okay. Then the pain would all be worth it. I was prepared to do *anything* to stop my bedwetting.

"You will need to come back tomorrow and every day thereafter for these treatments for another month until the bed wetting stops," the doctor told my mother as I stared off into the distance at the hospital counter, tears streaming down my face.

Electric shock therapy lasted for what was one of the worst months of my life. I was made to go every day, and every day I was strapped to that bed to suffer through 15 minutes of brutal treatment.

The pain got worse every day. Every night I wet the bed and cried myself to sleep from the injustice of it all. Sorrow overtook me until I refused to go again. Only two more sessions were scheduled but I could not stand it any longer. The pain and humiliation were too much.

Even my mother had to concede that the treatment was not working. She grieved with me at each visit to Dr. Kitzel in her own stoic, dignified way. After that, a piece of my innocence faded away, and I started seeing the world through all the wrong perspectives.

I was struggling with the overwhelming hopelessness that I would wet my bed for the rest of my life.

My sadness, which had always been a deep anger festering beneath the surface, started to ripen into rage. I found myself unwilling to follow the rules any longer. I wanted nothing more than to run away from my life and everything in it.

Even though I could still not stay over at a friend's house due to my bedwetting, I decided not to let that stop me from pretending everything was normal and that I preferred to stay at home when invited.

Soon after seeing Dr. Kitzel I decided to adopt a couldn't care less attitude. At school, I began disobeying the nuns every chance that I got.

I pulled off their wimples, sneaked out of the classroom, smuggled boys into the school, and made a ridiculous amount of noise during class and study times. I openly rebelled and reveled in it. While at home, I would live almost exclusively in my bedroom, never joining the rest of the family downstairs.

I was the worst daughter a parent could have. I only drew the line at trying drugs. I was offered marijuana a few times but never tried it. I think it was because I feared I *really* would be lost if I crossed that line.

The Red Door

"One of the greatest tragedies in life is to lose your own sense of self and accept the version of you that is expected by everyone else." – K.L. Toth

1974, Belgium, Age 15

My father's need to control everything extended to conversation over meals and the worst meal of the week was Saturday lunch, when we were all home from boarding school.

Instead of the normal chitchat, harmless gossip, or relaxed conversation, we were cross-examined by our father. It wasn't a relaxed "how was your week" type of questioning. He was searching for our most recent failings and when he found one (or imagined one), he pounced.

Whatever real or imagined shortcoming he seized would be the subject of a rant that would last anything between 2 and 7 hours and cover his reasons for deciding that each one of us was a useless embarrassment to his family name. He would go on and on about the same thing for hours, and he had a knack for opening old wounds.

Offences led to punishments. Roger came home one Saturday afternoon, and it was clear he had a few beers at the pub. In addition to the lecture, Roger was made to kneel on the kitchen floor for two hours, with an empty beer crate over his head while the rest of us remained at the table, trying to eat lunch, while our father raved about how Roger had shamed him.

A weight had settled in my heart, crushing all ambitions I might have had if I had grown up in a normal home.

There was never a relaxed atmosphere in our house when our father was home - always mental abuse, always arguing about something, always punishments, always somebody being put down.

My home was not normal, I knew that, and that made it okay for me to do the things that I was dead set on doing.

I had met two other girls, who I liked, through my brothers the last time we went to the bar, and I was scheduled to sneak out and join them there that night. There was no way I was missing out on that opportunity. Often my father came home drunk and slept in his chair, which gave me an opportunity to sneak out of the house.

There was plenty of opportunity for me to get to the pub, because he often worked late in his factory or went out to a bar himself. I could never sneak out of the house when my father was in his home office, as he had a security monitor where he could see the front and back doors all the time. He saw everybody walking in and out of the house, and he watched us all like a prison warden when he was home and sober.

At 9 p.m. I snuck out of the front door. It wasn't long before I arrived at my new favorite place—the local bar, called The Red Door. Night had settled on the street, casting everything in shadow and lamp light.

The bar was a simple rectangular building with grey walls and a red door. I entered dressed in my best casual outfit, wanting to look older than I was. Inside, the walls continued in reds and greys, covered with sports memorabilia. The broad oak bar featured several beer taps gleaming in the soft light, and people were laughing and playing pool. It was not a particularly fancy bar but a popular one in the village.

A lot of young people hung out there, and the heavy drinking had already begun. I met Lina and Elise in the corner, where the bar meets the center island that divides the pool lounge from the drinking area.

A huddle of older boys was already around them, and they were drinking in a haze of cigarette smoke.

"Christine! Glad you made it. Pull up a chair."

I became acutely aware that all eyes were on me; as if a pack of male wolves had just turned their heads and spotted a female lamb.

My clothes helped me stand out, as I always kept up with the latest trends but I still felt insecure because of my scar. I wanted to make a good impression and be cool.

A drink was slammed down on the bar in front of me and I drank it down in one gulp, eager to be rid of the nerves that kept me from breaking out of my shell.

The moment I had drained the beer, a second one was placed in front of me. I drank that one and several more before I started to slow down, sipping on the next. The music made the room swell, and a sense of joy and excitement overcame me. Whatever anger had been there was gone, replaced by a serene instability of my faculties.

Over the years, I lost the ability to deal with my emotions but now I was the strongest I had ever been; the brightest in my life. I could feel the eyes of everyone in the corner on me, and they were smiling and laughing—not at me but *with* me. My jokes were especially funny, so they said, and I had discovered the sarcastic wit of a disillusioned youth.

"Back to boarding school on Monday, so better drink while I can," I said, not too steadily.

"I can't believe your parents do that to you, dumping you in a boarding school from such a young age. That's messed up," Elise said to me, just barely slurring. Elise was stunning, and with her expert make-up and flowing blonde hair, she looked older than 16. Lina had the same mature style. They easily passed as 18. My father didn't allow me to wear make-up—ever.

"I know. I wish I could just run away sometimes. I'm so tired of it," I said without going into more detail.

In reality, most of these girls knew my brothers, who would be furious if I said anything bad about our home situation. Privacy and charity starts at home, my father always said.

I never understood why our home life was this big secret, for now, I kept it that way.

However, I knew everybody in the village was talking about us, so I guess it was not as big a secret as my father thought it was.

"Oh my God, I love this song!" Lina said, slipping off her chair and swaying to the music. One of the boys came up behind her and they danced together while they drank.

"It's one of my favorites," I lied, having never heard the song before.

I had to stretch the truth a lot back then in order to fit in. Without those white lies, I never would have had any friends.

The more I drank, the prettier I felt. It was as if my scar vanished when I was there; the boys didn't seem to mind it at all, after a few. I was hit on a lot, and eventually the harmless flirting became something more.

I won't say that Elise and Lina had a bad reputation but they were loose and free and did whatever they wanted to do. It was the way of the seventies and I learned it quickly. That evening, I danced with a few boys. One of Elise's friends, Leon, had taken a particular liking to me.

He had shaved hair and wore sunglasses in the dark bar, and he drank like each beer was his last. I confess, I was very flattered by his attention. As I had grown into a young woman, more and more boys had let me know that I was not an unattractive woman—quite the opposite. I always thought of myself as unappealing because the first thing I saw when I looked in the mirror was that ugly scar.

Receiving such lavish attention when I had been starved of it all my life was exhilarating. My new friends seemed to love me, and their male friends even more so. My head was thick with beer and liquor when midnight came around and I was feeling free and beautiful.

Leon had pulled me out onto the dance floor and was grinding up against me while kissing my neck.

I had never had sex before but I remember feeling like all I wanted to do was get rid of my virginity because it stood in the way of my rising popularity.

Leon was very drunk, and his hands were everywhere—I could barely keep track of them. A tray of drinks blew past us and we all saluted our youth before downing a couple of vodka tonics.

I want to tell you that I remember it clearly but I don't. The alcohol eventually dulled my senses, so clear memories of that first instance were lost forever.

Lina and Elise told me that I disappeared into the woods behind the pub with Leon for 20 minutes. Snapshots of it trickle in sometimes: the rustle of a slight wind, his hands down my pants and then the rough drunken movement as he held me in place and finished.

When I got back to the bar corner, Leon high-fived his friends, and Elise and Lina chatted to me with broad smiles on their faces. It was the first night of many for me. Once my virginity was gone, I became fair game for any man that showed me even the slightest bit of attention.

Sometimes I would take a boy to the bathrooms and have oral sex, or we would run off to his car and have sex in plain view of the street, or in the woods close to the bar, or behind a house—I didn't care. Everyone loved me down at the bar and I did whatever I wanted to there, with my friends. I rarely paid for drinks, as the boys did and I never really suffered from hangovers.

I channeled a lot of my anger and my rebellion into those nights at the bar; I did a lot of things I later regretted. At the time however, it made me happy to get out there and flirt with a bar full of people. I was even happy to have sex with the men around me as long as it made me popular.

I was so desperate for human approval and affection, that I had no idea that what I was doing was wrong, nor did I have any interest in right and wrong. I didn't understand the kind of reputation I was building for myself or the kind of life I was setting myself up for. I was just having fun—for the first time in my life.

Dirty, alcohol-fueled, self-hating fun.

Christine Clayfield

Men from the bar started to take me to their homes but it was never a pleasurable experience for me.

The entire time this was going on, never once did I get sexual satisfaction. I wasn't having sex for *my* physical pleasure. It was my aim to please the men, nothing else!

I wanted to do things to them that *they* liked, so they would like *me* for it. I wanted them to like me. Most of the time the sex was so quick that it was over before I was ever aroused and the alcohol dulled my senses anyway.

When my brothers became aware of my new social life; they were not pleased. They would come to the bar but they couldn't stop me. I had already decided that the less my family liked my actions, the better.

I was a messed-up kid looking for approval and love in broken places and anyone who interfered was my enemy. I began to view my brothers as junior versions of my father: cruel, judgmental boys, eager to control me.

We have never been a very close family, as we were never shown what a loving family was. Since we were in boarding school, we were always separated; there was not much time to get to know each other well. When we did come home for the weekend, it was always misery with our father.

Like Lina and Elise, I became an easy target for predatory men looking for a hook-up or a one-night stand. I thought that sex was what love was for a long time and no one around me knew or told me any different. The looser I became, the more I lost myself in the alcohol. I had never done well at school, except for languages. Now I was positively awful.

After a lifetime of social rejection and failure, it was intoxicating to discover that people thought I was funny. They liked my jokes and laughed with me.. They even liked my laugh, which they said was very contagious.

No one laughed at home. In the pub, I was the center of attention and appreciation, the life of the party. At boarding school, I was an ugly, bed-wetting girl, and at home, I was a failure.

But at the pub, I was two of the best things possible: pretty and funny. At the time, I thought these two things were the most important things to be.

Studying cut into my time for sneaking out and drinking all night, so I stopped studying. My father would come home and I would be staring at a page in a textbook I had never read before.

My report card punishments were frequent but they hurt me less because I had my own life now. Besides, my grades had never been very good, so it was only a small increase in the punishment.

My father started to change the punishments for my bad report cards. I vividly remember that mum had booked a weekend trip to Rome with the whole family. Many of her friends with their husbands and children booked the same trip, as it was organized via one of the women's organizations mum attended regularly.

We were all looking forward to it. The day we were supposed to leave, my father told me I wasn't allowed to go and I had to spend the weekend in boarding school as a punishment for my poor grades. The rest of my family went without me.

As twisted as it sounds, I actually felt happier hanging around bars and discotheques than I had been in my entire life. I thought I had it all figured out but I had not counted on the toll, on what sleeping around would eventually do to my self-esteem and my already fragile heart.

My bedwetting stayed with me, so I never slept over anywhere and was always home in time for breakfast, after having sneaked into the house.

I started dating boys and had loads of boyfriends but there was never any love between us. It was purely sex. A boy would meet me, date me, sleep with me for a while, and then I dumped him. I always left before any actual sleep could happen, afraid of the damp mornings that plagued me. That was how it went.

I could have found a nice boy, one who would treat me well and really care but I was not looking for one.

I didn't think such boys existed, and if they did, I knew they weren't likely to ask a girl who frequented pubs and slept around out for a date.

Along with my ever-increasing tolerance for alcohol, I started smoking cigarettes because most of the friends I hung around with did. Smoking was part of my new persona as a carefree bad girl.

I modelled my new self so closely on my new friends that I never even considered what I actually liked myself. I liked the bands they liked, the clothes they liked and the drinks they liked. I even started playing football because some of the girls I hung around with did. I secretly dreaded the games because I hated football. It was a price I willingly paid to belong.

Deep down, I knew I was a phony. I knew I didn't like these bands, clothes or drinks. Some part of me remained detached. I felt I just couldn't be the person that was inside me but I feared losing my new popularity. I didn't have the strength to live without it.

At home, my brothers teased me, as siblings do, but they took it too far. They never really thought about how it hurt me, and I didn't have the same emotional resilience as those who grew up happy and well adjusted. They joked that I was fat, and although I wasn't, they constantly called me "Fat Bum!" It stung. It added to my low self-esteem and even today, you will hardly ever see me wearing clothing that doesn't cover my bum.

My grades at boarding school started to slip and the nuns were becoming a relentless hassle that I didn't want to deal with anymore. I retreated into music and partying and shut everything else in my life out as much as I could.

My father saw the rebellion in me and didn't like it, the tyrant that he was. However, he didn't know the truth because I was getting pretty good at hiding everything I was doing.

With every bottle I drank and every man I was with, I was getting my revenge against the childhood that he and the nuns took away from me. I didn't think about the electric shock therapy when I was drunk, something that I found difficult to forget without the alcohol.

There was a perverse sense of justice there that I did not understand. All I knew was that when I was drinking and partying, it made the painful present less painful.

I was numb and resolved to ignore my father's commands. I took every beating and punishment. I watched disembodied, as if through a TV screen, as my father smashed the sunbed with a hammer, simply because mum enjoyed getting a tan. My brothers received their punishments regularly too, but it was all a cold reality to me now.

As I grew older and increasingly disillusioned, I found it disgusting that a man could subject his daughter to such prolonged punishment over what I chose to wear, when often, rumor had it, he crept off to visit the "girls of pleasure" in the red-light district in Antwerp.

He preached decency but then pooped on the carpet in his friend's house and cleaned himself off with the curtains because he was so inebriated.

He lectured us endlessly about the value of hard work, but he treated those who actually did manual labor with pure contempt.

He once threw a handful of diamonds on the floor in a local pub popular with working class people then laughed and jeered at people scrambling for them.

He punished us for doing anything he felt harmed the dignity of his family name or his precious reputation—which was not at all what he thought it was.

Yet, he also once pulled out a cigar along with a 5,000 Belgian franc note (the average weekly wage at the time was approximately 3,000 Belgian Francs) and set the note on fire and then used it to light his cigar, just to show everyone how powerful and rich he was.

He was nothing like the standards he held for us, and while no one spoke up against him in the town because of his wealth and power as an employer, over the years, the stories about his behavior grew and buried whatever good reputation he once had. He was the only one who didn't realize this. Or, perhaps he did.

I went "ice skating" often, which was my code word for the pub.

I had found a few new popular pubs, further away from my home, and I started to see Maddie more and more.

Maddie often used to come "ice skating" with me, as did another neighbor Annie, who lived across the road from us.

Her older brother used to drive us around to the bars and discotheques and when he was not available, we took our bikes.

Annie's house was often an escape for Lucas, Roger, and me, as Kane never joined us. We used to hang around in her house, eating biscuits and being silly. It was a haven to us because we could relax safely out of our father's sight and we could be "normal" kids in her house.

Having friends made going to church a completely different experience. My brothers and I had all hated going to church with our parents every Sunday; I already had to go to church every single day in boarding school. I sometimes managed to sit at the back with my friends Maddie and Annie by simply walking into the church behind my parents and then joining my friends at the back, while my parents continued up the aisle to their usual pew.

We girls would start whispering about boys and giggling and we really were disruptive on occasion. The priest would sometimes even stop the service and say, "Will the three girls at the back please quieten down and listen." On those occasions, I knew a brutal punishment awaited me but I was determined not to let that control me.

He had always punished us so severely at the slightest excuse and as a teenager, I realized nothing I could do would stop the punishments, so they were no deterrent for me. If I was going to get them, I might as well earn them and enjoy myself when I could.

Scandalous Business

"I love those who can smile in trouble, who can gather strength from distress, and grow brave by reflection. 'Tis the business of little minds to shrink, but they whose heart is firm, and whose conscience approves their conduct, will pursue their principles unto death." – Leonardo da Vinci

1975, Belgium, Age 16

The days streaked by in blank spaces, gaps in my memory from the drinking that had become habitual. I awoke one morning from a dream that would become familiar; I woke with the image of two identical twin girls fresh in my mind, a dear dream that would recur when I was feeling stressed or unhappy.

I just wanted love in my life, so I regularly dreamed about having twin girls, hoping that I would have them when I was older and give them the love I never had. That night, I dreamt that I had taken them on an island holiday, and I had lavished them with love and attention.

My imaginary twin girls were tiny babies in my mind and they gave me such a sense of comfort. It was always a good day when I woke from a dream about my girls. I started those days with the aura of the love that filled those dreams.

By the time I had lived the bar life for over a year, I was well and truly into it, rebellious to my very core and outwardly uncaring, like the world wanted me to be—or so I believed.

I started to pay more attention to how I looked "because of the boys." Mum was always paying for my clothes so I was mostly dressed very smart in expensive designer clothes. However, when hanging around the bars, I wore tight trousers, jeans or a short skirt.

I was no longer thin, as I started to put on weight because of all the drinking and the eating between drinking. We used to believe that the more you ate, the more you could drink.

The way I dressed was different now, and I hid my choices from my father, quickly putting on makeup and changing at Annie's house before going to the bar.

Eventually, I did not see any reason why I should be trapped at boarding school all week with the cruel nuns lording themselves over me, snorting at me in disapproval. I hated them. I was still a pariah at school—the nuns had made sure of that—and so I embraced the label.

Luckily, I was not the only one and managed to make a friend or two. It seemed like some girls just wanted drinking buddies and they weren't bothered about my past *or* present situation. Kate was my best school friend at that time, a nun-hater like I was. Together we hatched a plan to take the afternoon off one Monday, and we planned to head into town to hang out with a gang of rough, local boys we had met the weekend prior.

"See," I told Kate, who had doubted my expert forgery skills, "I've been writing my own notes for a long time. The nuns would find it suspicious if one of my actual parents gave me one, as the writing would be different," I said, showing her my freshly written note.

"It's really good," she admitted as she kept watch for Sister Henrietta's imposing silhouette down the hallway.

"Permission for Christine and her friend Kate to leave on Monday afternoon for a dress fitting in town. Special occasion for an important meeting," I read aloud.

"Aren't the nuns going to call your father and check?" Kate asked me, her brown hair perched in a half-bun, half-pony at the back of her head.

"No way. They would never bother a man as important as my father. He nearly bit their heads off the last time they called him," I reassured her. "All I have to do is look frustrated by it when I give them the letter, and they will believe it," I grinned.

"You are a genius, Christine." She pried open the dorm door a little wider. "Let's get it done then."

I decided to go alone to make it more authentic. One upset teenager could be believed but two...the nuns might have become suspicious.

The exchange went as planned. I handed the note to Sister Henrietta and she scowled at me momentarily. When she established that I was suitably put out by my father's wishes, she signed the note and off I went. Kate was amazed by my boldness.

"All done," I said proudly. "Old square head said we're free to go at 2 p.m."

While the other girls were hard at work in class that day, Kate and I counted down the hours to our orchestrated freedom. At 2 p.m., we rose and took the note to the sister in the front of the classroom, who was blathering on about the First World War. With the flick of a finger, we were allowed to leave. The pair of us grabbed our pre-packed bags and fled the grounds.

A taxi picked us up a short while later and we changed our clothes en route. Good thing mum always gave me spending money.

I wore a tight white top and denim shorts; Kate wore a tight summer dress. Neither outfit would have been acceptable to my mother; she would have been disgusted if an assistant had shown them to her on one of our shopping trips.

We arrived at the bar and to celebrate, we both ordered double vodka tonics and lemon. The boys showed up at 3 p.m., late but ready to party. Damien and Jason were as rebellious as they came and up for anything. They both wore brown leather jackets and insisted on doing four shots each of cheap whisky.

We watched in wonder as they entertained us with their confident smiles and insane hometown stories. When 6 p.m. came around, I knew that we had to head back to boarding school or Sister Henrietta might suspect something was off.

The pair of us did what any drunk, irresponsible teenagers would do; we invited the boys back with us.

They found the idea extremely exciting and followed us into our taxi for the ride to boarding school.

I wasn't worried about my bedwetting, as I knew, if smuggling the boys inside worked, we wouldn't sleep all night anyway, and the boys would have to leave before 5 a.m.

It was easy enough sneaking the boys inside; we knew all of the patrol routes the nuns habitually strolled each night. After signing back in, we doubled back and smuggled Damien and Jason into my dorm room.

From the age of 14, I had my own room in the boarding school, no longer a large room with 50 beds lined up in a row. I still had to do the walk of shame every day—that had never changed during my stay at boarding school. The walk became a routine task during which I just swallowed my feelings and pretended I didn't care.

Damien had brought along a bottle of whisky and some glasses, and we decided that the party was only just getting started. Kate, the boys and I started drinking—fooling around and having a blast. The room might have had flimsy cardboard walls, but at least it was ours.

"Why don't we play strip poker?" Jason recommended, beaming at his friend, who nodded vigorously.

He slammed his cards down on a makeshift table we had fashioned from the trunks at the end of our beds, and the game began.

First, Kate lost her trousers and all eight pieces of jewelry because she insisted that they counted. It wasn't long before the boys lost each of their jackets and their shirts too. The game wore on, a fierce battle of boys versus girls.

"Do you have a smoke for me, Jay?" I picked the boy I liked best, his naked chest staring back at me. He handed me a Camel and quickly lit it with his slick silver Zippo lighter.

It had the word "Fireball" emblazoned on the front, with flames encircling it. I puffed on my cigarette and checked the time: 8:14 p.m.

"The nuns will be coming round in 1 hour for final checks. You'll have to hide under the bed until they're gone."

"Just under the bed?" Jason put his hand on my calf.

"For now," I said, promising a good time.

Kate surfaced from an over the table kiss with Damien; she had just lost her top to a pair of aces. "You too, Christine. Come on, take off your top" Damian insisted, showing me his cards.

I leaned forward and stripped off my tank top, revealing a black satin bra underneath it. "You'd better open the windows and get the deodorant out; it smells like a bar in here," said Kate.

"Last one then, and we can clear away the smell," I said, on my knees now. Jason came up behind me and started kissing my neck. I reached for the bottle of whisky, now less than half full, and poured us each one final shot before we would have to prepare for Sister Henrietta's check-in. Some nights she didn't open the door; she just waited to hear our voices after our name was called. We hoped it was one of those nights.

Jason's hands were all over me now, the excitement of being caught piquing his interest.

"I can't wait," he mumbled to me, ignoring the shot I held for him. I turned and kissed him, topless and exposed, his hands sliding up to my satin bra. Then the door opened.

A cigarette burned helplessly in an ashtray on our trunk-table as Sister Henrietta stepped inside. We all froze for a moment, the two half-naked boys drunk with lust and the two nearly naked girls motionless with the shock of an early visit. I was still holding two shots full of whisky.

"Out! Get out!" Sister Henrietta yelled at the boys, who unfroze, grabbed their clothes and hightailed it out of our dorm room at top speed.

Kate and I were left with the outraged nun, whom we both rightly feared.

"Jezebels from hell!" she boomed, reaching for the cigarette and swishing away the smoke. It was heavier than we had thought. We dressed quickly, though drunkenly, and found ourselves sitting in the headmistress's office ten minutes later, our ears nearly torn off from the march there.

"You will both be expelled for your actions." She crossed her arms and seethed.

Christine Clayfield

"Drinking, smoking, and consorting with boys in the dorm rooms are strictly forbidden. I will be calling your parents in the morning to pick you up and take you from this school. You will not be allowed to return here. That is all."

Kate and I returned to our dorm rooms with another hailstorm of comments from Sister Henrietta.

"You will both end up dead on the street if you continue like this," she snapped. "Now pack up your things. You are gone from here at first light."

With that, she marched back down the hallway, taking her anger with her.

Kate then slipped back into my room looking shocked.

"She took my smokes," she said after a lingering silence, and the two of us burst out laughing.

"She forgot to take the whisky, haha," I replied.

"Shit! I didn't hear her at all. The hardest footsteps in the school and we get caught on the night she decides to wear slippers! Oh my God. I'm in trouble. My father is going to kill me," I told her, flopping down onto the bed.

"Mine too," she admitted, producing a second packet of cigarettes from her bag and lighting one.

"Might as well. We're already screwed." She had a point.

After a few more drinks, Kate returned to her own room.

The morning came and with it my mother, who picked me up and drove me back to the house in silence.

"I'm not going to tell your father...the details." She spoke carefully as we pulled up into our yawning driveway. "You were caught drinking, and that's that."

Good thing my mother had more sense than I did. My father never had time to go to school meetings due to his busy schedule.

I did not even consider what it might do to my father's mood if he discovered that his daughter was ruining his family name by sleeping around town. I nodded and faced the music inside. My father was furious but I could see that he understood the lure of liquor therefore, surprisingly, my punishment was light as I was sent to my room for just one day.

Turns out that being expelled from that hellish school was a pretty great thing. My father pulled strings to get me in at another boarding school in the area, and the matter was put to rest. I never heard from Kate again though. I suspect her parents believed I was a bad influence on her, which I probably was.

My father made sure that the whole scandalous business was hushed up, even though he did not even realize what had really transpired that night. It was the only thing keeping me from a week in the cellar, which I could not bear nearly as gracefully as Oliver did. I would sooner run away than deal with that.

A new school also meant new classmates who would laugh at my scar and my bedwetting. I no longer cared. I didn't plan to spend much time with them anyway. Now I had a magic potion to take the sting from their words and I could get it at any pub.

At home, my mother was keeping a closer watch on me than ever before. She did this with such vigor that my father started paying more attention to me as well, which I did not want or need in my life. My new school had different nuns. I soon found out that this did not mean that they were better, nicer, or less cruel than the others had been.

One thing was good: I no longer had to get up every day at 5 a.m. to attend church, as we only had to go to church once a week in this school. Another difference in this school was that one week was from Monday morning to Friday afternoon. This meant more time for me to get to the pub.

The biggest and best difference: my friend Maddie went to the same school. She had been there for several years, so she had an already established group of friends and I didn't want to demand her attention. Nevertheless, it felt good that she was there too and we did see each other on and off. When we did spend time together, we told each other everything, we enjoyed each other's company, talking and laughing.

I settled into a familiar misery, as my bed-wetting became a novelty among fresh judgmental hearts. It renewed a longstanding pain that had dulled in me and my behavior only became more erratic and careless.

Because of the hawk-eye I had on me, sneaking out was difficult for a while, so I would sit and listen to tunes in my bedroom, crying my eyes out. Such was the depth of my despair that my body would fall into a fit of uncontrollable trembling as I heaved, rocked, and cried until my head pounded and I felt completely dead inside.

Being a teenager is hard enough without an abusive father, a prominent scar and an inescapable bed-wetting problem. My self-esteem was so low that I found it difficult to make friends in my new school and I was back at home on the weekends without any escape. Music was my constant friend, a melodic companion that brought me through those rough times when I just wanted the world to end.

One week at my new school was particularly brutal. A gang of four girls entered the toilet room, where I was washing my hands. All of a sudden, without warning, they began pushing me around and proceeded to kick and punch me several times.

They forced me into the last toilet cubicle, wedging a chair between the door and the sink. I was trapped. One of them jeered at me, with a clearly hurtful tone: "You can wee as much as you want in there. If you wee enough, you might not do it in your bed tonight, for a change." The last thing I heard as they walked away was them giggling to each other. I was stuck in there for two hours before I was found.

I was burning with rage inside. I held myself together with a promise that no matter what, I was going to sneak out to see Elise and Lina that Friday night. My father was home and in a foul mood but was permanently connected to the phone in his office because something terrible had happened at work.

I arrived home with my mother that Friday to his voice roaring through the passageways of our house and resonating through every bedroom. I greeted him by nodding before running upstairs to claim my normal private space.

I could not wait any longer; I would sneak out and make a crazy dash for the pub. I popped downstairs to check on things; mum was already making dinner.

My father was in the lounge and railed on about a diamond deal that Oliver had interfered in now that they were working together. Lucas and Roger were the unlucky listeners.

Delicious smells permeated the kitchen –it was chicken soup, my mum's special recipe, tonight. Hungry as I was, I wanted out. I made a show of getting some juice, purposefully yawning widely to convince everyone that I was tired enough to go to bed without supper.

"You're not fooling anyone," Kane said to me as I passed him on the way to my bedroom. "If you try to sneak out, dad is going to catch you."

I scowled at him and brushed him aside, opening my door and slamming it on his negativity. Since the expulsion, I had used every trick in the book to get away from this house but few were successful. I would have to wait a few minutes to make my escape.

I had to get away—another moment of living in that trap was going to make me want to strangle myself. I went downstairs as quiet as a mouse, opened the front door, and let the early night air in. It was cool and brisk and I could barely see where to place my first step. All I could hear were the sounds of night: insects and their predators.

I sneaked out the door. As I turned, I nearly leapt out of my skin. There stood my father, smoking a fat cigar, the wisps of smoke curling upwards into the wind.

"Heading out tonight, Christine?" A simmering volcano under his offhand query.

"Just going for a walk," I lied, my breath catching in my throat.

"A walk? Without supper?" He squinted, already knowing the answer.

"I'm not hungry…just need some air." A small lie that I hoped would get me off the hook.

"Well then, you can trim the grass tomorrow to get the exercise you need. That will give you some fresh air! For now, go upstairs and straight to bed. Without supper." He eyed me menacingly behind his smoke.

"Yes, Dad," I said, crestfallen that I could not get away. I went back into the house, and he followed.

"And Christine, don't think of going for another walk again. I am not stupid, and I know exactly where you planned to walk. You are never allowed to go to the pub again. I heard about the people you are hanging around with. They are not the sort of people we associate with in this family. Of course, you are so selfish and so foolish that you would not think of that. You'd be happy to associate with any lowlife. You lack the intelligence to understand the consequences. Lucky for you, I am the head of this house, and I won't tolerate any more of this idiocy from you. All the fun at the pub is pretend fun; all the friends you hang around with are pretend friends. You are just too stupid to see it."

My heart dropped onto the floor, flopping around like a dying fish—at least that is how it felt in my stomach. I dared not challenge my father or admit that I was sneaking off to the bar.

I would not let my father impose his rules on me. I might not be able to go to the bar tonight, but I was going to find something to eat. I went to my bedroom and came face to face with Kane, who had been leaning in on my door.

"What are you doing?" I asked him in a dead tone.

"Dad told me to watch you. You are not to eat anything until after your punishment tomorrow," he recited back to me like a military commander instructed to keep a prisoner in their cell.

"I'm your sister…you're just going to let me starve?"

Kane smiled an ugly smile. "I told you he would know if you tried to sneak out tonight. He's on to you. He'll find out about all of those boyfriends you keep stashed away at the bar. Then you'll get what you deserve."

"You are just like him—a cruel bastard!" I hissed, slamming the door in Kane's face. Three thuds on the door let me know he wasn't going anywhere.

"Call me all the names you like, Christine. I'd rather be like him than like you. Slut." I fell back against the door and cried for some time. My own brother couldn't tell right from wrong.

I pulled myself together. I gathered my wits and went to sit at my second window, the one facing Annie's house. Annie and I had come to an agreement after a previous punishment of bed without supper. I would signal her with my flashlight: three flashes meant that I was being punished.

She would signal me back: three flashes meant that she would go to the chip shop and get chips for me. She would put them, in a plastic bag, in our little makeshift rope system, and then she would tug to let me know to pull it up. We had never actually tried it out until now, so I wasn't even sure she would remember. I had carefully explained to her how to avoid being detected by my father's security cameras. She couldn't go near the front door but had to creep along the side wall of the house. And of course, she could not make any noise.

I flashed my light at her three times, and then I waited. A few minutes passed, and I was starting to give up hope when I saw the three flashes in reply.

I scurried to the back of my closet, where I had stashed the rope under a pile of clothes that I was sure my father would never notice.

It wasn't long enough by far, so I stripped my bed and tied the sheet to the end. I waited for what felt like an eternity, sure that Kane or, worse, my father would come in and catch me with the rope hanging out of the window. I was already in enough trouble and I didn't want to get Annie in trouble as well.

Finally, I felt a little tug on the rope and carefully pulled the chips up. A while later I saw Annie back at her window, flashing her torch once and I flashed the torch once more, as my silent thank you to her.

From that day on, I never went hungry in my bedroom again because of Annie. It was a small victory but one that kept me going when nothing else did. I was satisfied that I could achieve things without my father ever knowing. That was my rope line to freedom.

The Tiny Dirty Room

"It's never easy to leave one's home, especially when there are only closed doors ahead of you." – Nadia Hashimi

2016, Belgium, after visit to hospital, Age 57

With not much change in my mother's condition, my husband and I headed back to her house for the evening. Oliver had returned to the hospital to stay with her, and I told him I would be back first thing in the morning. The frantic travel and the intense emotion of spending the day with my unconscious, elderly mother in the hospital combined with the onslaught of horrible memories had left me completely exhausted and overwhelmed. Going to my mother's house did not help.

The old house was full of memories, echoes from our childhood and the memorabilia that we had collected over the years. My husband went in first with our luggage as I followed behind. Looking up at the house, it had never been a friendly or loving place, and I dreaded entering it.

We were greeted by Lucas and Roger, who told us they were heading to the chip shop. My slight sense of relief was short lived. I heard footsteps on the stairs and a man stepped into the room.

It was Kane. Of all my brothers, Kane had always been the most distant. Different from the rest of us, he was the one child my father liked, with his brilliant school results and sharp, hard countenance. None of us had been close to Kane or got along with him, especially as teens. He never drank and did not hang out at bars like the rest of us, and he had judged us harshly for it.

He was also quick to throw us under the bus as far as our father was concerned, telling on us or leading father with questions meant to incite his rage.

Worse still was his moral compass, twisted by the man he had modelled himself on. Kane trotted down the last few steps and greeted my family with a formal "Hi, everyone."

His belly had grown wider over the years, fat from the wealth he had built on the shoulders of my father's fortune. Roger and Lucas seemed to shrink back when he entered the room.

"Let's put our bags upstairs," I said to my husband, leading him to my old bedroom. I walked over to the window where Annie had sent me package after package of food and took a few deep breaths to steady my nerves. I had nothing to fear from my family now. I was an independent adult woman but I still felt menaced by my past and seeing Kane was harder than I had expected.

"You all right, Christine?" My husband came over and took my hand. I must have seemed a different person to him in that space.

"Oh yes, just worried about mum."

After Roger shouted through the house that the chips had arrived, we headed down to settle in for a family dinner in my old childhood home. The chips were satisfying and laden with nostalgia; it always was when we ordered them. As kids, my father rarely allowed us to eat junk food, and so as adults, it became a luxury of the most special kind.

Kane spun a pen in his hand that our father had given him. He just studied his phone as we listened to Roger and Lucas swap stories of our mother when we were younger.

Kane didn't join in with the reminiscing. "She was never a mother to me."

I shook my head and tried hard to ignore him and how he blamed everything on our mother. It was misplaced of course, but for a man like Kane, life was easier if he could blame his problems on other people.

His less than perfect childhood was blamed on our mum. It felt like sea salt grinding its way through my stomach.

After doing everything he could to cozy up to our father, Kane once told mum that it was her fault our father was so abusive to us, as she never did enough to stop him.

"Why don't we put some music on?" Roger suggested, sensing the mounting tension.

"Don't bother. I'm going home," Kane replied.

Richard and I went back upstairs to my bedroom while the past beat inside me like a second heart.

1977, Belgium, Age 18

Despite my grades and lack of interest in school, I made it all the way through primary and secondary school. I don't know if my teachers detected some sign of hope in me that I didn't, or if they simply kept moving me along out of fear of my father. His name, his wealth and his wrath were no secret to them.

At 18, I wanted to become a veterinarian, as I loved animals but my father wouldn't allow it. He said I needed "a proper job." Instead, I drifted on to a two-year Public Relations and Communications course in Antwerp.

Lucas did the same course and Oliver was working in the diamond industry in Antwerp, so I saw both of them often in local bars. For me, that meant a lot of free drinks, as Oliver often paid for me, something that I took for granted at the time.

I had finally escaped the many horrors of boarding school. My father rented a room for me in a student house. I had the privacy necessary to conceal my bedwetting. Yes, I was 18. I was an adult and I still woke in shamefully damp sheets every morning.

I travelled home most weekends, as I didn't have a washing machine, to wash my sheets and clothes. Still, I was making progress as nobody would find out about my bedwetting.

I had been told by several specialists that my scar would fade with time but it never did. I had the first of three operations on my scar, so I was hopeful of at least removing that very obvious blight on my life. My optimism was misguided.

There was a slight improvement but the scar was still quite visible and would be for years to come.

The absence of love, for far too long, and all the misery because of it, had completely robbed me of the ability to love.

The next two years blended together; a cocktail of boys, sex and drinking that never seemed to end. I lived in utter open rebellion and found savage pleasure in doing so, causing trouble wherever I went, even though the only person I was hurting was myself.

Blind to the impact of my choices, I made these mistakes for quite some time. The drinking persisted and increased, as did my appetite for attention. When I got the feeling that a boy liked me, I would feel happy. It was only later in life that I realized they only liked me because I was easy prey. In the second year of the course, I won the "drinker of the year" trophy. One of my newly-found friends won the "mattress of the year" award.

Like me, Roger had always enjoyed music. It could not have been easy being the youngest, growing up in that house, and I believe Roger found an outlet that worked for him and made him happy: his record collection. I would sometimes watch him arrange them or play them when he needed to drown out the day. Music gave him a voice, and 16-year-old Roger wanted nothing more than to become a DJ.

One weekend while my brothers and I were home, our father had business in Antwerp and chose to stay there overnight. As a result, I woke up early and helped my mum prepare a relaxed breakfast, which Lucas, Roger and I enjoyed at the table in the dining room.

Kane was upstairs studying, not for any kind of test but because he liked to study in his spare time to ensure that he did well in his end of year exams at university. Of all of us, he was the only one to attend university, and he wore it as a badge of honor, which made my father very proud indeed.

After breakfast, we all retreated to our various spaces: Lucas went into the garden to play tennis, my mum started working on her needlepoint, and Roger and I went upstairs to play music.

I lay on my bed with the door open, reading a magazine whilst the music of Neil Diamond, a favorite of mine, was playing in the background.

Roger went to his room and closed the door to play his records on his stereo and to practice mixing songs together. About 20 minutes later, Kane was knocking at his door demanding Roger to be quiet so that he could study. The music from Roger's room was not loud at all.

"Turn it down! Now!" Kane shouted, hammering on the door again five minutes later. Roger told him where to stick his books and carried on playing his music with the door closed. Then the unthinkable happened. My father arrived home from his evening away in town.

Whenever he came back from one of these overnight stays, he was tense and on edge. I heard the front door shut downstairs, even though we were three stories up and playing music. The mood in the house changed instantly, as it always did when my father got home. Kane seemed delighted that our father had arrived in time to hear this fight.

As heavy, careful footsteps made their way up the staircase, Kane projected his voice even louder. "Turn off the damn music. I'm trying to study!"

The footsteps paused for a second then hurried a little until my father passed by my doorway. I could hear everything from where I was laying.

"What is going on here? What's with all of this shouting in my house?" my father demanded.

Kane was happy to explain.

"Roger has been blaring music out of his room and I can't concentrate on what I'm studying. I asked him to turn it down, but he's ignoring me!" He studied my father's reaction.

"Maybe he can't hear you," my father said, trying the handle. It was locked.

The fact that the door was locked and that he had tried to gain entry into a space in his house that he could not, enraged him.

"Boy! Open this door. Open this door. Now!" came his booming voice, no longer calm but instead brief and sudden like a bullet.

The music level dropped, and I hurried to my bedroom door to see what was happening with Roger. Click. The door unlocked. My father pushed it open the second it did, causing Roger to stumble backwards after the door knocked him off balance.

"What?" complained Roger, his face red and his eyes fearful. "Don't what me, boy. Your brother asked you to turn down the music. Now do it!" my father ordered.

Kane smiled smugly as Roger stood his ground. "It wasn't even loud. Did you hear it when you came up here?"

"That's not the point. You are disturbing him. Now turn it down, or there will be hell to pay."

My father switched off Roger's stereo and closed his door. I had the feeling that was not the end of it. My father had not made it down three stairs before Roger's music came back on, now at full volume. Roger, being 16, no longer listened to our father without protest, and he became very rebellious over the years. There was a scent in the air, whisky mingled with sweat and cigars, along with bad decisions.

My father detonated, stamping down the hall again until he reached Roger's door. It was locked. I could not help but feel like Roger had made a fatal error in judgment. I peeked through my door at the scene, hoping that Roger would switch off the music. A beating was coming; even Kane knew that.

The rage that infected my father propelled him against the door, which he shunted off its hinges by his shoulder ramming. It only took three tries before he was in the room with Roger.

The music was blaring louder than ever, so my father did what any unreasonable man would do. He grabbed Roger's stereo—his prized possession—and threw it out the window.

The glass smashed as the stereo plummeted hard towards the ground. I could not keep myself away any longer.

I arrived at Roger's doorframe to see my father half beating Roger, half-tearing through his record collection, smashing each and every album. The renewed silence was filled with Roger's shouting– and mine. I could not take it anymore.

"What the hell is wrong with you? That's his life! He loves his music! You are destroying his most precious possessions!"

I shouted at my father but Kane had arrived, and he held me back. "Stop! What are you doing?" screamed Roger, completely helpless as all of his music was shattered into bits on his bedroom floor. He did not even feel the punches when they landed.

At one point, my father had Roger against the back wall, and he saw where the stereo had landed...on his own car. Of course, he blamed Roger for this. He exploded again, beating Roger while instructing him to obey him. Watching the violence of the moment and the unjust outcome of the incident, my mind went blank with hatred. I had to get out of there.

I would not spend another minute of my life in that house, with that man. He was nothing but a force of destruction, ruining everyone's lives around him. I pulled free from Kane as he continued to watch my father work on Roger. Throwing my hands up, I tore back into my bedroom and gathered up what I could—some clothes and some personal items. I fled my room and nearly collided with my father in the hallway.

"And where are you going?" he demanded, his face burnt red from the anger and thunder he had shown Roger.

"I'm leaving. And I'm never coming back!" I declared frantically, taking three stairs at a time. I could hear him coming after me, but I was faster. I made it down the stairs quickly; then burst out of the front door.

"Where are you going?" my father called to me from the front door.

"Anywhere is better than where you live!" I shouted back to him, seething. It was the final straw for me.

After 18 years of living with his random moods and under the constant threat of violence, I was done with it.

I felt hysterical and angry, like the road beneath me would split with every heavy footstep. I walked for a time to let myself cool off. Then I stopped. Suddenly it hit me that I had nowhere to go. I had not considered my lack of real friends or the fact that I could not sleep in somebody else's house because of my bedwetting.

Not for one second did I think about what it would do to mum if I ran away from home. I have always regretted that.

There was no place for me to go. With my higher education course finished, it had only taken me a month to find a reason to leave my home forever. Now that I had done it, I was stuck with the consequences of my decision. I was desperate and desperately lonely. I had no money, no job, no food, no real friends, no love and no home to live in.

The only two friends that could have helped me were Maddie and Annie; but as they were my neighbors, that wasn't exactly a good solution as my father would have to walk just a few steps to drag me by my hair back into our house. I needed to get much further away than that.

I walked for what seemed like hours, wandering from house to house trying to find a pub friend who could help me. I begged them to help me. All of them. They all said no; one after another they closed the door in my face, like I was a door-to-door salesman. That was when I realized I was well and truly alone.

Friendless and penniless, my feet took me to a familiar place: the bar I had been frequenting over the last few years. Surely, someone would help me get on my feet. I pushed open the red padded door and stepped into my favorite party joint in the village. With nothing but a little bag of personal items with me, I felt foolish for not taking anything of real value.

"Hi, Mike, is Janine in?"

Saddling up to the bar, I waited for the barman to call Janine, the fiery-haired manager of the place. I had spent many evenings drinking with her and felt like she might give me a job if I asked, as she knew I would draw in the boys to her pub.

Janine sidled over from a back room, wearing blue cleaning gloves. I explained my situation to her.

"I need a place to stay for a while, until I can figure things out. Please let me stay here. I'll work to cover the rent," I said, wearing my sincerest face.

She considered me and then said, "Follow me. If you can live in here, you can stay. I could use a good cleaning woman."

Janine led me upstairs to a small, dark room cluttered with mops, buckets, empty bottles and other junk.

"Start by cleaning this room. This is where you sleep." I thanked her and did as I was told. The room was positively filthy and much smaller than I had hoped once all the stuff had been moved out of it. The windowless room was cold and dark. It stank of old cigarettes and spilled booze, and some of the stickiness would not come off the walls.

One single, bare, flickering bulb hung from the ceiling. So this was the place that would be better than home, this tiny, dirty, filthy room. I settled in as best I could. A man I met at the bar gave me a second-hand mattress, and I used the bar toilets.

An old tin bucket became my bath, and I had to hand wash myself with water fetched from the sinks in the toilet rooms each morning. It was no hotel, but I was free.

After just 2 days working as a cleaner, Janine told me to serve drinks. She told me that her customers liked me, males and females; she thought I would attract extra customers to her pub.

A week into my new life at the pub and I was drinking like there was no tomorrow. I found the only way I could sleep in that place was to be drunk.

I covered my mattress with tons of plastic bags to protect it from my bedwetting. At home, I had a plastic cover for my mattress but I didn't bring it with me, and I didn't have any money to buy a new cover.

I also didn't have any money to buy decent clothes, so for the first time in my life, I started to dress pretty scruffy—but I didn't even care.

Even though I lived in impossibly dirty surroundings, in constant contact with men that wanted to take advantage of me, I was free—free from fear, free from violence, and free from being told how useless I was.

For a while, it felt good. Filth was an improvement over fear. Janine gave me some old bedsheets. My new upstairs paradise smelt like urine after a few days because I was forced to save up my wet sheets and take them to the launderette when I had time and money.

I never let Janine find out that I wet the bed and hid it from everyone at the pub. I obsessively sprayed air freshener around the room and would spend my last penny on a new can. Luckily, Janine gave me her only key to my room.

Although I was drinking a lot, I wasn't eating very much, so I lost weight and returned to a size small.

One Friday morning Oliver walked into the bar. He was working for my father at the time but was looking to make his own way in the diamond industry. He wore a suit and had a brown briefcase that made him look very affluent. That morning, Oliver was not there to see me—he had come to drink.

"Hey, sis, I heard you finally got out of that place." He waved as I approached him at the bar.

"Yeah, I couldn't take it anymore."

"Dad's furious. I'm glad I found you here. Mum has been worried sick. Can I get you a drink?" Anxiety oozed from his pores. I nodded.

"Where are you staying now?"

"Here. I'm living upstairs." I was concerned as Oliver was talking rather seriously, unlike him.

"Are you all right, Oliver?"

He blinked furiously, wiping nervous sweat from his face.

"No, no, I'm not all right. I'm still getting over the shock. Last night I was held at gunpoint in my house. The robbers threatened to kill my family if I wouldn't open the diamond safe. They stole my diamonds. I was handcuffed, thrown in the boot of a car and dumped in the woods."

It was rough news of the worst kind. The diamond industry is built on trust and reputation, so Oliver had diamonds in consignment from another diamond dealer.

I knew that a blow like this could end Oliver's career. He looked like a man sentenced to death.

"Oh my God, Oliver! Have you filed a report with the police?"

"Yes, but it's not going to bring them back. They're gone. Millions. Gone."

My situation was bad but I felt deeply for Oliver. He had been working hard to make a name for himself in the industry, but he did not seem to have my father's killer instinct. That he had passed down to only one son and it was not Oliver. In many ways, he was too kind to be in diamonds, where business was often dirty and strategic.

People used to call us the "Ewing family" from the Dallas TV series, which was very popular at the time. It was an American soap television series revolving around a wealthy family with intrigue, money, scandal, seductions and family crises. What happened to Oliver could have been a storyline in one of the episodes in that series.

Life at the bar was grueling and hard in a way I had not yet experienced in my young life. The living conditions were so poor that I was sick all the time from breathing in that smoky filth all day, every day. Because I was there all the time, I also started drinking more and more.

A customer would come into the bar in the morning and buy me a round, and I would gladly drink it. I drank anything anyone put in front of me, desperate to wipe out my childhood and the situation in which I now found myself.

In a way, I was grateful for the alcohol because it helped suspend the reality of living in a dirty closet, without anything in the world but my skin. As soon as I was tipsy, I became funny, people told me. So, … I was often tipsy.

At the pub, as soon as I was tipsy, I always told funny stories, said odd things, acted silly and was quick with jokes; people were cracking up with laughter.

Janine told me I had a dry sense of humor and her customers liked that. She knew that especially the male customers loved hanging around me.

Very often, during my breaks, a man would break through the crowd, I would kiss him and often I would end up having sex with him somewhere. I couldn't take him to my room above the pub because of the urine smell that persisted despite all the air freshener.

I became a whirling, drunken wreck of a young person—consuming more alcohol than should be legal, and sharing myself with men who didn't care about me at all.

I did hang out a lot with Annie and Maddie, and we constantly found new pubs to visit on my days off. Each time we went out together, we competed to see which one of us would kiss a boy first that night.

By now, I was pretty good at seducing men and I knew what they liked, so I was often the winner. I thought at the time that I was a winner, but 'winning' looks very different in hindsight.

Funny how you can go from being one of the richest people in the village, to someone who cannot even afford a square meal. That was me.

I was turned out and beaten down by a life I had never asked for but in all of this rampant suffering, I genuinely thought I was having a blast. Rebellion rested on me like an iron casket over the next few years.

The freedom that tiny, dirty closet-room gave me was of incalculable value. For as long as I live, I will never forget that dingy room.

Gradual Incline

"What you believe is very powerful. If you have toxic emotions of fear, guilt and depression, it is because you have wrong thinking, and you have wrong thinking because of wrong believing." – Joseph Prince

1980, Belgium, Age 21

I thought I was living a life of freedom, but in reality, I did not have the slightest notion what it meant to be free. I stumbled into every trap that was set around me, looking for the familiar prisons that felt like home.

I moved from boyfriend to boyfriend, my self-worth constantly teetering on the brink of no return.

Then Harry walked into the bar one day with stride and attitude. He had light brown hair in a quiff, blazing eyes, perfect figure and a black leather jacket. At 21, I could not have resisted him, even if I had been sober.

Soon we were drinking and chatting together, flirting and laughing. For every funny bar story I shared, Harry had five, each funnier and wilder than the last.

"I like cars and having fun as much as anyone," he told me, flashing his charming smile at me.

Janine rolled her eyes from behind the bar and continued stacking glasses. I could see she wanted to tell me something. I had just finished my shift and was a little too drunk to understand her dubious glances. A few more people joined us, and Harry turned to engage a few other girls who had pulled up their chairs.

Feeling slighted but in a good mood, I staggered off to the bathroom to freshen up. I returned to find Harry facing me squarely as if waiting for my return.

"There she is!" He showed me my seat, a wide smile on his face. His sudden change in attitude had come from the conversation he had enjoyed with the other girls while I was applying my lipstick in the bathroom. He asked them who I was and they told him.

"Her father's Frank Lemmens, the richest man in Keldonk," they said, Janine told me later that evening. By then it was too late. I was hopelessly smitten. He didn't need to make any further effort but he did anyway. "I like you, Christine, you're special."

It was the first time a man had ever said that to me. It was as if I'd been struck by lightning. The air was electric and I was floating. I grew besotted with Harry and everything he was.

I loved the fact that he liked me even more than I liked him. Everything was a whirl; he said he needed me, he said he loved me and I believed him. We drank constantly but he treated me like a queen—and that left me more drunk than the alcohol. Some girls might have been suspicious of Harry's instant devotion but not young me.

I wanted to ask Maddie for her opinion about Harry, as I heard that her boyfriend knew Harry well, but I completely lost contact with her. I heard that she also ran away from her home. I asked around but nobody seemed to know where Maddie was living, so I was constantly left wondering if she was okay.

"I love you," Harry said to me one day over a drink. "We should move in together and get you away from this horrible bar." Harry was my longest relationship ever.

It had been the best year in my memory, or at least a year without abuse from my family home. I started drinking less, as I didn't have to impress the boys any longer now that I had a "proper" boyfriend. I detested living in my tiny closet in the bar, so I jumped at the chance to move in to a proper house with my boyfriend.

At last, I could have a normal life! I imagined Harry and me getting married and eventually having children. I was more than ready to leave the bar behind.

The first thing I did was apply for a "real" job at a company called Agfa. Despite my terrible study habits, I had a functional level of fluency in five languages, and that landed me the position. Today I can speak five languages: Dutch (Flemish), Spanish, German, French and English.

I used my language skills constantly, developing them and expanding them where I could. Thanks to Lucy and our imaginary language, learning languages was easy for me. I got the job at Agfa. I was secretary to the sales manager for France, Germany and Spain for a specific type of camera film and took pride in my work.

We found a small, one-bedroom house in Berden, a small village, three kilometers from where I used to live with my family. It was an old house that we could afford with my salary and Harry's unemployment money that he received from the government.

He spoke often about getting a job but never seemed to get to that point. Instead, he would tinker with cars, hang around in bars, go to the casino and complain about money. Any work he did do on his friends' cars was rewarded with a pint instead of any real cash.

I had to start paying more attention to my appearance because my job was in an office environment. I was no longer dressed scruffy but I dressed as you would expect for a secretarial look. I had to spend some money on some nice, but cheap clothes. Anything I could wear around my neck or in my ears to draw attention away from my scar, I did.

I found out that my father heard about Harry and disapproved of him, of course. That didn't bother me, but Kane's reaction did. He was eager to stay on my father's good side because he believed that would help him create his own diamond empire. Kane got married shortly after I moved in with Harry, and when I arrived at his wedding reception, he threw me out.

"You are not invited. I don't want you here!" He charged across the party hall at me. "You are not welcome. Get out now, or I will call the police."

I stood frozen for a moment with the guests staring at me. My father was drinking at the bar, my mother and my other brothers looked as helpless as ever. I left without a word, deeply hurt.

Because my father disapproved of Harry, Kane threw me out of his own wedding, in the hopes of scoring more points with our father.

Things changed the day Harry and I moved into that house. It was as if someone had flipped a personality switch in his brain, and he now believed he could treat me however he wanted to.

I told Harry about my bedwetting before we moved in together. He seemed fine with it and didn't act like it was a problem. Then came the first day that he actually woke up in wet sheets at 6 a.m.

He snorted. "Looks like living together is going to be a lot of fun! What the hell! Is this how it's going to be every day? It had better not be! It stinks and it's disgusting! Take these sheets off the bed immediately, put clean sheets on and you go downstairs so I can sleep a few more hours in a dry bed."

I lived with him now, and that meant—in Harry's mind— that he owned me. "You're getting fat," he'd comment often, then "You're revolting," or "You're a stupid cow," or "You're a lazy bitch."

It was a gradual incline until, in that first month, his taunts became, "You're a waste of space," and "You're not working hard enough," and "Who would put up with you?" The more Harry drank, the nastier he was towards me, like deep down inside he actually loathed me.

I was confused, tired and worried about my situation. I knew I'd need to be self-sufficient, I didn't want to go back to the bar. Having that brief glimmer of hope changed something in me. I decided to study and improve my education, so I went to evening school to study accountancy.

I had grown up in a wealthy environment, in a big house with staff and I wanted the same for myself as I aged.

Harry loved the idea of having more money to spend but disliked the fact that I was studying in order to make that happen. He would say as much and then would go out gambling and drinking all night with my hard-earned cash.

Harry spent his days tinkering with every car in the village but refused to check mine. I drove my old banger of a car to and from my classes, frequently running late because it would simply stop in the middle of the road. I would have to get out of the car and start pushing it whilst holding the wheel. I could rarely manage to get the car to the side of the road on my own. It was deeply embarrassing. Sometimes people could see I was struggling and would stop to help. The times when nobody stopped, I had to beg them to help with waves of desperation and my hands in a praying position.

That was when I decided that if I ever had children and I could afford it, I would buy them a brand-new car. Sparing someone you love the indignity of poverty and embarrassment is a priceless gift to give.

Strange things started to happen whenever I left the house to go to my classes. After pulling into a garage because my car kept cutting out, I was told I had salt in my petrol tank and that the fuel had turned to sludge. The carburetor needed replacing, fuel lines, and tank too—a total mess.

When I complained that kids had put salt in my car, Harry just said, "You shouldn't go to those classes anyway." I should have realized that he had done it, but I didn't. We started arguing and fighting all the time but each time it would get bad, he would apologize. Harry was a master at apologies and I always believed him. I wanted things to get better.

Despite his apologies, his drinking and penchant for humiliating me became worse and worse the longer we lived together. He hated that I earned more money than he did. He simply could not cope with that at all.

He came from a lower social background and his parents were on benefits. He couldn't stand that I found a job, that I was more successful than him.

The humiliations became unbearable—"good for nothing woman," "bitch," and "selfish runt" were his favorite slogans to hurl at me regularly.

Eventually, insulting me at home wasn't enough for him. One evening when we were drinking down at the pub, he announced to the entire room that I wet the bed every night. "Yeah, she does, imagine that!" he beamed, sending my heart plummeting into my shoes.

"I have a medical condition," I lied, choking on the judgement of the people around me. I pretended not to care but at the same time, I was deeply ashamed.

I came back from a class on another evening and he was very, very drunk. He started swearing and wrecking the house. Before I could say anything, he grabbed me by my hair and threw me out onto the road.

This became a regular occurrence. Every time he threw me out, I would go to the bar and sit there until he came to find me and apologize. I knew the atmosphere was getting worse but I blamed myself for it. As a Catholic, I was taught to forgive and forget and as someone who grew up being abused, I just wasn't that shocked by his behavior.

Harry always seemed so sincere and so I forgave him. I was either numb to it or too deep inside of it to see how closely it mirrored the treatment I fought so desperately to escape from my own father. Everything I had done as a child provoked the man, who needed little provocation. My father was a ticking time bomb of abuse and I bore his torments in silent resignation until that day when I had finally had enough and ran out. Here I was, plunged neck deep right back in the exact same thing.

A few more of Harry's greatest hits included his growing gambling problem and rubbing my face into my wet sheets every morning like I was a dog that needed better training.

"Look at this!" he would shout at me, holding my neck and forcing my face down onto the wet sheet. "You need to stop this! Look at this. It's not right! You are disgusting!"

When I did manage to go to evening classes, he sometimes travelled to the school and simply removed my car and took it home, so when the class was finished, I reported the car as stolen to the police only to find out later that Harry had picked up the car just to give me hassle. The next evening my car wasn't there, I no longer reported it to the police but took the train home instead.

I was breathing the familiar air of shame and fear. He said he loved me. I made excuses for him and believed I could change him. When he wanted sex, I agreed—whether or not I wanted it. Not that he really asked. It would be more accurate to say I complied without fighting back. Harry was becoming sexually violent. Instead of wanting to give me any pleasure, he instead seemed to take pleasure in treating me brutally.

Months rolled by as Harry's disdain for me grew. I excused away the verbal assaults and angry outbursts. He was just drunk. He was just upset. He didn't know what he was doing.

At the end of every month, he demanded my pay check. "Give me your money," he would say brusquely. "Give it to me or you're going to make me hit you."

And so, I gave it to him. I never saw a cent of the money I spent all month earning. Harry took it all and used it to go out drinking and gambling. We often didn't have food in the house, and I lived in a manner that was scarcely better than the pub closet; but at least there, I could keep what I earned.

I believed Harry would change—his apologies filled me with hope and comfort. I saw flickers of love and kindness in him but eventually they became like rare butterflies drifting off with the morning wind.

No Longer a Daughter

"Denial, panic, threats, anger -those are very human responses to feeling guilt." – Joshua Oppenheimer

1981, Belgium, Age 22

Outside of the movies, I hadn't really seen anything better growing up. Harry was better than my father was. At least Harry apologized. My father was a well-respected man in the diamond industry. For all of his faults, he was much loved by the community for what he did for the small village of Keldonk's economy, employing over 500 people. And yet, at home, we saw something very different. So, I grew up assuming most fathers were like mine and that what happened at home was nothing like what happened in public.

Amidst all of this stress and turmoil, one day, out of the blue, my father knocked on my door. I had not spoken to him in years, yet there he was standing on my doorstep.

"Dad?" I said to him, noticing the thinning hair and skinnier-framed man that stood before me.

I opened the door and in he walked. It was like having an ice sculpture come to life and decide to visit you in your home. I did not know what to say to him. I had not said a word to him since the day he beat Roger and I ran away. He sauntered over to a chair in the lounge and sat down. My heart convulsed with panic. At any moment, a drunk Harry could arrive home and two of my worst nightmares could collide.

I could not think of a single word to say to him. We just stared at each other. A deathly silence hung between us like mustard gas, playing on our nerves.

The man who had made my childhood so unbearable was here.

The man who had tortured his children enough for each of them to run away, one by one. Everyone but Kane of course. They all went back home, after a while, except for myself. The silence grew thicker and more oppressive.

Perhaps he expected me to say something. I didn't. I expected him to say something. He didn't. I bustled around, walking back and forth from the lounge and the kitchen, my mind paralyzed by shock. My father stared at the ceiling until an hour passed…and then he left. We never spoke a word after I opened the door for him to come in.

Only a few minutes after my father left, Harry arrived home. He was in a very jovial mood after winning some money at the casino. Once again, he asked me to marry him. He had been asking for weeks now. Each time I skirted around the subject. This evening, he became positively insistent about it. He wanted an answer.

Afraid of him turning nasty, I conceded, and we were officially engaged. I suppose I was also feeling lonely after such a strange visit from my father. It reaffirmed that I would be alone in my life and that Harry was all I had.

That evening, we had sex as usual. It was heavy and uncomfortable, rushed and without passion—almost bestial. Harry had become a selfish lover, if you could even call him that. He climbed on, went through the motions, and finished. That was Harry.

In the days that followed, my father's visit continued to play on my mind. I got up early that Saturday, after having my identical twins dream. I saw both of their faces clearly, nestled in my arms in a beautiful nursery in a home I did not recognize. Both girls were smiling and happy, suddenly sitting as toddlers on the floor playing with an enormous mound of toys. I wanted them so badly. The lingering feeling of sadness manifested in a new ending: my father was there and he was angry with me.

I couldn't go back home and I wasn't happy with Harry; I was stuck between a rock and a hard place.

After a lot of soul-searching, I decided that I should go home that day and patch things up with my father, ask him to forgive me and let me come home again. As I got ready, I felt apprehensive. Some wounds don't ever heal, that was what it was like with my father and me.

The door invited me to leave, but instead, I chose to stay and phone instead. I thought about it for quite some time and hardened my resolve.

Picking up the receiver, I dialed my childhood phone number. It rang three times, and then my father answered. "Yes, Frank Lemmens here."

I took a deep breath. "Dad, it is Christine…your daughter. I am calling to see if we can talk. I know I have been wrong in the past."

I heard him take a deep and long breath.

"Christine? I don't know anyone called Christine. I no longer have a daughter."

He hung up.

The surge of pain that I felt from somewhere inside my stomach, heart and chest gripped me. I collapsed onto the floor, clutching the phone and broke down into heaving sobs. Through all the pain I had experienced as a child, nothing hurt me as badly as that phone call. Being abused is horrendous, but hearing that I had ceased to exist to my own father crushed the breath from me; it flayed my heart.

I cried and felt a constant nausea for two solid weeks, then I called my mother. I had to try. Surely if he had come to my house, he was hoping I would speak to him. I didn't tell a soul about my father's visit, or my phone call to him. Not my bar friends, not Harry—no one.

I was ashamed that my own father would feel that way about me. Then, cruel news. My mother told me tersely that my father was dying of lung cancer. Only my mother knew. I asked her if I could come and see dad. She responded that he wouldn't want to see me, as he had told her I didn't exist anymore, in his eyes.

Christine Clayfield

The guilt of this singular moment would haunt me for the rest of my life. It is my single biggest regret that I did not talk to him when he came to me that day.

He had been right all along—the people I hung around with were bad people, and they had a negative impact on me as a person. He was right. Everything that I was about to endure I had brought on myself; my poor judgment and my worse behavior led me to my fate.

I deserved to marry Harry. When I had agreed, I really didn't plan on going through with it. I just wanted to avoid his anger. Knowing that I had failed to make amends with my father convinced me I wasn't worthy of anything better. We set a date for the wedding.

1983, Belgium, Age 24

I was called to come and see my father just before he died. I raced to the house and stood trembling and panting at the foot of my father's bed. He glanced in my direction but I couldn't tell if he saw me or not. He looked disorientated and drowsy; side effects of the morphine.

He closed his eyes for the last time. He was gone, forever. He was only 57. We all stood in a suffocating silence and I started to cry until Kane turned to me and said, in a rough voice, "It's no good crying *now*! Now it's too late." A moment I will never forget.

Sometimes the people you have worked hardest to love in your life are the ones you miss most when they are gone. It was like that with my father and me.

Now, a gaping hole existed where he once was. The man I had blamed for everything bad that had ever happened to me was forever beyond reach. He lived his entire life without ever once seeing any good in me.

Harry insisted on moving forward with the wedding and I sensed he wanted it to be over and done with. I was drifting around in a cloud of guilt and shame, so I let it happen.

The loss of my dad drove me into Harry's arms, such was the significant absence left behind in his wake. I felt the keen rejection of those last days in my soul.

I knew that marrying Harry would make me unhappy, but I was lost and felt like I deserved little better. I figured "at least he doesn't hit me," so I agreed to go ahead with the wedding.

I saw no choice other than to make the best of what I had. It was familiar to me. This was what I thought love was all about, at that time.

I did not want to end up in a pub closet alone again, and none of my friends cared enough about me to help. I had only one option, and I clung to the hope that marriage would change Harry, as I believed I could change him. It crossed my mind to leave Harry and move in with mum, but this hope for change stopped me from doing so.

None of my brothers approved of Harry, least of all Kane but they all came to the wedding, which was little more than a meal between two families. Harry's mother and father were decent people, although extremely poor. They carried a wholly unrealistic view of who their son was. Of course, they were happy that their good boy married the daughter of the richest man in the village!

So, while Harry's family ate and drank in happiness, mine did so with the weight of our father's death freshly draped over our shoulders. There was no happiness for me on my wedding day—a big part of me knew that marrying Harry was a mistake. I desperately needed somebody—anybody—to be with and Harry happened to be that person.

Marriage did change Harry but not in a good way. He immediately became nastier and more violent than ever before.

Low on money, we had booked a two-week stay in a two-star hotel in Spain for our honeymoon, which was all we could afford. We drove to Spain by car, as we couldn't afford to fly.

I sensed something was off when we arrived at the hotel that first day. The hotel umbrellas were like red stars imprinted on a blue sky. Everything would have been wonderful but Harry's mood was off. He started drinking heavily and did not stop.

I was lying by the pool in my bikini, Harry was helping himself to cocktails directly next to the hotel bar, where he decided we should sit. It was a muggy, sticky day—the kind you had to enjoy with liberal dips in the swimming pool to stay cool.

I laid on a deck chair with my sunglasses on and my straw hat shading my face as the sun baked my skin. Harry settled on a chair next to me, turned, and with the straw still in his mouth blurted out, "Now that your dad's dead, you can ask your mum for money so that I can start a garage." I looked at him through my sunglasses, faintly outraged that he was so crass about what he wanted. Harry had always wanted to own a garage where he could repair people's cars.

"I can't do that," I replied offhand, "and I wouldn't want to do that. We should both work and save up our own money if you want to start a garage." I watched as Harry's jaw clenched around the straw and he drained his fresh cocktail.

"Okay, I've had enough of the sun—let's go and get a drink and relax in our hotel bedroom."

I had been laying in the sun for long enough, so I was also ready to go inside. I thought that what Harry had said to me was just him taking a chance and didn't consider it again.

We lazily ordered another round of drinks and made our way down the white passages into our bedroom—a small room with a bed, a table, a bathroom and a television. The moment Harry shut the door behind me, I was overcome with a sense of dread.

"Now that your dad is dead, you can ask your mum for money so that I can start a garage." He opened up again, in a sturdy and angry voice. He stood tall, both arms over his chest.

"Harry, I just told you I don't want to do that," I reiterated, growing more fearful. Harry moved to the door, locked it and pocketed the key.

"I am telling you, you useless bitch, that you *will* ask your mum." He looked at me, his cruel eyes filled with hate. Then he pointed his finger at me and marched towards me.

I was cornered. I shook my head and stepped back, but he seemed to grow in size and fury at the sight.

He grabbed my arm and pulled me down onto the bed, raising his hand. "I'll beat you if you don't ask her, Christine."

He had never struck me before, so I pushed my luck. The threatening hand came down onto my head and face with the force of a mallet. The next ones were not slaps but hard follow-up punches in my stomach. He grabbed me by my shoulders. I struggled against him but I couldn't break free; he was too strong. The pain shot through me, and I was winded. I rolled off the bed and hit the floor, wide eyed and terrified.

"You *will* ask." He raised his fist and towered over me. "No, no, no," I gasped, writhing breathlessly on the floor in pain. He hit me and kicked me—connecting with my stomach, my arms, my chest, my legs and my back. My mouth was wet with the taste of blood, my head was pounding. I was dizzy. He meant to hurt me badly. I curled up into a ball and held my hands over my head as blow after blow stole my breath.

Then he stopped and stormed out of the room. I tried to be brave but was soon overcome by a wave of my emotions and I broke down. Hugging my knees in my chest, I rocked back and forth, shivering in disbelief. It was my first real beating from my husband Harry.

I agreed to marry him because he didn't hit me and I hoped he would change. My belief in him not hitting me was now shattered. I realized what an enormous mistake I had made by marrying him.

I sat there, humiliated and wretched on the floor for what seemed like hours. I was in pain and felt lower than the lowest insect and had no idea what to do. So, I did what I had done for most of my life and cried myself to sleep. He did not come back that evening.

I woke in agony with dark bruises covering my arms, my legs and much of my body. Later that morning, Harry gingerly walked through the door, puffy eyed and somber. He collapsed on the floor at my feet, begging for my forgiveness.

He begged me not to tell anyone, because he loved me and would never do it again. He'd been drunk.

He had big dreams for us. He just wanted to have his garage so he could take better care of me.

I wish I knew then that they always say this. I wish I had known what real love was supposed to look like or how a marriage was supposed to work.

Harry was a textbook profile of an abusive spouse, but this was before that textbook was written. No one talked about abuse then. Wives of abusive husbands were isolated and ashamed. I had no idea how cliché an abuser Harry really was.

My brother Lucas and his wife were in Spain, and he planned to come and see me for one day. When Lucas arrived, we decided to sit in the sun by the hotel's pool. My brother asked me why I was walking strangely.

I laughed at him and said, "Too much sex. You know how it goes on a honeymoon," and he laughed back. I tried to ignore the pain and walk normally.

When we arrived at the pool, everybody took their clothes off to reveal their swimming gear, except me.

I couldn't let anyone see my bruises, so I lied and said I had sunburn from the previous day. Sweet Lucas. He knew something was wrong. As soon as he could maneuver a moment alone with me, he asked if I was really okay. I was ashamed and afraid he might confront Harry, which would only lead to more punishment for me, so I assured him I was fine, just sunburned and hung over.

The next day Harry was drunk again. He grabbed me by my hair and dragged me into the car shouting, "Get in, now! We are going for a ride."

"You can't drive, Harry, you are too drunk!" I yelled.

"I can do what I want," he replied smugly and stopped me from getting out of the car. I had no choice and was hoping for the best. We were driving with speeds in excess of 200 km per hour.

Harry always used to show off how fast his Mazda sports car could go. "Please Harry, slow down, you are going to get us killed," I shrieked.

"That's the plan," he screamed back at me, "if you don't ask your mum for money, I don't want to be alive, so I am going to kill us both. I am going to drive into a car at full speed."

I was petrified. All of sudden, he swerved his car to the left, hitting an oncoming car sideways.

It was a loud bang and our car swerved from left to right a few times but Harry got control of the wheel again. I knew he just wanted to scare me; otherwise, he could have hit the car head on.

I looked back through the window and could see in the distance that the other car was swerving left and right and ended up on the side of the road.

When I pointed out to Harry that we should stop to call the police and check on the driver of the other car, he just ignored me and kept driving at a very high speed.

I was scared for my life; clearly, he was too drunk to see reason. I did not see any other option but to try to calm him down.

"Harry, I love you. Please slow down. I don't want to lose you," I pleaded with him and lied.

"Will you ask your mum for money?" he screamed at me.

Thinking I would die if I did not tell him what he wanted to hear, I replied, "Yes, I will ask her for money!"

Harry slowed down and eventually drove the car into a car park. Twisted as he was, he then hugged me as if nothing had happened. "As soon as we are back home, you will ask her, yes?" he demanded.

I nodded and begged him to let me out so I could drive us back to the hotel. He agreed and fell asleep in the passenger seat soon after.

That evening, after another day of drinking, we got back to the hotel bedroom and Harry locked the door behind us.

"You promised me today and I want you to confirm it. Are you going to ask your mum for the money for my garage?" His words hit me in my chest like ice.

I stood frozen in terror, I said yes earlier, as I was too scared after the car crash incident.

I could not bring myself to say yes again. I just felt too proud to do that. I felt I had to earn the money myself, and I was not about to ask for a handout.

"No," I said with finality. Again, he attacked me. He punched and kicked me until I lay in a crumpled heap on the floor.

Every single day, for the entire duration of our honeymoon, he asked me this question and tried to beat me into submission when I said no. Every day I felt the nagging, creeping fear of violence suppress me. I stayed silent. I was afraid, locked into the worst prison yet—with a man I had married.

On the eleventh day of our honeymoon, we were having breakfast together in the bedroom when he asked me the question again. "No," I replied, the same as before.

He grabbed me by my hair and pulled me off the chair, dragging me by my hair around the table, making sure that this time the message would sink in. He pulled me back up, forced me to sit on the chair; his hands became fists. I was fighting a desperate battle to try and get up but he kept me in place. I gripped onto the table for support, my whole body started to shake as I was taking the punches.

He beat me hard and for much longer than he had before. By the time he left, I had blood trickling from my head. I was trembling; a plethora of salty tears fell from my chin, soaking my clothes. He vanished again, as he always did—leaving me to find the strength to get up.

He did not return this time. The next day he still wasn't back at 10 p.m., so I called his parents. "Harry is here right next to me," his mother said in a matter-of-fact tone, as if I had done something to seriously upset her boy.

When I spoke to Harry on the phone, all he said to me was, "You didn't do what you were told, so I came home."

Harry had beaten and abandoned me on our honeymoon, leaving me in Spain all alone because I would not concede to his wishes. I had to find my way home on my own. That was the end of my honeymoon from hell.

No Reason to Smile

"With violence, as with so many other concerns, human nature is the problem, but human nature is also the solution." – Steven Pinker

2016, St. Vincentius Hospital, Age 57

It was 6 a.m. when I woke up, too early to go back to the hospital but I could not sleep. After a brief encounter with some buttery toast, I got to work flipping through some pages in my Filofax and swiping through a multitude of notes on my iPad. I had a speech to write and deliver on Saturday for the charity fundraising event. I had dreamt of Harry last night and woke to a familiar sick feeling in my stomach.

These memories kept invading and all I wanted to do was get some work done. I sat on a swivel chair in my old bedroom, my husband still asleep and snoring lightly—the only sound purring intermittently through the crisp silence of the morning. The sun blared into the room, dashing white light across my old desk. More than once I had to reposition the curtain to limit the glare it was making.

I managed to cobble together some thoughts on a piece of paper, but it would need serious planning and effort. My mind was elsewhere. It had been over 20 years since my father's death, yet I remembered him clearly, like he was still in the next room. His passing, and the circumstances around it, had changed the course of my life.

If he had not died, I would not have married Harry—I was blinded by the grief of my circumstances. I was a mouse in a paper bag, trapped by my own inability to recognize that I wasn't just a mouse but a set of teeth too.

I lingered on a sentence, scratching at the margins with my pen, until I plopped it down, frustrated.

It is in those solitary, quiet moments when the memory of Harry and my father hangs in the air like dust—immovable and never-ending. I needed distractions. Eventually, my husband woke, and we had breakfast together as time sped up to its natural pace. We left the house and headed back to the hospital early. There was no change in mum's condition.

I returned to my seat in front of my mother, her eyes closed and still. She was fighting, holding on to life, and I respected that. There is no honor in giving up on yourself, no matter how old you have become.

The memories of my life glistened like droplets on a winter leaf, collecting their weight and spilling into my mind and I was powerless to prevent it. My mind continually flitted back to Harry after he left me on our honeymoon.

1983, Belgium, Age 24

I made it back home to Berden, rattled and spent, my bones aching and my mind scattered. I was hurt and angry with Harry for leaving me in Spain, even though when he left, the beatings stopped. Harry arrived home shortly after I did and made a big show of an apology. He seemed genuinely sorry and ready to make amends. Everybody in my family told me to leave Harry and immediately get a divorce.

After I left home, I had stopped going to church but was still, in my heart, a Catholic. To me, this meant I should strive to be a good human being and to be able to forgive and forget. I just couldn't divorce him, because my conscience told me I had to forgive and forget. So, that's what I did: forgive.

I truly believed that forgiveness was my only course of action, and so I gave it humbly and foolishly. The nuns drummed it into me that you have to forgive people. Harry was my husband, for better or for worse, but he didn't make it easy, and the constant abuse quickly escalated to all-out daily torture.

His abuse added another layer of pain and anger to my already traumatic experiences and my fragile heart.

Rarely a day went by when Harry was not actively trying to run me down, beat me down, or tear me down emotionally. Once again, it was normal to me to live in a constant state of fear, expecting the worst and then being surprised by the new levels of cruelty that he would inflict on me.

One evening I suggested to Harry that I would find an evening job, on the days I didn't go to evening school, to earn more money so that we could save some to build a future. This set him off, and he shouted that I should be home with him in the evenings so that when he wanted sex, he could immediately have it. I was sick of scraping by, sick of him complaining about not having money to start a garage and sick of the increasingly brutal sex.

He leapt up and began beating me. I tried to run upstairs to our room, but he caught me near the top of the stairs and threw me down them. I broke my arm. At the hospital, I told people I fell down the stairs. No one asked about the bruises; people simply didn't those days.

At the end of the month, we were short of money as usual.

"There's no money. You need to find a better paying job," he would say to me, wearing nothing but a white t-shirt and boxers, his feet on the kitchen table as I helped myself to my morning cornflakes.

"I'll try to find a different job," I told him, irritated. "*You* should go to work too," I muttered, reaching for the blue pot of sugar and spooning some into my cereal.

"I know you don't have money for going out," I tried to say cautiously, "but I really need some to get a binder for my class project. I want to do well, and this presentation matters."

"Get a binder then." Harry smirked at me.

"You have all of my money," I said, raising a spoon of cereal to my mouth.

"There's none left," he said coolly, watching me. The second my spoon touched my lips, I knew something was wrong.

"What the hell?" I exclaimed, moving to spit out the salty mixture, but Harry lunged at me, holding my hand over my mouth.

"You are going to eat your breakfast. All of it." It tasted like I had poured the entire saltshaker into my cornflakes. It reminded me of the taste of the TUC biscuits.

"Chew it. Swallow it," he said, smiling at me. I choked and spluttered but still Harry held my lips closed. I did as I was told. Then he released me.

"You put salt in the sugar container? Why the hell…"

"Because it's funny."

I could have seen how it would have been funny, really I could have but Harry would not let me leave for work until I had finished my entire bowl of salty cornflakes. I got into my car to leave for work as Harry watched me out of the living room window, still smirking. The car would not start. It continued to turn over, until BANG! Something shot out of the exhaust.

In a panic, I opened my car door to investigate the sound. There lay a potato a few meters away from the car. Harry had stuffed a potato in the exhaust pipe. He clutched his ribs as he was laughing so hard.

"Serves you right, you stupid woman!" While he bellowed from inside, I got back into my car, hoping that no neighbors had heard him.

My mouth was dry with salt and my stomach felt queasy. I just had to get through the day and do the best that I could do. I had no idea that fighting against Harry was like fighting against an oncoming tsunami…and I was just a person staring at it on the beach.

My father would have been so disappointed in my situation. It seemed that I always came back to that thought that I was either about to do something that would have disappointed him or I had already done something disappointing.

Work flew by in relative happiness and soon I was on my way to my evening class to continue my accountancy studies.

"Don't forget that tomorrow is the last day you get to hand in your class project, or you will receive a zero grade," the teacher called out as the class settled in for the lesson. Another reminder after the lesson had my stomach in knots.

I was paid in cash that month because of a computer problem at work. So I planned to go directly to the shops after class to buy that binder I needed, before Harry could take my money again.

He was one step ahead of me. Waiting outside in the parking lot was none other than my husband himself.

"Give me your money." He snapped his fingers.

"I don't have it yet," I tried to lie, but it was useless. He grabbed my bag and emptied it on the ground in front of some classmates, who were leaving for home. He found my wallet and took my cash from it, not leaving a cent behind.

"Please, Harry. I need to get a binder!" I begged him, scrabbling around on the floor while trying to gather up my stuff.

"This shit is a waste of time," he shouted at me, pointing harshly at the building. Then he left. At least my car started that night, and while I cried in the car, a crazy thought occurred to me: I should just steal a binder. Without thinking, I pulled into the mall parking lot and prepared myself for the act. I needed that binder. The project was a vital part in the course, and without it, I could not graduate, and consequently I couldn't build a better future.

I was a very bad, very obvious thief. After smuggling the binder under my coat, it took me three steps out of the store before a security guard caught me. The police were called, and I was held in a cell for questioning.

"Why did you take the binder, missus? It's not even worth anything," an officer asked me.

"My husband wouldn't give me any money," I said flatly. "I begged him for it because I want to build a better life for us, and he said no."

They called my next of kin: Harry.

He arrived, heavily intoxicated but trying to remain civil because of where he was—a police station. To my horror, they carted him off to another room to have a chat with him. He was silent and brooding all the way home. I knew what was coming and prepared for it. The moment the door clicked shut, Harry exploded.

"Don't you dare ever tell anyone I'm doing anything wrong again!" he bellowed at me, slapping my face and shaking me. "Do you hear me, Christine? I won't come the next time they call me. Don't you *ever* tell anyone anything!" he said, throwing punches now. It was a quick beating and not a particularly bad one.

Harry did not care that I'd been arrested; he was only worried about his name, as he wanted everyone to think that he was a good husband.

When Harry was finished taking his frustrations out on me, he opened a bottle of whisky and carried on drinking. I watched as he drank. He drank away my dreams of having a binder for my class project. I had so little that even though I worked hard all day, I could not have the one practical thing that I needed for class and I was too ashamed to ask somebody for help. Harry stood up unsteadily.

"I'm sick of your stupid classes," he announced. "I'll decide what you turn in, and what you'll turn in now is nothing." I felt helpless and hopeless as he threw all of my course work into the open fire. All my hard work was mere ashes in seconds. For the rest of the evening, Harry was happy to scold and humiliate me from afar, muttering about the evening and how stupid and useless I was to get arrested.

I never got my diploma for accountancy. Instead, I had a criminal record for stealing a binder. At least I had the accountancy knowledge. I returned to evening school to study something new: computer programming. I had to find a way to earn more money, and more importantly, I had to stay out of Harry's way for my safety.

Harry and I never agreed on anything; our points of view were different on absolutely every aspect of life.

A war of words was a daily occurrence. I assumed arguing was part of love. My view of marriage was that it was a constant battle where couples argued and husbands beat up and dominated their wives. I did not expect Harry to agree with me or respect my views.

My bedwetting was a constant source of conflict, and I expected that. Who besides my mother and brothers had ever failed to shame me and attack me for it? One Saturday morning, Harry woke still drunk from the previous night.

"For God's sake! I've had it with this bedwetting. I am totally and utterly fed up with it. Put new sheets on. Now!"

I was getting out of bed when he kicked me in the back.

"Do it quicker!" He followed me to the linen cupboard, pushing and slapping me. "If you keep wetting the bed, you will have to sleep on the sofa from now on. I am not taking it any longer, you disgusting woman!"

His words hurt far more than his blows that day. He went on and on, shouting about how disgusting and dirty I was. I was ashamed to my core of my bedwetting problem. I was isolated and embarrassed, and a lifetime of trying everything to stop it had failed. His cruelty about the bedwetting was so much worse than his abuse about my intelligence and looks because I had no comeback, nothing I could say to prove to myself that he was wrong. I knew I had no control over it, but there was the damp sheet every morning, reproaching me.

This man who begged me to marry him did not love me. I felt broken, hopeless, beaten down and totally alone.

A few days later, I discovered I was pregnant. I knew in my heart that I could not raise a child with Harry. I could not bring a child into that violent home. I had to get it done.

It was the hardest decision I ever had to make, and I battled with my conscience for a good few weeks before I settled on a course of action. I took the train to Holland, where abortion was legal and I had it done there.

I never told Harry; I was only gone for a day so he thought I had gone to work. He never asked me where I went, and so it was a secret I managed to keep.

After the abortion, I grieved. It took me several months to get over it; I felt isolated and couldn't tell anyone. I didn't think anyone would understand. I had to grieve alone. I began to resist Harry when he wanted sex. This prompted him to develop a new habit, asking me if we would have sex. Every morning when he got up out of bed to go to the pub, he would say, "Are you good for sex this evening? If you are, I will be home at 9 p.m.; if not, don't wait up because I will come home tomorrow morning instead."

I was puzzled because Harry would always stay out late. He usually wanted sex at some insane hour of the morning when he was blind drunk and barely able to comply, which made it awkward and horrible. I could not enjoy sex with Harry. He was so cold blooded about it.

I was certain that if he were getting up every morning to go to a job instead of to the pub, he would change. I believed I could change him. I *had* to change him, to turn him back into his old self, the man who adored me and was so thoughtful and sweet to me when we first met, or so I thought. He came home before midnight one night, and I decided to seize the opportunity to try to talk to him.

I waited until we were in bed, and I thought he was relaxed. I told him we could be so happy if we could buy a house, and I was sure we could if he would get a job. He seized me by the hair and slammed my head into the metal bed frame.

"You don't give me orders, you stupid bitch," he hissed at me, continuing to bang my head against the bed frame. "Do you hear me? Do you understand? You stay out of my business."

I couldn't speak. I was stunned and frozen with pain and terror. He continued to pound my head into the metal frame. Blood began to flow down the side of my face and drip onto the pillow.

He stopped when he saw the blood, pushed me off the bed, and strode out of the room. I sat on the floor with my hand pressed to my bloody head and listened to him stomping and slamming cupboard doors in the kitchen.

He returned with a rubbish bag and stuffed some of my clothes into it. I watched in silence as he opened the window and threw the bag of my clothes out. He grabbed me by my arms and feet and dragged me, bleeding, down the stairs.

"You're rubbish," he screamed, flinging open the front door. "You belong out with the trash, you worthless slut. You can *never* tell me what to do!" He shoved me to the ground, and I sat stunned, barefoot and in my nightgown, as Harry slammed the door.

"Look, you are bleeding," a voice said softly behind me. I realized all of the neighbors were standing in their doorways, staring. One had come over to me.

"My wife has called an ambulance," he said, helping me to my feet.

I said nothing. I was choking on shame and fear. I required 15 stitches, had a concussion and I spent five days in the hospital. The most shocking thing to me was that Kane was the first person who came to visit me in hospital. He sat next to my bed offering to bring me anything I needed and asking me over and over about what had happened. I evaded his questions but I was deeply moved.

Maybe he *did* care! I wondered if perhaps, underneath the hard persona he portrayed to the world, there was a soft, caring side of him too. I am not at all sure whether it was in his heart to help me or just to take over from my father and be the one in charge but I would like to think that there was a flicker of conscience and empathy inside him.

When I was released from hospital, I returned to Berden. It never occurred to me to go elsewhere. Harry apologized as usual and life was quiet for a couple of weeks.

Then one night when I got home from school, I found a note on the kitchen table in Harry's writing. It said, "I am in the attic." Confused, I went up the narrow stairs.

Halfway up, I saw Harry hanging from a rafter. I screamed and nearly fell, racing down the stairs to call an ambulance. I was too scared to go back upstairs, as I thought Harry was dead.

The ambulance arrived a few minutes after I called.

The ambulance crew told me that Harry had disguised the fact that he was actually standing on a wooden crate.

He didn't really hang himself but wanted to give me the impression that he did. They told me that there were no signs of rope marks on his neck at all but decided to take him to the hospital anyway.

Whilst I was grabbing some things together to drive to hospital, I found a letter in the kitchen. "My suicide note" was written on the envelope. I still have his letter; here is just some of the content:

My darling Christine,

I begged you to love me but I've learned that you cannot love. You are just the same as your dad. I have helped you and allowed you to move in with me because I love you but you constantly have to hammer on the past and you never forgive me for a few mistakes I've made.

A lot of people would be angry and wouldn't be able to bear the pain that I had to endure from you and that's why I made mistakes. Please forgive my mistakes because I love you so much.

I hope that you have learned a lot from me otherwise you will never be loved, by anyone. I can't handle it any longer. Pray for me, my darling. I forgive you for all that you did to me but I cannot hate you although I know I said I hated you in the past.

My last will is that my car will be given to my friend David and the rest is all yours. Please ask my parents to forgive me and to forgive you too.

Your loving Harry

The letter was clearly written so people would think it was all *my* fault. Harry told the hospital psychiatrist that I ignored him, that I stayed out all night and that he was miserable, lonely and very unhappy.

He wanted to tell the world that it was *my* fault that we were not happily married. He was the one who was suffering, so he said.

He faked the entire thing shortly after I was released from the hospital, after he pounded my head so badly that I required stitches. And of course, he shared the entire phony story with everyone at the pub. He constantly joked around the house and in the pub about how good he was at faking his death, he found it incredibly funny that I fell for it.

A few weeks later, I arrived home from my evening computer classes to find him sitting in the lounge with blood dripping from his wrists. I called the ambulance and when the medics arrived, they cleaned his wrists up and bandaged them. They were annoyed and told me he was in no danger at all from such minor cuts. He told his newest tale with the same gusto with which he had shared the previous one, and it was all because I was so terrible.

One evening, Harry decided to have Sammy and David over for dinner, a couple that he regularly hung out with at the pub. They owned a big garage in the village and would talk "shop" all day if they could—Harry loved his cars. He drove his second hand sports car, whilst I drove an old banger.

I arrived home from work to a frustrated husband, who was tidying some stuff away for once.

"You better start cooking, and make it good. I like these people," Harry said to me coldly, shunting me into the kitchen.

I did the best I could, but we had almost no ingredients and I had never learned how to cook. I had little reason to cook. I usually had my warm lunch at work, which was free in the company's staff restaurant.

We rarely sat down to dinner together like a happy couple would. Harry was usually at the pub and I had my evening classes.

I thought I could manage a roast chicken, and they arrived while I was making a salad. I heard them chatting and laughing in the lounge as I struggled on in the kitchen.

We had no herbs or spices and I knew very little about oven times. In the end, the chicken was slightly burnt, the potatoes were undercooked and the salad was dry. Nevertheless, I was pleased with myself.

It wasn't that bad really, especially considering I had no chance to plan ahead. I set the roast chicken on the table, Harry stopped talking and glared at it.

"What sort of food is this?" he asked, horrified.

"It's a roast chicken," I said to him, feeling the heat rise in my face.

"I can't eat this. No one can eat this!" he said. "Please excuse my wife. She is usually better at this…God."

I stood hovering over the food as Harry took a big swig of his drink and started sweating. Not knowing what to do, I began dishing it onto Harry's plate first.

"What are you doing?" he demanded, pushing the plate away from himself. "I am not going to eat that shit. You're just flipping embarrassing me now. Seriously."

Sammy, an older woman with curly black hair, spoke up for me. "It's not that bad, Harry. I'm sure it tastes better than it looks. Besides, we have all had kitchen mishaps, haven't we dear?" David nodded jovially but I could see Harry was not settling down.

"A mishap? This is a bloody disaster. I mean, when my friends are over?"

"I didn't do it on purpose, Harry," I implored, more and more humiliated by the moment.

"Of course you did. You did it on purpose. You nasty bitch." Harry was quickly becoming dangerous and I think Sammy and David sensed it.

"No need to be so hard on her, Harry," David said, trying to help. "We can always get chips from the chip shop."

At the word "chips," Harry slammed his fists down onto the table, enraged by my bad cooking. "Just look at this muck! She does this to me on purpose." Harry reached for the roast and threw it on the floor at my feet. It splattered there, a mangled carcass of wings and legs.

Then he took handfuls of potato and salad and threw it at my feet. That was when the mood completely changed. Sammy and David both stopped smiling and trying to be nice, but Harry was committed already.

"That's where your food belongs. Now pick it up," he commanded me. I stood anchored to the floor, like a shrine decorated with offerings of food. I could see that Sammy and David were getting upset, preparing to leave. I didn't want them to.

"It's all right," I repeated, dropping to the ground, "I'll clean it up. It's all right."

I felt their eyes on me and their pity and anger. It felt terrible to be exposed like this, for people to see how my husband treated me. For years I had wished that people would see how I was being treated and to care in some way but now that people were seeing it, I just wanted to be invisible.

"Pick it up now!" Harry demanded. My hands were shaking, and I kept dropping bits of the food I was picking up.

"We should be going," Sammy said, rising quicker than a window blind. They made their excuses and left quickly. Harry came back from seeing them off and was furious. Whilst I was cleaning up the food, he put his foot firmly on the back of my neck.

"Now eat it, bitch. You think it's funny, embarrassing me? Then you can eat your dirty food."

He pressed harder on my neck with his shoe and I put a piece of floor chicken in my mouth as my head was held against the ground. He made me eat piece after piece, nearly all of it. It tasted like dirt and sand. I wanted to vomit.

That night, he was in tears, apologizing and heaving with regret. "I don't know why I did it. I was so humiliated in front of them," he sobbed.

"They had all of these great opportunities for me at the garage, if only the food had been good…I'm so sorry. Please tell them I have never done this before and I am a good husband."

He was so upset, and I was so touched at the idea that he was considering getting a job. I had to forgive him. I was married to him, and I believed it was my duty. I still wanted to live up to my Catholic beliefs about forgiveness.

The next evening, Harry was drunk again and back to his old ways. This was how it always was with him; his apologies never lasted. At home, I never knew when he might creep up from behind and punch me with a word or a heavy fist. At night, he would often grab a pillow and suddenly, without warning, slam it down over my face to suffocate me. He would only stop when he saw I was clearly in distress and panicked. He threatened to kill me on a regular basis.

Most of what he said were lies. He constantly lied about where he was going, whom he was with and what time he would be home.

Around that time, he also became violent with the furniture and other household items. He would get upset about something and get his hammer to smash apart a chair, an ornament, or whatever he spotted. We only had necessities as furniture, so each item he smashed needed to be replaced, which got quite expensive. I owned nothing aside from my clothes and my schoolbooks. I never knew when things would be destroyed. I spent months in that war zone, never knowing when the next attack would take place.

Living with Harry was a nightmare, I didn't know what to expect. I cried during the day and at night. My life was full of tears. I had no reason to smile; it seemed as if there would be no end to my tears.

Harry mostly went to the pub without me. Sometimes, on Saturdays, I went with him and we drank a lot. On one of those nights, we staggered home around 3 a.m. and Harry was angry and shouting at me the entire walk. I went straight up to bed as soon as we entered our house in the hope of avoiding a beating.

In the morning, I came downstairs to start breakfast and found the lounge and kitchen destroyed. The windows were broken, and the curtains were strewn around the floor with broken dishes and vases. All of the chairs had been smashed to pieces. Harry was behind me on the stairs.

"You see what you did yesterday, you drunk slut!" he muttered.

I couldn't believe I had done any of it as I always acted funny when I was drunk, not aggressive. I had no memory of much of the evening. I knew I went straight upstairs but Harry insisted I came down again.

The fact that I *might* have done it myself and didn't remember it troubled me. I will never know whether Harry smashed our house to pieces or I did. I made a decision right then and there: no more heavy drinking, *ever*.

That was the end of my heavy drinking. I *never* drunk whisky, vodka or spirits again. I had learned that day that those kinds of drinks can mess with your brain, give you blackouts and make you lose control.

Instead, I would occasionally have a beer or glass of wine, but I have not been *drunk* since that day. I absolutely hate being out of control.

The next weekend Harry invited his drinking buddy, Marcel, over for a few before they went out. Marcel had a huge beer belly and a beard—but he was nice enough. So nice that he invited me to go with him.

I thanked him and said I would rather stay at home, but Harry cornered me in the bathroom a short while later and insisted that I come along. I was exhausted from a busy workweek and determined not to drink, but the alternative was a beating and I was desperate not to be humiliated in front of anyone else again.

We spent hours in the pub, and they drank heavily while I sat there nursing an orange juice. When closing time was announced at 4 a.m., Harry and Marcel stood up and told me we were all going to see Nicole.

"Who is Nicole?"

Neither replied.

Ten minutes from the pub, we arrived at a small house with a little red light in the window. Nicole, I realized, was a prostitute.

At first, I assumed we were there for Marcel; after all, he did not have a wife or a girlfriend. The three of us got out of the car, and Marcel continued up the porch steps and into the house, where a half-naked woman who was waiting for him, smiled and said, "Hi Marcel, are you back again for a bit of fun?" She dragged him lightly by his sweater and closed the door.

I sat and waited with Harry on the steps. Some fifteen minutes later Marcel came out with Nicole and high fived Harry. "Your turn," Marcel said.

I looked from Marcel to Harry and back to Marcel again, feeling my heart implode in my chest. I had never considered the possibility that Harry was unfaithful. Stupid, stupid, stupid me.

"You stay here with Marcel," Harry said to me. "Don't you dare go anywhere. I'll be back soon."

I felt lower than I ever had before, as I watched my husband embrace the prostitute, smiling as he followed her into the house—leaving me, his wife, on the steps outside.

I didn't say a word to Marcel. At that moment, I detested him and my husband too. Harry was not even kind enough to keep it a secret or do it behind my back. At least when my father did it, he did so discreetly and he'd never actually made mum sit outside a brothel while he was inside.

Harry came out 10 minutes later, more drunk than he was before. We all walked back to the car and piled inside.

"What's your problem?" He grunted as I shot him a sad look.

"Are you kidding me?" I shook my head.

"If I want more sex and you are in your stupid school, I have to get it somewhere, don't I?" Harry sneered. "This is where I get it, from my favorite prostitute and there's not a damn thing you can do about it!"

Something inside me clicked and rage like I had never known before took hold.

Harry had taken everything from me: my dignity, my integrity, and my sense of self. I would not let him get away with this anymore. He would never spend my salary on prostitutes, drinking or gambling, ever again—not as long as I was breathing. The prostitute was the last straw. He had gone too far!

Marcel drove us home. Harry and I got out of the car and we were already fighting by the time we stepped inside our house.

"Don't you ever embarrass me again in front of my friends! You cannot tell me what to do! So what, you've met my favorite prostitute. No big deal is it! Tomorrow, I'll take you to the other 4 prostitutes I visit!" he smirked sarcastically.

"You don't love me at all, do you?" I reacted, still in disbelief of how stupid I had been, thinking he was faithful.

He had a horrible smirk on his face. To shut me up, Harry started beating me, one punch after another, his fists flying into every part of my body that he could lay his hands on.

He put his body weight on me and I plunged to the floor. I shouted and screamed and told him exactly what I thought of his behavior. The louder I became, the harder he hit me. My voice rang throughout the street and through our flimsy windows.

Everyone in the street heard that fight. They heard me finally standing up for myself against this monster of a man.

"Stop!" I shouted with all of my might. "Stop hitting me! Help! Someone help! He's going to kill me!"

I wasn't going to hide in shame anymore. I wanted the world and everyone in it to rain down on Harry, destroying his sense of safety, as he had destroyed mine since the day we got married, eleven months ago.

Pain erupted from every place on my body like being wrapped in a blanket of nails. I remember I shook uncontrollably and my legs were twitching. There was blood on his knuckles and blood was oozing out of the top of my head. My head was hurting and I felt tremendous pain in my gut and ribs. "Please, Harry, stop hitting me, please," I kept begging but to no avail.

"I am going to kill you, you bitch!"

His feet and fists were everywhere. For every blow I took, another was to follow. The speed of the blows escalated. Fist after fist collided with my head and I gagged as blood splattered from my mouth.

Still, I screamed until it felt like my voice box would be wrenched from my throat. All of a sudden I was unable to speak or breathe. Everything around me became a blur.

Then...the final punch. I lost the feeling of feeling. I saw a glimpse of twin girls. One minute I was dizzy and the next there was nothing but darkness and silence.

I heard later that the police arrived moments after I stopped screaming. On many previous occasions, the neighbors called the police but they eventually stopped doing that, as the noise of arguing and shouting became the norm on our street.

This time, the shouting was so loud that the neighbors had been afraid to come near us, but luckily, they phoned the ambulance and the police. They found me lying in a pool of my own blood on the floor of my house. Harry was sitting in his chair, drinking.

I had been hospitalized twice before thanks to Harry's temper. This time, Harry beat me nearly to death. He knocked me unconscious. I was barely alive.

The Purple Frame

"Progress is impossible without change, and those who cannot change their minds cannot change anything."
– George Bernard Shaw

I was in hospital for ten days, deep in a coma and completely unresponsive to the world around me—I couldn't see, hear or feel the doctors, family or friends who came to visit me. I was alive, but no one knew how; my injuries should have ended my life. The doctors told my family to prepare for the worst, as permanent brain damage was possible.

Harry, that selfish, violent bastard, had beaten me to the point of death—because I objected to him bringing me along on one of his prostitute visits.

You never think of the person you grew to love for what they do but for what you think they are—and perhaps that was my biggest downfall. To me, Harry had always been my first love, the man who had liked me back, and the guy who told me he loved me, even though he lied.

None of his actions and violent behavior were a part of him, and I did not think of them that way. He had been kind early in our relationship and I believed that was the real Harry. It was the alcohol that drove him to violent madness.

Even in my attempts to understand my husband and do right by him, a voice in my head would sometimes shout, "What about you?" I suffered because I chose to suffer. Everyone in my life had told me over and over again what a useless, good-for-nothing person I was.

The nuns. The girls at boarding school. My father. Harry. Even the teachers at my second boarding school told me I would never make anything of my life.

I was a raw nerve of insecurities, lower than the lowest creature, deserving of nothing. My main problem was not that Harry was abusive and violent; it was that I was too afraid and full of self-doubt to leave him.

Loneliness is the cruelest of all emotions and I avoided it to the brink of my own death. As a little girl, I was isolated, left to exist in the gaps between people, never really with them. People shunned and mocked me. The pain—the enormous, devastating pain of that memory—had kept me with a man who nearly took my life from me.

I let it happen. By staying with Harry, I was staying away from loneliness. That night, when he took me along on his visit to Nicole, the voice inside my head cried out. The loneliness I had been so afraid to see again was still in my heart, only dressed in something different: indifference. I knew that I had fooled myself for too long and that things had to change.

I believe that every soul is born with a fighting spirit. The kind that lifts you up when others try to pull you down. The kind that screams, "Enough tears!" when your heart is a drum solo away from total collapse. There is a reason why people die from heartache and despair. Without hope, there is no voice left inside you to fight back against the madness of the world. There comes a time when you can either break away or break into a million pieces. I felt my breath rising and falling, slowly and softly.

I heard a rhythmic beeping noise and felt a hard mattress beneath my body. My nose was stuffy; there was something inside it. A dull ache pulsed in my head, trickling down my neck and into my shoulders. Enough was enough. I had cried a lifetime's worth of tears. No more. I could take it no more.

My heart had been stabbed, played, burned, cheated and broken, but it still worked.

The darkness grew lighter, a pale brown with the faintest hints of light-shocked red. My eyes fluttered, and then…they opened.

"She's awake!" I heard a nurse say. "Doctor!" It was an echo of a voice, as if from a distant memory.

The room was bright and stark, even more so because the morning light shone directly on my face. Suddenly a pair of doctors were at my side, both wearing looks of great concern. The first, an older man, bustled around me, the sound of his clothes chafing and swishing as he moved. Everything was amplified—the light, the sounds—and as I licked my lips, I found them to be like two dried up slivers of crispy bacon left in a frying pan.

Then the pain rose inside me like a rearing beast, every movement caused pain and I cried out.

"Pain?" the second doctor said, picking up a button and pressing it.

Instantly, my arm felt cold and my pain eased. It was a wonderful feeling. I felt like I could have sprung out of bed and cooked everyone breakfast. A light hit my eyes as the doctor shone a torch into them.

"Looking great, Christine. You had us worried for a while." He leaned in to tap on my chest. "You were admitted unconscious 10 days ago. Do you remember?"

He looked at me as the memory of Harry's beating glimmered in my memory like hot coals in a dark night sky.

"Yes…" I swallowed; my mouth was so dry. A nurse handed me a glass of water. I took it and drank. "I remember, my husband…" I managed to say.

"Yes, I know. Your contusions were knuckle shaped. Your family and your neighbors told me about your husband." The older doctor sighed.

"That is something for the police report, I believe. I'll leave you in Nurse Amy's capable hands; your vitals are strong." Nurse Amy stayed with me for some time that morning, monitoring me and taking my blood pressure every hour.

During that first hour of being awake, I felt a surge of energy course through my veins. A renewed purpose. I knew I had escaped death.

"It seems you have all your faculties," the second doctor remarked. "You are a very fortunate woman."

I didn't feel fortunate; I felt angry. Harry had done this to me, and this time no apologies were ever going to make me take him back.

"Enough is enough!" I kept thinking, shaking my head. I was disorientated and weak but glad to be in hospital and alive. My decisions had brought me to this place, my weakness. I allowed this to happen to me. The bitter truth of this thought caused my jaw to clench. Enough! I said to myself again as tears threatened to well up. The time for tears and sadness was over. All that remained was outrage and change.

In that hour, a strange thing happened to me, as if in my coma I had been dreaming about all the bad things that had happened to me in my life. I thought about the cruelty of my father, the uncaring nuns, and the laughing children. I thought about all the so-called friends who had slammed their doors on me when I needed help and the men who had used me so savagely in my teenage years.

I laid in bed and thought, "What's that noise?" It was me, screaming, but in my head, it was as if the sound was coming from somewhere else, not from my mouth.

Then I overcame the embarrassment that tempted me to silence.

"I've cried enough tears!" I said aloud to the nurse, who smiled at me as she scribbled on her chart.

"Having a moment?" she asked, and I could see she knew what I was thinking. I nodded, my eyes glistening.

"I'm so tired. Things have to change," I croaked, my voice still finding itself.

"That's a great sentiment," she said slowly, "but it's only useful if you act on it. We see women coming in here all the time with relationship 'problems.' Some of them never leave their partners and sadly die because of violence. If you have any strength left, I say reclaim your life."

I thought about her words. If almost dead is what forgiving and forgetting got me, then I didn't want to do it anymore. I had to change my life, everything about it, *right now*, or the next time I would be dead.

This was it. It ended now! I felt anger, pain and sadness inside me but I also felt strength, resolve and hope.

I knew I couldn't change where I came from, but I could change where I went next. I had to find a way to overcome my fears and move forward with my life. I had to cross over to the other side. I needed to find the courage to rebuild a meaningful life and change the course of my life forever.

I was going to meet my fears with the same resistance that a rock shows the wind. I promised myself nothing was ever going to be the same again. I saw an image of my twin girls in front of me and remembered all the dreams about them.

My toxic levels of shame and guilt did not dissolve as soon as I awoke, but I'd found my survival instinct. I began to see that my father, the nuns, the other children, and Harry had all been wrong about me. I was not useless or worthless. I would prove them all wrong and show them what I am really made of. A fighting spirit like I had never known before reared up in me, casting its head back and roaring at the world. My Catholic upbringing all of a sudden didn't matter; I said to myself that I had done enough forgiving, that there was a limit how much forgiving I had to do and that I must have reached that limit. I finally understood the truth. This was my defining moment.

All my life I had been insecure, full of self-doubt and thought I was a useless person. I believed I would never amount to anything. I had been trained from the age of five what and when to eat and when to go to the toilet; in boarding school, that's how it was. They told me when to sleep, how to act, how to speak, and even how to dress. I was told what to say and when to say it. They told me what they expected of me and refused anything beyond those expectations.

I was never shown any love or affection, and I wasn't even aware that a person could love oneself, but I was about to change all of that.

I no longer feared anything. I'd been beaten to the brink of death and survived. For the first time, I saw strength in myself. I was alive.

Harry had done enough damage to kill me and yet, I was alive. This was my rock bottom. I kept telling myself I was lucky to be alive. I had big plans for a new life. I felt broken beyond repair because of all the abuse I had endured but I told myself I was going to pick up the pieces of my shattered life. It was the end of my life as I knew it.

I cried a river of tears because of my abusive dad, I cried a river of tears at that cruel boarding school, and yet another river was shed because of my slave master husband. And so, I made a promise to myself, *No Fourth River*. I was determined that no matter what, I would never cry a fourth river. It is time for change and no more tears for me! Like a mantra, I kept repeating to myself: This is enough – No more tears!

I felt an overwhelming urge to find the person I truly am, the real me hiding beneath the layers of misery, emotional pain and physical abuse. Now, I was going to live for real. I was going to let my inner fire burn brightly and enjoy life. I wanted to become the woman I knew I could be. I was going to rise above Harry and anyone else who tried to hurt me.

I had an unbelievable zest for life in that moment. I wanted my children, if I would ever have any, to see me as my true self and not as everyone had painted me to be my entire life: a failure.

I all of a sudden realized that if someone treats you badly, there is something wrong with them, not with you. It is not normal for people to go around destroying other people's lives.

You cannot hide yourself in a life you hate, waiting for the life you want to come along. I was done with insecurity and rejection; all it had gotten me thus far was a deathbed. I made the ultimate decision. I realized that nobody was going to come to my rescue, I needed to rescue myself from the bad place I was in. "I am my rescue and it will never end unless I end it," I thought.

I would divorce Harry and move out to pursue happiness for myself! He had chipped away at what little there had been left of me, bit by bit. Going back to him was certain death.

If I would hold on to my pain, I would allow him to steal even more of my life away. He didn't deserve that. I'd made the mistake of letting people stay in my life longer than they deserved. Not this time.

I told myself that I only have one life and I was going to ride it until the wheels fell off!

As I rested against my pillow, I saw my dad's face and begged him to release me from Harry.

Somehow, I wanted my dad's approval. "Is it okay if I leave? Please, Dad, let me leave him. Will you approve of what I am doing?"

I never did get an answer. I realized that dad was right in what he had been saying all the time: I was hanging around with the wrong people, and I would have to pay for that. I did pay for it, almost with my life. The morphine-induced mirage vanished, and I was alone again with Nurse Amy, who was casually sitting on the chair beside me.

A life filled with failures can still be very rich inside. Deep down, I had dreams. I did want to be happily married, to love and be loved. I wanted joy and freedom and laughter—the real stuff, not what is found amongst drunks in pubs.

Harry had no part in these dreams, and he'd have no further part in my life. I knew that, but he didn't. That afternoon I woke to Harry nudging my shoulder.

"Hey, Christine…hey…how are you feeling?"

"Harry? Harry!" It took me a moment to orientate myself. "I just wanted to say that I'm really sorry about this. I totally overstepped, and I know that. I've been to talk to a priest about it, and I'm going to go to counselling sessions to control my anger. I promise I'll never hit you again," he whispered to me, glassy eyed from the beer he had been drinking.

"Harry, I…" I began, but he cut me off.

"I know, I know. I am really sorry. We'll work on it, okay?" He thumbed my hair but I smacked his hand away. In that instant, I saw the anger flash across his face. It would never be over with him, not until I ended it.

"Don't touch me. Monster! Get away from me. You nearly killed me. I am not ready to die!" I said, my voice rising.

"Shh, Shh, Christine. Be quiet!" Harry moved to hold his hand over my mouth like he had done so many times before, but I bit him.

"Help! HELP! I want a divorce. You are never going to hit me again. You've laid your last fist on me, you bastard!"

I shouted. Nurse Amy pressed a red emergency button on the wall and tried to pull Harry away from me.

"You don't mean that," he wailed. "You don't mean that! Christine! Excuse me, I'm talking to my wife! I'm talking to my wife!" Harry bellowed as Nurse Amy was joined by two large, burly security guards, one of whom hooked Harry underneath both his arms.

"Get him out of here!" I shouted as best I could with my rusty voice. "He's a monster. Everyone's going to know, you bastard. Everyone! I want a divorce!"

Harry was screaming and fighting against the security guards, but they were forcing him backwards out of the room.

"I never want to see you again!" I shouted after him, and then to myself, "I'm starting over. Without you. Free."

A wild sense of triumph settled on me, and I felt like I could do anything. A fresh start. One free of the nuns, the bullies, my father, and Harry. When the nurse offered me anti-depressants, I cheerfully refused them. I wasn't depressed. At last, although I was almost beaten to death, I was I truly alive!

I visited Harry's parents the moment I was released from hospital. I brought pictures showing them how their son had beaten me; one of bruises after one time he had strangled me, as well as one of my accounting class textbooks that he set alight. They didn't want to believe me, but it did not matter. I was leaving their son, and they could have him. He was never going to hurt me again.

I quit my job at Agfa because I wanted to change *everything* in my life. I always hated that job anyway because I was constantly being bossed around.

At Agfa, I decided that one day I would set up my own company so I could set my own rules and nobody could tell me what to do.

Mum seemed much happier after dad died. She went on holidays, hung out with her friends each afternoon in local taverns and did coach day trips. She smiled more and stood up straighter. I was delighted to see her so happy.

I moved back in with mum. I had been an awful daughter over the last few years and it was time to make amends.

I apologized to mum and told her that I would prove to her what a great daughter I could be. From that day onwards, I have always been in contact with mum. I hated myself for leaving her when I left home, but she forgave me and said she understood why I did it.

I had another important issue to take care of; I had to get rid of my criminal record for stealing that binder. I wrote to the court explaining the circumstances of the theft, my abusive marriage and my desire to build a better life and how much I regretted the incident. A few months later, I received a letter that my criminal record was withdrawn due to good behavior, extreme circumstances and regret. I was so relieved. One more obstacle to my future success had been removed.

At the same time, I decided to start my own business. I did not know what or how, but I knew it was the right course of action for me. Never again would I take orders from anyone. I made a promise to myself that nobody would *ever* control me again and tell me what to do, when to do it, and how to do it. I would be completely independent and free.

Unfortunately, Harry made it hard. He took the divorce badly and was now essentially destitute without my income. He began stalking me, following me every time I would leave my mother's house. Eventually, one evening he broke into the house. My mother awoke to a drunk Harry standing over her. She was terrified.

"You had better tell Christine to come back to me, or this time I'll kill her. You hear me, woman? You tell her that!" He said his piece and left.

Christine Clayfield

At the commotion, I burst into my mother's room, but Harry was already gone. She was clutching her nightdress, frozen in fear.

"He was in here, glaring at me. He said he would kill you if you don't go back to him," my mother said, her lips trembling.

"I'll call the police. I'm never going back to him," I told her.

"Good," she said, still in shock.

Harry was still rumbling around downstairs, drunk and smashing things. I locked the bedroom door and called the police.

They arrived some 5 minutes later to find Harry screaming at the top of his lungs.

"You better come back, Christine! I'll kill you!" he said, swigging from one of my dad's aged whisky bottles from the pantry.

The police caught him quickly and put him in cuffs.

"You can press charges if you like, ma'am; he seems to have secured a key to your front door somehow. You say this man is your ex-husband?" a police officer asked as my mother and I stood outside and watched Harry being loaded into a police car, lights flashing all around us.

"Yes. My violent ex-husband. The divorce isn't finalized yet though. No, I don't want to press charges." I thought that would do more harm than good. Even then, I wanted what was best for Harry, and I did not think a prison sentence was right for him. He needed help for his aggression and violence under the influence of alcohol, and perhaps he also needed to attend Alcohol Addiction counselling.

I called his parents instead of pressing charges. They thanked me and swore to me that he would no longer be a problem and that it would be quiet until the divorce was finalized. They were wrong, very wrong.

I hated that mum was now involved, as Harry had broken into her house and terrified her. I offered to move out and find an apartment on my own. However, mum insisted I stay with her. I agreed but told her if Harry upset her again, I would have to move out.

Throughout the divorce process Harry shouted and screamed whenever he saw me. Each time, I could hear in his voice that he had been drinking.

I would come home to him on the front lawn and wake up to him on the front lawn.

It started as begging. He would shout, "Please come back to me, Christine! I love you!" as always, it progressed. Eventually, Harry was threatening again to kill me.

"You are at the end, you slut. If *I* can't have you, nobody can and I *will* kill you! You love this, don't you?" He'd shout outside the house as my mother and I looked on from the window. "I'm going to shoot you in the head!"

By the third night of these threats, he was waving a gun around like a lunatic. I became scared to leave the house and I was afraid for my life. I called the police on him constantly, and I *did* press charges, fearing for my own life. The police convinced me to do so.

"He hasn't done anything but threaten you," the police would tell me, "so we can't hold him for longer than 24 hours. Maybe you should move away," they suggested. Believe me, I considered it, but I had my heart set on starting over in Keldonk. *I* had to move away whilst *he* got to stay and behave like that? I wasn't prepared to do that.

One evening, he managed to break into our garage, steal my mum's Mercedes and drove it around the village like a lunatic. For about 10 minutes, the whole village could hear the sound of the horn and the screeching tires. I watched through the window as he purposely crashed the car into an electricity pole. The police arrived and he casually got out of the car and walked straight to them.

After I pressed charges and the situation got really terrifying, the court issued a Domestic Violence Injunction and Harry was not allowed to be within one mile of my mum's home.

My family members were really worried, and so was I. It got so bad that the police gave me 24-hour protection.

My mum called Kane and my other brothers to come over one night and talk about what they could do to help. Kane seemed to be the most worried after I told him what Harry had been doing to us. He listened and nodded.

"If the police don't sort this out, then I will," he said calmly. Kane kept it short and sweet, something that my dad never did.

The next day, Harry was not outside. I have no idea what Kane did. Harry never caused trouble for me again.

I had to pay Harry alimony, since I earned more than he did during our marriage. Talk about injustice. I was the first woman in Belgium ever to have to pay alimony, so my lawyer told me. The only way to make it stop was to catch Harry in bed with another woman. So, I started following him with my friend Annie for months. It seemed to take ages, but eventually I got my revenge.

The police caught him with another woman and the alimony payments were cancelled by the court. It was the first step to me regaining control of my life. The divorce was finalized.

Around the same time, Kane was sorting out the inheritance money from my dad, which he mishandled and hid from my brothers and me. We were all so naive at the time; none of us knew how to challenge him. My oldest brother Oliver sounded the alarm and revealed how we should have inherited more, but we were all too timid to do something about it.

Kane inherited our dad's business rigor, something Oliver was no match for, so we all just settled for what we were given. Oliver was the oldest at 32 years of age and the only one who knew about doing business in diamonds.

He knew that something was wrong with the inheritance figures that Kane said he would pay us. I was too stupid and so were my other brothers. Oliver didn't have the hard character Kane had so Kane simply ignored his comments about the money. Kane had the advantage of the benefit of the doubt therefore we had no choice but accept his decisions.

Kane took over dad's diamond business and kept most of the money for himself, paying all of us hardly anything, spread out over a period of years because he "didn't have the money."

He said that the business was making big losses; he added that there were lots of debts and the dollar currency was against him.

He paid us all peanuts compared to what we should have inherited. We could all have been millionaires but instead, we received as good as nothing.

We found out later that Kane used the inheritance to move most of dad's industry over to Sri Lanka, where labor was cheaper and where he built a fortune for himself. My father had fought this change in the Belgian diamond industry for years, encouraging other companies to keep all the manufacturing in Belgium as his company did.

Kane started building factories in Sri Lanka, employing more than 2,000 people to produce diamonds. Kane had an empire of diamond-related businesses, in some 15 countries all over the world.

Kane felt like he had to carry on dad's legacy—in every way. On one occasion, Roger's girlfriend was in our house and dad never approved of her. Kane decided to drag her out by her hair, which caused a huge fight between Roger and Kane. Roger was so furious with Kane that he reported him to the police.

I hardly saw any of the inheritance that Harry had expected me to get. It was funny in a way because that potential inheritance was what drew Harry to me in the first place.

His first real interest in me had come only after he had found out who my dad was. Janine, my old boss at the pub, had tried to warn me, but I hadn't listened. How ironic that I was nearly killed by a man to get at money that I was never going to get in the end!

I had to get my life together on my own, without any financial help from anyone. I stepped out into the world like a child on their first day of school, bright eyed and nervous. My self-esteem was super low and I worried a lot about my appearance.

I started by working for Kane in his diamond company, which was just across the road from my mum's house.

Kane kept part of the local diamond factory going for a few more years. I did all the staff's wages and secretarial work, counting and sorting diamonds too. It was a transition position, one to get me on my own two feet while I researched options for starting my own business. It gave me strength.

While I still dreamed of living happily ever after with the right man and my future twin daughters, I wasn't sure he existed or that I'd be able to identify him.

Alcohol wasn't clouding my judgment this time; I stuck to my vow to never get that drunk again.

To say I had trust issues was an understatement. I had trouble trusting even myself! Aside from the impact of my abusive father and abusive husband, there was the money. My identity wasn't my own. I was my father's daughter and my father's company and my family's wealth were known throughout Keldonk.

1984, Belgium, Age 25

I had zero tolerance for any man who might use me for either sex or money. Although my three brothers and I hardly received any money after my dad died, everybody in the village assumed we all had a limitless pot of money. I had zero willingness to trust any man enough to let him prove he was genuine.

I also realized that I had to pay more attention to how *I* felt about someone instead of worrying whether or not they liked me. I stopped doing things I didn't want to just to get people to like me. I no longer hung around with people I didn't like, and I no longer did what I thought people wanted me to do, to be liked.

Instead, my view was "If they don't like me as I am, they can go away. I am going to be myself from now on." I was trying to be brave, to live bravely, but inside, I was still afraid. I was very careful about what I did and where I went.

Things still felt precarious. I was determined but I knew how easily life could slide out of control.

I was not going to give myself or anyone else a chance to derail my plans. I wanted a loving relationship with somebody who would truly love me. So far in my life, nobody "really" loved me; it was all pretend love and pretend pleasure, just like my dad told me.

The first few months after the coma, I went out for business related meetings for Kane, but rarely for pleasure.

During this time, I made a list of qualities I would like to have in a man. First and foremost, absolutely NO drinking. I had seen enough trouble with alcohol from my dad, Harry, my friends, and…myself.

He must be loving, sophisticated, caring, charming, trustworthy, and non-judgmental; have a good sense of humor; respect me; no bossing me around; not wanting to change me in any way; he should have a good job; and our opinions on life should align.

Those were my rules. Oh, and no sex for the first six months, so that ulterior motives were removed from the equation.

I realized I had to love myself first before I could love someone, but it was difficult to forget my past. I soon wound up in hospital again. My insecurity combined with my determination to keep my life under control rapidly turned to an unhealthy obsession with limiting what I ate. I developed an eating disorder, Anorexia Nervosa, and my starvation caused a lump to form in my groin.

It had to be surgically removed, and this was an eye opener for me. I started trying really hard to eat again and get over my fear of food. As this was happening, I started dating again but my trust was scarred forever. Most men were instant let-downs.

When I met new people, it was like that first-day-of-school feeling all over again: social anxiety. Would they laugh at me? Would they reject me? Would I sit alone and be ignored while everyone else was chatting and laughing?

For a while, I played some sort of revenge game: seduce men, then dropping them like a stone. Now I was in control instead of people controlling me!

1985, Belgium, Age 26

In boarding school, we had swimming once a week and I used to enjoy it. I also used to swim a lot in the pool we dug ourselves in our back garden. I loved swimming when I was younger so I decided to start swimming again.

Then in 1985, at 26 years old, I met Luke. I started swimming competitively and loved every second of it. Luke swam too, and he bashed into me doing lengths one day.

We met formally in the coffee bar and struck up a relationship—he swam professionally for a club, and I joined the same club. Long distance swimming, 5 and 10 kilometers, was where I excelled.

Luke eventually convinced me to compete in the long-distance race for the team and a few months later, I won my first trophy! I stood on the highest step on that podium accepting my trophy, happier than I had been in my life. Just a year previously, I would have laughed if anyone had suggested I try swimming competitively. Because of my success, I grew more confident, and Luke and I grew closer. He respected my six months no sex rule.

I swam in several competitions that year, winning most of them. My name appeared on the top of the swimming races results in the sports sections of several newspapers. The feeling of achievement rested in my bones and I was obsessed with finding more of it. I started training for a triathlon. It was tough. I trained for six hours a day sometimes: two hours before and four hours after work.

The training for the triathlon was not only good for me physically but also mentally. It confirmed the fighting spirit I had in me. I felt I could achieve anything. I was developing the new me I'd decided to become when I awoke from the coma.

After all the bullying and abuse I had experienced, I was determined to now be the best in everything I did.

Behind my guarded, confident exterior, however, there was a timid girl, afraid to make friends for fear of rejection and ridicule. That became my next hurdle to overcome.

I even managed to open up to Luke about my bedwetting, which was still plaguing me. While he said he was fine with it, he didn't seem to be very happy about it when it actually happened, I could judge by his face. We never spoke about it.

Luke and I travelled to The Canary Islands for three weeks, and stayed at Club La Santa in Lanzarote, which is a sports and holiday resort with an Olympic size swimming pool. We trained for the triathlon from early morning to late at night.

A few months later, I came 32nd out of 200 people in the triathlon. Not good enough, I told myself. I knew I could do better, and I set my sights on coming in first next time.

Two months later, I did. I won a triathlon! I was a winner now. I stood on the number one spot on the podium when the golden trophy was handed to me.

It felt great, and nothing could stop me! Race after race, I received trophies and medallions; I still have them all today.

Soon, Luke began to reveal some traits I did not want in a partner. He liked hanging around in pubs, drank too much, and sex was never passionate enough for me. Not to mention, Luke was a diamond polisher and I often felt that he didn't really love me but was also after the money he thought I had. It was fun hanging out with him because we were both into sports, but that wore off; so, it was time to say goodbye.

Winning the triathlon and swimming taught me that I could win at anything with enough effort. I was ready to move on.

On my way to the post office one day, I bumped into Janine, the pub owner who gave me a place to sleep. She told me that Harry was spending his days drunk in her pub, telling everyone that his plan to get a lot of money out of me didn't work. This was confirmation that he did marry me solely for the money. I guess I had already accepted this but hearing it from Janine just validated that Harry never loved me.

I was glad I had not run into her sooner. Having my athletic victories under my belt, discovering my confidence and breaking up with Luke had all softened the blow.

My next goal was to open my first business, all on my own. I wanted to nurture my mind with information and knowledge providing me the building blocks I needed to teach myself and to build a better life.

I attended several business courses and read a ton of books about life, business management and entrepreneurship. I went to typewriter training, motivational classes, sales courses, and telephone techniques courses. They helped me get in touch with what I really wanted from life. I started to realize that success is all about planning and preparation, and I was ready.

I remember a quote I read in a book by Napoleon Hill: "Whatever the mind of man can conceive and believe, it can achieve."

After reading that quote, I made my list of things I wanted to achieve in my life:

- A man in my life, who would love me purely for who I am and accept my past.

- 10 children to shower with love, including identical twin girls.

- My own successful companies so nobody would ever boss me around.

- Multiple streams of income.

- A big house with a lot of land and without a mortgage.

- A marble bathroom with a TV in it.

- A study in my house.

- A big entrance to my house with a big metal automatic gate, as I was always scared that Harry would find me. For this same reason, I also wanted:

- Security CCTV cameras so I could see what was going on outside my house, whilst I was inside.

- To speak on stage to overcome my fear of being a useless individual.

- Household staff so I could concentrate on doing business.

On reflection, I noticed that a lot of things on my list, my dad had also achieved. Perhaps I was subconsciously realizing that I had thoughts in common with him.

I typed the list neatly on a piece of paper. I read in a book that purple was the color of the independent woman, so I bought a purple picture frame to put my list in and hung it in my bedroom.

Next to the frame, I hung a few pictures of the things that I wanted to achieve, to visualize my dreams. I was going to devote the rest of my life to achieving all the things on my list. I knew I needed a lot of money but I was prepared to work hard for it. I was going to be a survivor of the unfairness of my past.

I told myself that the joy I was going to create in my life would make me forget all the pain I had been feeling. I refused to play the victim. It was my mission to be so busy loving my life that I had no time for hate, regrets, negativity, worry or fear.

I wanted to be my boss, own my own set of companies, and command respect from people in the business world. I wanted to earn a lot of money so I would never have to drive an old banger again or beg anybody for money as I did with Harry.

Any money I earned would go to my loved ones—the future love of my life, and the twin girls that I had always dreamt about.

From that day on, I looked at my purple frame daily to keep me focused on how to achieve it all. Writing down everything I wanted in life made me realize I was never the person I truly was inside.

My circumstances never allowed me to be the *real me*. The person I thought I always was could finally come to life. I wore my coping mask for so long that I didn't even know who was really underneath it.

I met the stranger who was inside me all my life but never had the chance to appear. The stranger I knew well became the new me. I found myself.

The Invitation

"There are no secrets to success. It is the result of preparation, hard work, and learning from failure." – *Colin Powell*

1986, Belgium, Age 27

After my victories in sport, I knew that I was unstoppable. Anything I decided to do could be done, and I was going to make sure that the world knew that. I started putting some serious thought into my future and what I wanted.

When I was practicing to compete in the triathlon, I had to constantly tell myself, "Keep going, keep going, and you'll get there." I was going to apply these exact principles in my business life as well. I was going to work until I made it.

By 1986, a new technology had emerged that was sweeping the nation: personal computers. Everyone wanted a computer, but nobody had one. In Keldonk, this meant one thing—demand without supply.

Spotting an opportunity, I let it stew in my mind for a few days before formulating a plan. I didn't have a lot of money and was not about to ask my mum for any. Kane had only given her a fraction of what she was supposed to get, and I would never touch it. I wanted to do everything myself, without handouts.

Thanks to a bank loan, I was able to change my old banger for a new car, of which I was very proud.

I didn't know much about computers but I was planning to turn what I didn't know into my greatest strength! I had strengths I never knew I possessed.

The new me, a businesswoman, was born.

I knew how much presentation mattered, so I dressed up and drove my new car to the Apple Computer Headquarters.

I was building up my confidence, and only people who knew me well knew that I lacked self-esteem.

In the Apple offices, and in all of my subsequent business deals, I was bursting with energy and good ideas. I was determined to become an Apple dealer and wouldn't take no for an answer. I had a meeting with the Apple Dealer Recruitment Manager and two other sales people. Together, they would judge my suitability to open an Apple dealership. I assured them that I would work my socks off to become the best-selling dealer in the whole of Belgium, and I would exceed all the sales targets.

I blew them away with the detailed market investigation I had prepared and presented, complete with colorful handouts. I gave enough information for them to paint a picture in their mind of how the interior of my shop would look: welcoming, professional and prestigious. I simply spoke my mind in a very direct and honest way. It worked. I became an approved Apple dealer.

Next, I went to the bank with the business plan I had put so much time and effort into researching and drafting. I could see that personal computers would be the next big thing—maybe even the biggest, and I wanted to get in on it right away before the market got more competitive.

The bank's loan manager sat back in his stiff grey suit and surveyed me with mild disinterest. He was, however, impressed with the way I presented my business plan: in a professional-looking binder—the same binder I had in mind for my accountancy course project. He read over it carefully, looked up, smiled and said: "OK, We will give you a loan for this business, but you need to pay the loan back in 4 years instead of 6." It wasn't ideal but I thanked him and I was determined to make it work.

I went from a "nobody" to a business owner. I had an Approved Apple Dealership, some money from the bank and a head full of dreams. I found a perfect location for myself in a small shop, with some storage room. The rent was affordable and I settled in with my bits of office furniture. I would do whatever it took to make this business work.

The morning the "AM Computers" sign, my newly established business, erected on the wall outside the building, was one of my proudest moments. This was me. I was forging my own path, making my own rules. All I had on my side was a fax machine, a desk, some pads of paper, a telephone, and the Yellow Pages. My wits would have to take care of the rest.

My first day in the office I put my head down and I worked. I called close to a hundred people that day looking for leads. Just one computer sale would earn me more money than I had ever earned in a month, as computers were much more expensive back then, so I was motivated to land that sale.

"Hello, this is Christine from AM Computers. I'd to talk to you about the benefits for your business, with a Macintosh computer from Apple…" Call after call I was either rammed up against a wall of resistance or the customer would hear me out, thank me, and then put down the phone.

The rule of 10 for cold calling, which I read about, applied: For every 100 phone calls I made, 10 people would be interested, and 1 person would buy.

Then it happened. My first sale! I had convinced Apple to lend me a computer so that I could demonstrate to people how it worked and understand it better myself. Every time I landed a lead, I jumped in my car and headed to a sales demonstration to prove the computer's worth. I was literally selling computers out of the boot of my car.

Two weeks of demonstrations and calls eventually resulted in that coveted sale. I sold a Desktop Publishing system—an Apple Macintosh—to a printing company, along with Aldus PageMaker, which was graphic design software. On top of that, I also sold them a LaserWriter printer. I made a tidy profit and basked in the enormous earning potential, like Superman charging in the sun.

After that, I called more often and drove to more appointments. Thanks to my persistence, I sold more computers! It was not an easy game to be in. I made mistakes but I learned quickly.

Some weeks into my rigorous schedule, clients began to call me with problems—the computer would not start, or the printer was making a noise. I had no staff to deal with these issues, so I dealt with them myself.

The knowledge I had picked up during my computer programming courses saved me. Programming wasn't for me but I was glad I had taken those classes. I learned what I could and became my own engineer.

Armed with a new bag of screwdrivers and software testing tools, I would handle these callouts on my own. I opened the computers up, investigated the wiring, pushed a few buttons and always managed to get them to work again. Often, printers that did not work were simply not plugged in. It was the dawn of the PC, during the days of the typewriter, when plugs were scarcely used in an office environment.

As the months rolled by, I wore many different hats: a sales hat, a computer engineer hat, one for software and warehousing, one for accountancy and secretarial work, and one as my own receptionist. I juggled them all in a team of one, delighted to find that I could manage it all. Each day I worked from 9 a.m. to 1 a.m. in the morning, loving every second.

During this time, I developed a personal approach to selling, and my customers loved me. I showed interest in my customers through engaging them about their lives, their children and their interests. Someone's interest in me is something I longed for my whole life, so I wanted to show others that I cared.

The rule of 10 now became the rule of 40; so, for every 10 potential customers, I sold 4 computers. That was when I realized people bought from people, not from brands. I had two options: struggle or expand. I chose to expand.

An important part of running an expanding business is realizing that you cannot do it on your own forever. No one is that talented. So, I took on a few staff members.

People asked me for other types of computers, the Olivetti PC and the Commodore PC, and I wanted to provide them.

I found myself not only to be good at selling, but also at buying. Suppliers told me I was very good at squeezing good deals out of them.

As a woman, running a company sure has its disadvantages. I remember one incident very well. It was the end of the day. Members of my staff were going home. Night approached fast and I was alone in my office, staring out of the window, only the hum of the air conditioner breaking the silence.

I was waiting for my meeting with Bruno. Bruno used to do business with my dad and then with Kane. The doorbell rang. "Hi Bruno, come in." I swung the door open. Bruno, his wife Donna and I had been out to dinner a few times when he often ignored my attempts at friendly conversation.

He looked scruffier than usual, with bushy brown hair and unusually shabby clothing. He hadn't shaved his beard for at least a week.

He looked 60, although he was only 50. Donna had become a bit of a gossip, which is why we rarely had meals together anymore.

Bruno was out of work for more than a year and was interested in discussing the possibility of us working together on business deals. Donna told him to come and see me with his ideas. I never particularly liked Bruno, but I agreed to see him as a favor to Donna. I forced a smile.

"Long time, no see." His voice was rough, altered by years of smoking.

"I heard you had some ideas about us working together?" I folded my arms and waited.

"You could say that." He licked his lips.

"Well...what kind of—"

"Donna and I have been separated for a few months now."

"Separated? As in divorced?"

"Not yet. I've been living in a motel."

Bruno took a step forward. I instinctively took a step back, for reasons still unknown at that point; I didn't feel comfortable with the way Bruno looked at me.

"You know, you're all Donna talks about," Bruno said, taking another step. "Successful Christine! Why can't I be more successful?"

"Why did you come here?"

His hands were all of a sudden on my waist and he pulled me close. "It's been a while for me."

He then forced me into a violent kiss, proceeding to hold his hand on my mouth. "I can't touch Donna, not even just for a cuddle, so you see, my darling, I thought of you."

He withdrew momentarily, only to grab me by the hips. "That's all it takes to make me hard," he whispered, his lips brushing my ear. "You, saying my name. Now say it! Say my name!"

"Let me go!"

My heart pounded. I felt a sudden thud as my body was slammed against the conference table. Bruno began tearing at my clothes.

I was screaming inside my mind, stuck in denial. This wasn't happening. This was a dream. A nightmare. My thoughts rang loudly in my mind.

Hot, shallow breaths flew over my ears as a voice said, "I always loved you, Christine," moving his body slightly up and down in jerky movements.

This is far from a business meeting; my mind screamed at me, this is sexual assault!

He grabbed hold of my breasts through my blouse and began to fondle them, tugging painfully at them, squeezing them, while attempting to drag the neckline of my blouse down to expose them.

It was this pain that delivered the final blow to the fear that had me immobilized, and I fought with Bruno.

I bit his hand. He seemed surprised and jumped off me, but he immediately put his hand between my legs, grabbing my privates.

Furious now, I pushed his hand away, but he returned it to the edge of my skirt and started attempting to pull it up.

Somehow, he unbuckled his belt during the fracas and with a few jigs and tugs amidst the struggle, his trousers were soon around his ankles and the possibility of rape was even closer. He kept me pinned against the table within his grasp and I had nothing to hold on to, hit him with or even throw at him.

I struggled violently as he clutched me; he glided his hands up my skirt and grabbed hold of my buttocks whilst grinding against my body. I could not match his strength and was tiring from the strain of holding myself up against his attempts to push me down to the table and onto my back.

My panic rose to new levels as he tried to rip my panties and I shrieked, a scream so raw, hoarse and filled with fear that even I was surprised at how loud it was.

The screech filled the office and echoed through the walls. "Stop that," he barked with a voice that quivered slightly with fear. Encouraged, I drew breath again and let loose another yell.

Panicking, he covered my mouth with one hand while the other returned to fondling my breasts. I bit his fingers deeply until they bled; I spat out the coppery tang of blood and continued shouting for help. Muttering incoherently now, he hurriedly let go, drew up his trousers and ran out of the office. He knew the building we were in had security guards and it wouldn't be long before they would turn up.

As soon as he stepped out of the door, he was caught in the light of a torch and he froze for a moment like a deer caught in headlights.

Then, turning abruptly, he took to his heels. From my fetal position, I saw a security guard pass by the door in hot pursuit. Another guard ran in and pointed his torch around until its beam fell on me. As soon as it did, he rushed over to me and kneeled gently by my side, asking quietly, "Are you okay?"

It was an awful, petrifying evening. I was almost raped and escaped just in time. I filed a complaint with the police and never heard from Donna or Bruno again. Years later, I heard that they got back together and moved to Sri Lanka.

I fought against sadness, and struggled on my own like I had done many times before.

Each day my resilience grew, and each night my resolve hardened. I was going to be a success.

Later on that year, amidst my growing company and my insane work schedule, I met Louis, an Olivetti sales manager, from the French part of Belgium. He had a cheeky smile and was tall, bold, slim and sweet, with a French accent and a very sensual nature.

Not only was I attracted to him, but he respected my six-month rule. Only five years older than me, we started seeing each other regularly. He would chat with me for hours at the office about computers and life. What began as an interesting friendship eventually turned sexual months later.

I could tell that Louis had been a womanizer and that he had been with many different women in his life. He was very charming and seductive, wearing his attitude like a confident badge of honor. Naturally, I was suspicious.

"Would you mind getting an STD test before we spend the night together?" I asked him one evening.

"Oh…uh, sure. That's a good idea!" he said after thinking about it for a minute. I did everything right.

We both got an STD test, although he never saw mine—I did it in private just to make sure I was all right for myself; which, I was. My hormones were raging, so when the tests were finally done and the night came, it was amazing.

Louis had an apartment in Antwerp, which is where we would spend time. We had no hope of being discrete enough to stay at my mum's house. We had loud, youthful, lusty sex, the kind that leaves you feeling like you deserve a gold medal.

When we were apart, Louis and I would have phone sex, and we were very good at it. There was something about his sensual tone that turned me on, and his seductive nature was always very verbal, so phone sex was a natural progression for us during those times apart.

Things in my life seemed to be going incredibly well. I had a growing business, my first staff members, and a budding name for myself in a trendy new field.

Plus, I had the attention of a French lover who was able to give me sexual satisfaction like no man before him ever did. I truly believed that my life was finally pulling itself together, like a magnetic puzzle that only needed to be flipped in order to come together again.

Then one Friday, quite suddenly, things changed. We were sitting around the breakfast table in Louis's apartment, when a white envelope with silver writing slipped through the mail slot of his door. He swaggered towards it, wearing nothing but his black silk underwear, leaned over, picked it up, and in five steps had settled back at the wooden kitchen table, tearing it open. "An invitation to my sister's wedding," he said, scanning the card.

"Oh wow, a wedding! When is it?" I asked him, assuming I was invited.

"Oh, don't worry about it. It's just a little thing, and you are so busy at work," Louis said apprehensively.

I could tell by his lack of eye contact that he felt uncomfortable.

"What's the matter? Am I not invited?" I asked him, confused. We were as close as a couple could be, or so I believed.

"You are invited but…listen, you don't have to come." I stared at him and leaned back in my chair.

"What if I want to come?"

"I would prefer it if you didn't." He just scratched his naked chest. I was, in truth, surprised by this revelation.

"Why not?" I asked him sincerely, scanning his face for emotion. What deep, dark eyes he had.

"Listen. It's not me, okay? My mother heard rumors about you, and she doesn't approve of you. She doesn't want you to be there." He grew more agitated, taking long swigs of his coffee.

"Your mother? I've never met your mother! What has she heard?" I asked, horrified. I knew I had not had the most tasteful past.

Louis sighed heavily. "She told me that you have a bad reputation. That you have been with a lot of men and that you are a drunk."

The words crashed over my head and shoulders like the ice water wake-up from my childhood years. I measured my words carefully, my defenses immediately going up.

"You know about my past…I've told you."

"Yes, but now my mother knows too, and she doesn't like you! I'm sorry about that," he added.

"Where did she hear these rumors?" I folded my arms.

"I don't know…rumors travel fast. I can't say, but she knows."

"How long has she known?"

Louis was grinding his jaw now and tapping the table with his fingers.

"A few months."

"So," I shook my head. "Just so that I am clear, you are too embarrassed of me to take me to your sister's wedding because your mother believes I am still a slut and a drunk?"

"YES! Yes, I am embarrassed! I don't want you to meet my family," he exclaimed, although I could see the words rolled around uncomfortably in his mouth.

That was when I knew. It was over. I broke up with him there and then and told him, "If you want to love me now, then you also have to learn to love and accept my past because the struggles I went through in the past made me who I am today."

I told him I could never be with a man who did not respect me and feel proud of me for who I had become. I was worth more than that. We parted ways, sadly, but exercising my right to dignity in a relationship filled me with renewed hope for the future.

It hurts when you realize you aren't as important to someone as you thought you were. I suddenly understood why he didn't want to walk hand in hand in public; he simply didn't want people to see that we were a couple. I was no stranger to disappointment and frustration, so I coped.

I decided that we would remain business friends as he sometimes gave me company names I could sell to. If he didn't succeed to sell the company an Olivetti computer, I tried to sell them an Apple Computer.

In a way, I was taking advantage of him by using him for business leads and I actually took pleasure in doing so because of the way he treated me.

Any future man would have to accept me for who I am, realizing that I come with my baggage of past problems. If this would ever be a source of arguments, it was not acceptable for me. I knew love could be better and I always believed that one day, I would meet a man who would *really* love me.

The Magical Handshake

"In life, you have to take the pace that love goes. You don't force it. You just don't force love, you don't force falling in love, you don't force being in love—you just become. I don't know how to say that in English, but you just feel it."
– Juan Pablo Galavis

1987, Belgium, Age 28

When one door closes, a window opens. Don't waste time staring at the closed door and risk losing the life-changing miracle that is watching you through the window. The latch is always on the inside. After Louis, I threw myself deeper into my business, specializing in typesetting and graphic design.

I was starting to earn good money, and since I was used to dressing smartly when I lived at home, I returned to my roots in order to impress business people, to ultimately score the business deals I had set my sights on.

I needed customers and suppliers to think of me as a professional businesswoman, and it was important to reflect that in my appearance. I usually wore a business suit with high heels.

To compliment my image, I purchased a top of the range Mercedes, which I thought at the time was important. Perhaps I just wanted to buy one because my father had one.

I bought some stunning jewelry sets with sparkling diamonds. Mum said I was allowed to wear her jewelry, but I felt too proud to do that and wanted to make a point that I earned enough to buy my own jewelry.

With my shoulder-length hair, combed back with a stylish curl, giving it a coiffured look, combined with diamond earrings, people's eyes were never drawn to my scar, making me feel better.

I had to do everything possible to feel comfortable in my skin and that way, close a lot of business deals.

As a businesswoman, I was constantly meeting new people, mostly men. Countless men asked me to go out for meals with them, to discuss business, or to go on a date. Most of the time I declined. However, I did have a lot of short-term boyfriends, from all walks of life.

None of them met enough of my requirements to become serious though. Furthermore, in each relationship I was in, there was constant arguing: "I don't like it when you do that" or "You can't say this or you can't do that," etc.

I just wanted to be myself, do what I want to do, and I certainly didn't want another relationship with constant arguments. There was no longer space for toxic people in my life. I told myself I was done wasting my time trying to get people to love me for who I am.

I realized there was still one thing that gnawed at my self-esteem, and I had the power to change it. Medical treatments and technology were always improving, and I decided to find another specialist plastic surgeon to help with my scar. It was well worth the expense. My scar was not completely gone after the procedure but it was significantly less red and less obvious.

I was thrilled. It was the best it had ever been. I became very skilled at camouflaging it with special make-up so you could barely notice it.

My confidence was improving in all areas of my life. I soon had the chance to try my English on the job for the first time. A customer asked me if I could get hold of some software created by DP Digital in the UK and I was ready to make it happen.

Up until that point I had only studied English at school, and had bits and pieces that I picked up from movies and music. It did not matter; I made it work. I called the company at their branch in Essex.

It turned out the software was lucrative and I stood to make a healthy profit on each sale, so we set up a meeting. A week later and I was in the UK with two of my staff members, my sales manager and my technical engineer.

We arrived at DP Digital offices, wearing my best business clothes to make a good first impression. We were waiting in the lobby when the receptionist stood and beckoned to us.

What followed was one of those moments that sneak up on you, completely unexpected, and take you by total surprise.

"This is Richard, our sales manager," the receptionist said as my eyes travelled upwards, meeting his eyes. They were soft and kind. I immediately noticed his ever-so-cute smile. I held out my hand to shake his, and the second my skin touched his, I felt a surge of energy leap from me into him and from him into me. It startled me—so much so that I nearly lost my balance.

I could see in Richard's face that he had felt the spark too— the kind that exists in storybooks, written by fanciful romance novelists and children's authors, a connection to another human soul that jolted my insides and sent flutters through my stomach.

We greeted each other and he showed us to the meeting room before he was called away. Richard was immaculately dressed in a grey suit and tie and shiny black shoes. He was a bold, slim man with a beard and moustache.

My heart hammered discreetly in my chest as I barely heard the technician who was addressing us. My staff peered at me curiously; they were not used to seeing me so distracted. A few minutes later Richard returned and told us all about the software. I listened as hard as I could, trying not to portray my obvious attraction to him.

"This version of the software sells very well because of its powerful built-in features," Richard said to me, his presence taking up the room.

"I can see why; I'd love to sell this in Belgium. I'm sure it will sell there too. Graphic designers will love it," I said knowledgeably, although my thoughts were on other things.

"Forgive me for saying so, Christine, but it's so refreshing meeting a woman who knows about this kind of software," he said to me. Those days, a woman talking about computer software was unusual.

I blushed. "It's good for me too. I've learned some interesting things here from you."

"Can I ask...are you going to the Apple exhibition in San Francisco this year?" I could see he was nervous, and I became excited.

"Yes, definitely," I replied, something inside told me I wanted to see him again.

"We have other products available that could be suitable for the Belgian market. Can we arrange to meet there so we can continue this conversation?" he inquired.

"Of course, I'd be happy to learn more about the software and other products," I said to him, keeping it formal.

We exchanged business cards and Richard told me he would fax me details of where he would be staying in San Francisco.

The meeting was signed and sealed that same day, and I told Richard I would see him again at the Mac World Apple exhibition in San Francisco.

"I'll see you there," he told me, perhaps interested in closing more sales with my company.

When I arrived back in Belgium, there was a fax from Richard. He was obviously a man of his word. The fax gave details about his trip to the exhibition so that we could meet up...and we did.

I counted the days until the exhibition. My thoughts stayed focused on Richard and those sparks. I met him at his hotel in San Francisco, and we decided to go to the bar to talk. I wanted to get to know him on a personal level, to find out why I had suddenly felt so strongly for this strange man.

Two minutes into the conversation, my heart fell.

"I'm married with four kids, so they are a handful," Richard told me. That was it. Whatever feelings I felt would have to dissipate. Richard continued and added, "I haven't been happy with my wife for a long time. I'm planning to leave her soon; I just haven't had the courage to do it because of the kids. They will be devastated."

He sounded sincere and genuinely remorseful. I could not explain it, but I believed him. That night we spoke mostly about computers and software but also about our lives.

I found out that Richard was a drummer in a band and loved music as I did but that he could not focus on it because his wife insisted he get a "real" job. She was mentally unstable and had been hospitalized often.

Six engrossing, entrancing hours slipped by as I listened to him talk. I knew that I was falling in love and I rebuked myself for it. After all I had been through, I should know better. How could a stranger have this effect on me? By the end of the night, a slow song played and Richard invited me to dance with him.

Feeling his arms wrapped around my body was ethereal. I felt that I had stepped into a movie, my heart was bursting. No matter how hard I tried, I could not resist him. All we did was dance. He was the perfect gentleman.

When the slow music stopped, he said, "We can't do this. I am still married...but we can be friends."

I nodded, knowing that I would rather be his friend than nothing at all.

True love—when it hits you—takes your heart, mind and soul by surprise. You suddenly belong to someone, even if it is impossible, as it was with Richard and me. Your mind thinks only of them and you long for the next time you get to stand in their presence. Whoever Richard was, I felt that he was made of the same things I was.

Sometimes when you lock eyes with people, you know at that very moment they will affect your life. That's how it was with Richard, the very first time I looked into his eyes.

We spent the next six days together in San Francisco and we behaved impeccably. He was eleven years my senior, lived in another country, and had a wife and four children back home. It was an impossible situation. And yet, the San Francisco trip was the start of something. I could feel it in my bones, more than that, I knew that he felt it too.

It was a mutual "love at first handshake" that descended on us. I left my heart in San Francisco! I told myself that Richard had too many complications and that we could never be together. Life had to go on and so did business. I would not get in the way of his marriage or his children's upbringing.

Some weeks later, Richard visited me in Belgium for one day to assist our customers in upgrading the software we had purchased from DP Publishing.

We went out for a meal, burning with desire for each other but unable to act on it. I would not kiss him or cross the line; I wanted his decision to leave his wife to be all his own. We agreed to stay in contact and we started faxing each other every day. He lived in the UK, and I was in Belgium.

We were apart but together. In love but unable to love. I learned a lot about him and he did the same with me. Every now and then, Richard and I spoke on the phone. He spent long hours telling me that I could do anything and that I was an extraordinary businesswoman.

"I believe in you," Richard would say to me. Those words became more important to me than "I love you" ever did. Somebody believed in me!

It was the confirmation I'd always craved, and I could finally completely believe in myself. Nothing could stop me now. Richard gave me the greatest gift anyone could give me: he believed in me, when nobody else did. Nobody *ever* told me they believed in me.

Richard gave me the confidence I needed and I started to make a lot of new friends that I met through business. I have never liked the small chitchat, but I love talking about business—all aspects of it.

I tried as best I could to put my feelings for Richard aside and invested every penny I had into expansion and a big idea. I needed extra computers, extra staff, and a large showroom to bolster sales. I was alive with ambition and drive. Time management became extremely important to me.

I spent the next few weeks knocking on every computer manufacturer's door, persuading them to give me show stock for free. I got each and every one of them to agree by leveraging my state-of-the-art showroom and its sales capacity. The new premises, located in Duffel, were fifty times bigger than anything I had managed before, and I hired eight new staff members, mostly sales people.

On the massive opening day, 800 people walked through my showroom. I ran promotions and closed a lot of sales. My investment in a magnificent marble showroom paid off big time. For the first time in my life, thanks to Richard, I believed in myself and it worked. I was unstoppable. I set myself goals and I wouldn't stop until I achieved those goals.

The showroom looked absolutely stunning. I had instructed the architect that I wanted the best of the best. Average was never good enough for me. I was not Mrs. Average.

My brothers only knew me as a "rebel" and "the sister who drank a lot and had many boyfriends."

They didn't know the new me, the ambitious, successful businesswoman, because I was working long hours, seven days a week, and had little contact with them. However, they all came to the opening day of my new showroom and were very impressed.

They congratulated me and they were all shocked by the massive size of the offices and showrooms, as well as the striking interior. They thoroughly enjoyed the evening and praised me for how well it was organized. It was very clear that they were amazed by the transformation of who I had become. My mum attended the reception with a few of her best friends and she was extremely proud.

With the best computer merchandise in the world, my two-story showroom was the talk of the town—a luxury spectacle of unparalleled beauty.

Richard found time to come to the opening day; he told me that he would not have missed it for the world. He stayed from opening to closing at 11 p.m., and told me many times how proud he was of me.

Richard recognized the businesswoman in me and he encouraged it. Still we had not crossed the line and become physical. Richard, the kind-hearted and devoted person he is, couldn't cheat on his wife, even though his wife had already been unfaithful to him—a few times. Richard even found some of the love letters from the men with whom she was unfaithful.

She had pushed him away so completely that, for a long time, they were just two people under the same roof. There was no more love, no more unity, no more companionship. Their relationship was no longer a marriage.

Richard was fraught with guilt over the unexpected love he had developed for me. He blamed himself for giving into it, even though all we had done wrong was feel something for each other. We never even kissed but somehow we both knew we were meant to be together.

The Question List

"The greatest gift that you can give to others is the gift of unconditional love and acceptance." – Brian Tracy

2016, St. Vincentius Hospital, Age 57

Another day went by with nurses hurrying in and out of my mother's room, checking her stats and speaking in hushed tones over her. I spent most of my time there, perched on the uneasy tightrope that could pull me either way depending on my mother's response to the treatments they were giving her.

The next day, towards lunchtime, we; Richard, Roger and myself, had all relaxed into the silence and were regularly breaking it. Anything to avoid the stark reality of my mother's coma and her ever-present threat of slipping away.

Richard had just left the room to catch some fresh air and get a bite to eat. Then, from the corner of my eye, a snatch of movement drew my eye. Turning my head quickly, I realized it had not been my imagination at all. My mother was moving her arms and hands. My eyes immediately darted up, and I gulped down a breath of air, bringing new life into my weary bones.

Her eyes were open!

"Mum? She's awake!" I said to Roger. My mother's voice permeated the silence, lifting it finally and gleefully from the room, which seemed to change color as she spoke.

"Christine?" She grasped for my hand. I gladly took it, a warmer version of the icy grip I felt just yesterday.

"You've been very ill, Mum. The doctors are coming," I said to her, searching her wrinkled face.

I could see she was alarmed and confused to find herself in hospital. Two familiar nurses swept into the room. As they took her vitals and spoke to her, tears rolled down my eyes.

"I thought I would never hear her again," I whispered to Roger so that no one else could hear me. He nodded silently.

I could not believe it. She had woken up. Despite her age and everyone's insistence that "it was her time," she opened her eyes and looked right at me. Not only that but she recognized me. For more than a year now, Mum had barely recognized me at all—her dementia was progressing, and it left her very quiet and subdued most days.

The doctors pulled Roger and me outside as the nurses tended to my mum. The older of the two addressed us, his eyes alert and sincere.

"The fact that she has woken up on her own is an excellent sign. I cannot say that we are out of the woods yet, but her vitals are strong and the infection is healing. Your mother is one tough woman; she may survive."

It was the kind of news we never expected to hear, not after days of watching her motionless in her hospital bed. It filled me with joy to know that my mother still had some life in her and that she was not ready to leave this world.

I listened politely to the doctors, but my spirit had already ghosted inside to hug my mother. The second the doctors stopped talking, my body reunited with my spirit and I walked towards her bed. She was tired but quite lucid, I hugged her lightly and carefully, channeling my love for her into that moment.

"I love you, Mum," I whispered. I had only once before told mum I loved her, but from now on, she would hear it regularly, I would make sure of that.

"I love you too," she responded and we fell into easy conversation like she had never been a breath away from the end.

After 10 minutes of talking, she collapsed into a comfortable sleep. Roger had left to go home and would return later that day. As my mum slept, I was overcome with inspiration and wrote page after page of observations about life.

I was writing the speech I would deliver at Saturday's event. Assuming mum would get better quickly, I would be able to attend the event. Whilst writing parts of it, memories flashed through my mind.

1988, Belgium, Age 29

Richard and I remained friends as we both understood the love we felt for each other at the time was forbidden. We visited each other after discovering it was impossible to stay away. Yet still we could not be together. It was like walking under an umbrella in the most perfect sunlight of our lives.

We became good friends, and as friends do, Richard visited me one weekend. We met up in Brussels with a friend of Richard's, Clarissa. I got on very well with her; we had a lot of fun together. I thought she was funny and she thought the same about me.

On the evening of the first night, we all went to a bar with live music. Clarissa met up with some other friends and went to a disco bar with them, leaving Richard and me alone.

"Are you coming with me or what?" Richard grinned, gesturing to make our way back to his hotel room. "I have something I want to tell you." I nodded, my intentions pure.

We were exhausted from sightseeing during the day and hanging out together that evening, which was wonderful, wild and exhilarating. When we got up to his hotel room, we put on slow music and started dancing together. I rested my head on his shoulders and dreamed that he was mine. I could hear his heart thumping beneath my head, nervous like I was.

Richard stopped dancing as the music played on, held my hands in his and gazed deeply into my eyes. I could not recall loving a man more than I loved him.

"Christine, you know we share something special..." he began, and I listened raptly to every word.

"I have been dealing with a failed relationship at home, struggling to free myself of this guilt and make it right..."

A pause that seemed to last forever hung between our warm bodies. I spoke.

"You can tell me anything." Then he looked up and reached over, cupping my face in his hand.

"I couldn't tell you earlier, whilst Clarissa was with us. I love you. I know what I want, and it's you! I have finally left my wife and moved in with my mother. For you. For us. I can't live that way anymore when my heart belongs to you."

He was vulnerable in that moment and beautiful. He continued to say that he stayed with his wife for as long as she was on the anti-depressant medication so he could be there for his children. His wife had stopped her medication, so it was the right time to leave her.

I let him pull me into a profoundly sensual kiss, the months of our forbidden friendship erupting into passion and desire. The barriers separating us melted and the feelings we shared with each other captured us in an electric shock of emotions. I kissed him back—hard and desperately—and it was nothing like I had ever experienced before. I had been in enough relationships to tell the difference between love and lust and I knew this time it was love. In the past, I wanted to be loved so badly that I couldn't even tell that it wasn't love.

A natural unity overtook us, and things slowed down. Every touch was heightened; every breath was measured. The way that Richard kissed me and touched me was different from anything I had ever felt in the past.

Not sex, like it had been with so many others, but love. As it dawned on me that I was making love for the first time, my heart cast itself wide. I had known Richard for several months and was well within my six-month rule. That made it even better! This time, the six months didn't have to start counting from the moment we kissed but from the moment we met.

I felt loved, accepted and treasured in a way I could not have explained until that night. This was my future husband; I could feel it in my bones. The love I felt for him echoed inside me, guiding my hands and my body.

I did not have to think about anything at all—it was the most enriching, natural experience of my life.

At the end of our union, the earth shook hard enough to fly into the sun. It was perfect.

That night was the most romantic night of my life. I had sex with many men before, but never this kind of sex. This wasn't sex; it was an exchange of extremely passionate feelings for each other. I knew that night that all the sex I had before was just sex, nothing more than physical sex.

This was passionate lovemaking between two people who loved each other very much. The passion, the desire, the lust and the feelings were simply out of this world. All doubts were drained away because of this lovemaking session.

One thing I had learned in the past, because I had sex with many men, was how to please men in bed, so my sexual confidence was high. This time, though, for the first time ever, real love was involved. Richard never worried how many people I had slept with; he just accepted it and joked that he would benefit from my experience.

He didn't care about my past because he wanted to be my future. He always said, "What happened in the past, happened. I am not worried about it at all. I wasn't there. I look into the future, with you."

We lay together in bed talking for hours afterwards, our minds buzzing from endorphins and the euphoria of new love shared. In bed, vulnerable and happy, I shared my feelings about my dad with Richard.

"It's my biggest regret, not speaking to him that day he came to see me," I said as Richard listened intently. "I always thought that one day I would patch things up with him. I've wrestled with that day over and over again. He came to see me and I said nothing. I feel like the worst daughter in the world."

Richard considered my words carefully, then spoke: "You are far from the worst daughter, my love. You were young and troubled and finding your way. Your father was a sharp, brooding man with a lot of faults. I think, he loved you though. Why else would he bother to come and see you after he knew he had cancer and was going to die? It sounds like he regretted the past as much as you did."

"It's confusing," I mused, "now that I am older, I wonder if he was as bad as I thought he was. He punished us but perhaps that was all he knew. I didn't make it easy for him. I was very rebellious."

"Good intentions blossom from love. I think your dad just did not know how to communicate it clearly. The way he treated you all was wrong, even though he believed it was right."

Tears welled up in my eyes as I lay on the soft cotton sheets. "He always said I would never amount to anything. That I was useless."

"Useless!" Richard said, surprised. "Absolutely not. You are who you are—a wonderful, caring, intelligent woman with a heart of gold, a keen eye for business, and an attractive hunger for more from life.

That makes you perfect. You have been misguided and underestimated all your life. I can see your dreams reflecting in your stunning, green, distinctive eyes. Your eyes are the window to your soul.

You can achieve all your dreams. You can do anything! You are going to achieve extraordinary results in business. I look into your eyes and I can see your good heart. If your father saw you now, he would be proud of you."

Richard's words gave me enormous comfort. I leaned into them and wanted to fall asleep in his arms but I knew I could not stay. At 5 a.m., when Richard began to fall asleep, I told him I had to leave—and I could not confess why. At 29, I was still wetting the bed. I could not face telling him that after a perfect night spent together. The older I got, the more embarrassed I became about it.

A terrifying fear set in and I was afraid that Richard would reject me if he found out that I had a problem of this magnitude.

Perhaps it wouldn't be a problem for him, but it sure was a very big problem for me. I drove home, got some sleep and drove back a few hours later. That same day, Clarissa, Richard, and I said our goodbyes, and they headed back to the UK. Despite our awkward ending, as Richard wondered why I didn't stay the night, love bloomed and grew between the two of us.

Richard started faxing me love letters, confessing his love and declaring his deepest, darkest fears and struggles to me, like we now faced them together, which we did. Somehow, we both knew that we had found our true love. I was not prepared for this: suddenly I had so much love to give. I never knew how much love I had in me.

Richard wrote:

Rest assured that I will never knowingly hurt or embarrass you but will always be your most loving friend and confidante. I know that you said that we must both fight our emotions, but I will find this almost impossible. If am being presumptuous by assuming that your feelings for me are as strong as mine for you, please let me know now.
I must try to see my children often as I love them very much. I am prevented from doing what I want to do (work in Belgium somewhere so I can see you more often) because of my children, but they grow older every day.
During my life I have only fallen in love with two women, my wife and you, Christine. I still respect my wife but am afraid that over the past years love has slowly died between us, and me being the person I am, I cannot forgive past events. I now trust you as my closest friend and will talk only to you of these matters. I have gained a close friend for life, you, Christine.
All my love,
Richard

An extract of my reply:

You are not presumptuous by assuming that my feelings for you are as strong as yours for me. I love and respect you with all my heart. You are so far away, but sometimes I can feel you near me. I still think that I have to fight my feelings and emotions for you because of the impossible distance between us and because of your children. I never want to be someone who keeps you away from your family. I would like you to be my most loving friend, for now.

There are many people in life, but only a few will make a lasting impression in our minds and hearts. You are one of them. I will always treasure having you in my life, and I believe we can be friends forever.

I am very much looking forward to meeting you again soon because there are so many things I want to talk to you about. One of them is the situation with your wife and your children. I want you to know that I never want to be an obstacle and the last thing I want to do is hurt your children.
I love you,
Christine

Richard replied:

I cannot tell you how much I appreciate the sentiments that you express. I now know that my deepest emotions for you are returned, and words cannot express the passion and depth of my love for you, which is growing day by day.

Christine, you are definitely not an obstacle to my family. I can and will overcome work, money and family problems somehow in order to see you.

My main problem is how to keep from hurting my children. It's not their fault that I no longer love their mother and love a Belgian woman instead. I am, though, a man of honor, and I will support them no matter what (financially, emotionally, etc.). My wife is the mother of my children, and I do not hate her, I respect her. I realize that she has hurt me but I do not wish to be unnecessarily hurtful. My conscience is now troubled because of my children. Until I sort out my future, I do hope to support them and my wife.

I know that my love for my children will always be with me and that I face some heartache related to them, and I need you to help me get through it. I will overcome this and be as good a father as I can be to all my children, present and future.

You are not standing between us; it is not your fault. I am a grown man and can make my own decisions, and I need you. Please don't let your conscience trouble you; it should be clear.
With all my love and deepest affection,
Richard

Around this time, Richard had terrible conscience problems with his children but knew that if he wanted to build a future with me, he had to overcome them.

I have never influenced him to make a decision other than saying that I loved him dearly. His four children and their ages at the time were Nina, the oldest, 18; Clara, 16; Mateo, 12; and the youngest, Martin, 8.

I loved arriving at my office in the morning to see if another poem or letter was waiting for me on the fax machine. I had never experienced pure love before. It filled my mind and erased a heartache that had been with me for many years.

While he knew that divorcing his wife would involve a lot of conflict, it was his children he worried about most. During those months when we were forced to be apart, we romanced each other over the fax machine.

Words and declarations brought us together as our minds aligned with our hearts. That was the difference with Richard— he and I believed in the same things. Neither of us knew if a long-term relationship was possible because of his situation. Richard and I only saw each other a few times, but those few times were enough for us to realize we had something special, a very loving bond. Being apart for too long was impossible.

Richard had promised his wife a long time ago that if she stopped taking a certain medication for depression, he would take her on holiday. She did stop the medication, and because Richard was a man of his word, he booked a holiday to Corfu for one week.

I guess it was unusual for him to go on holiday with his wife, whom he had already left, but he wanted to go out of respect for her having stopped the medication. I didn't mind, as I supported Richard in whatever decision he made regarding his wife and children. Most of all, I trusted him implicitly.

They agreed to go as friends but all they did was argue the whole time. The holiday couldn't be over quick enough. They both admitted that they hadn't loved each other for several years and the best thing was to divorce. They knew it would be hard for the children, but they also knew they had to go their separate ways.

Some months later, Richard told his children about the divorce. It hurt them. Richard was incredibly torn up about this, but we both understood that it was necessary and that nothing could spare them from the pain of it. As he sorted through the remnants of his old life, I didn't want to interfere.

I knew that if I went over to help him, I would only make it worse and harder on the kids. They would not understand how deeply we loved each other or that our love was meant to be. Once the dust of his past had settled, we finally saw each other again.

Seeing him again set my heart free from its cage, and it was the best feeling I had ever felt.

In May of 1988, 2 months after the Brussels weekend, I travelled to the UK to stay with Richard for a short visit.

Richard had booked us seats to see one of his favorite comedians, Dame Edna, at the London Palladium and a classical concert at the Royal Festival Hall the following evening. It took a lot to say yes because it meant that I would have to face my biggest and most persistent problem. On the phone that afternoon, I was plagued with doubts.

"I'll stay with you, Richard, but there is something I have to tell you."

"That doesn't sound good..."

"It's just something personal I need to get off my chest," I said. "It's very important to me that before we continue, you should know about it. I will explain it when I arrive there."

Later, he would tell me how crippled with fear he was over that brief conversation. He thought I had cancer, or three hidden children, or that I was married. In any case, he was convinced our happiness was about to end.

Richard booked a room in the Liongate Hotel in Hampton Court for three days. There was no escape route. I loved Richard, and he loved me—but I could no longer keep him from my truth.

Fear gripped me. I was terrified that he would reject me or be disgusted by me. I had no idea how he would react. I felt like at any moment, I could lose the happiness I had found in him— the happiness I had been searching for since before I started school as a child. Richard was already struggling with his family and now I had more baggage to give him.

I agonized over the decision but decided to choose love over fear. Sometimes you have to trust that what you feel is strong enough to get you through anything. I flew over to the UK.

Richard met me at the airport and drove me to the Liongate Hotel. As we ascended the elevator to our hotel room, all I could think about was how I was going to tell Richard.

Once inside the neatly decorated room, with its white and red linens, he poured us each a soft drink, and we sat by the window. Richard's face was all business, and I was drinking adrenaline and fear.

I tried to get to the point where I could tell him, but the words did not fit in my mouth.

"Look, I, uh, there's something that...what I mean is that sometimes things in the past...no, that's not right." As I struggled to express myself, Richard drained his Coke all down in one gulp.

"What is it, Christine?" he pleaded with me, his hands on my knees. "You can tell me anything."

I took a deep breath and collected myself. I felt like a Disney princess about to battle the dragon before either dying at the hands of darkness or living with my happy ending.

"Okay. Here it is," I said, my heart thumping hard in my chest. "I am going to tell you my deepest, darkest secret. You should know it before our relationship goes any further. You have to promise not to laugh at me. It's a very sensitive matter that I have been dealing with for my entire life." Richard moved onto the couch with me and slung his arms over my shoulders.

"Of course I won't laugh, my sweetheart. I love you. I promise that I will not laugh at what you tell me." The sincerity in his eyes blew me away, but even then, I talked around it, and he could tell.

"Christine, you are not getting to the point. I know you are afraid, but I'm not going to judge you. Please, just tell me." His kind eyes shone back at me.

I blurted it out. I knew no other way.

"I wet my bed every night. I'm 29 years old, and I still wet my bed. Usually the more work you put into something, the better it becomes, but it doesn't apply to dealing with bedwetting. You could put in all the effort in the world and not have anything to show for it as none of the remedies I have ever tried have worked. I am very sorry but I really cannot help it."

A few moments passed as my eyes filled up with tears, decorating my dress with droplets of sadness.

Richard pulled me into a hug and held me tight.

"So what? That's not a problem for me. I still love you and everything that you are!"

His answer made me cry harder, and I retold him snippets of my childhood that still plagued me: the cruel nuns and the incessant laughing of the children. Then he lifted my chin and met my eyes.

"Once we live together, I will wash your sheets every day for you. For as long as you are with me, no one will ever laugh at you again, my love. I was afraid you were going to tell me you were ill or something but bedwetting is the least of my worries! I will live for the rest of my life to make sure you will forget your past and always be happy."

His eyes filled with tears too, relieved that I didn't have an incurable medical condition.

We went out that night and made love when we got back. It was the second time we had made love. I thought the first time we made love was out of this world, but this time it was extra-terrestrial, mind-blowing, mesmerizing!

It was extremely erotic and romantic. The attraction for each other, the kissing, the abundance of passion, the whispering, the shivers, the warmth! It was unforgettable and electric.

Richard brought out all the love I had in me. He taught me what real love is. I realized that I had never actually loved anybody before.

For the first time, I slept overnight with Richard. That morning Richard stripped my sheets for me. That was when I knew we were getting serious.

We both agreed in advance, before we decided to go away for the weekend, to make a list of questions for each other as we both knew our lives were about to change forever. Together we took a walk next to the water and made our way to a shady bench cast in the dappled sunlight of the mid-morning, near the hotel grounds.

The bench was set in beautiful surroundings in front of the river, the perfect spot for me to get serious about what we were getting ourselves into.

For months, I had been developing a compatibility list of what I wanted in a partner.

I had to break out my list and make sure that Richard was the one. On that bench, I spent the morning questioning and re-questioning Richard as my perfect partner, and he indulged me.

He left his wife and kids for me, and I wanted to make 100% sure we were doing the right thing. I grilled him—question after question—as if he was on a game show and the questions were tied to real-life rewards.

We spoke about the consequences of our actions. I asked Richard easy questions, hard ones and funny ones too. I had a total of 75 questions on my list. I asked him about politics, foods he liked and disliked, his health, his favorite music, how he folded towels and sheets, etc.

Here are a few questions I asked:

- We see each other only on the weekends at the moment, in a relaxed atmosphere, no pressure from work. How will we both be in a stressful work environment?

- We will only get to know each other 100% once one of us leaves their country, as only then will we be able to live together. Are you happy with this? Do we both really understand the consequences of our decisions we have to make?

- If you ever move to Belgium, you will have to leave your band. Will you not miss your music too much to be happy?

- What have you been the most depressed about in your life?

- What makes you happy?

- Although I have consumed a lot of alcohol myself in the past, I am totally against drinking alcohol, especially spirits. I have seen too much misery because of it. Do you promise me that you will not drink a lot of alcohol?

- I will never be a good housewife, cook or cleaner, as I hate household chores. I will always work hard enough to, as soon as possible, be able to afford staff to do this. Are you happy to do the household chores, until we can afford staff?

- What are your expectations in life?

- What if one of your children is totally against me or can't cope with the divorce? This is a possibility, and we need to be realistic about this. Will you want to go back to the UK, should you ever move to Belgium?

- I am a hard worker, and work comes before pleasure. Can you accept this?

- I have been laughed at for most of my life and will be deeply hurt if somebody laughs at me again. Do you promise never to laugh at me?

- I have been bossed around for most of my life, and I am now my own boss and never want to be bossed around again. I am a very independent woman and I want to be in control. We will, of course, make decisions together, both our opinions taken into account. Are you okay with that?

- I would like 10 children, and you already have four children. Are you happy with that?

- Our nationalities are different, which automatically brings different cultures, traditions, and habits. Will we always overcome this?

- Will you be able to accept and live with my past problems? I might get flashbacks that will bring me sorrow, and I will sometimes cry because of these.

- I will love and accept your children with open arms and help them as much as I can, but we have to be realistic, and the love for our children, should we ever have any, will be a different kind of love as your children are not my own blood. I am a realistic person and we have to talk about this now, as it is so very important. I will meet your children when your youngest is nine years old. I won't know them from birth, I didn't carry them nine months, I didn't give birth to them, and I didn't breastfeed them, so how can I love them exactly the same as I would love my own? Are you happy with my view?

- I earn good money with AM Computers but I am certainly not a millionaire and I have a lot of overheads too. My company might even go under and then I won't have any money. Can you accept this?

- What happens if we have no money for you to go to visit your children in the UK, should you ever move to Belgium?

- I have been lied to too many times, and I think trust is very important in a relationship. If lies creep up in our relationship, it will be the end of it. Do you agree?

- I am a very direct person and don't beat around the bush. Many people don't like that, as it is not a common characteristic, as far as I know. Can you accept this?

- How are your spending habits and what is your financial situation? (Richard couldn't stop smiling when I asked this question immediately after saying I was a direct person).

- If I move to the UK, I will want to set up my own company, which means, working long hours. Can you accept that?

- Because I wet the bed, you will have to wake up every day, often in the middle of the night, so that I can put fresh sheets on the bed. On top of that, every morning, the sheets need to be washed again. This is the norm for me. Will it not become too much for you?

- In case we can't have children together, for a reason unknown at present, are you happy to adopt or perhaps try artificial insemination?

- How important are birthday and anniversary celebrations to you?

- What makes you most insecure?

- What are the five principles you believe in most regarding the education of our children, should we have any?

He always had the right answer. Finally, I told Richard that while I wanted 10 children, I mostly wanted twin girls.

"It's been my dream to have identical twin girls for most of my life. I've been dreaming about them since I was a young girl and I want to investigate how to maximize my chances of having them," I confessed to him that morning. "That dream has gotten me through some pretty rough times," I continued.

"Then we must try for them one day" was his response. After the question session, we laughed together.

It was Richard's turn.

"What are your questions for me?" I asked him.

"I have only *one* question. Will you always love me?" he asked his eyes full of warmth.

"Always. Yesterday, Today, and Tomorrow." I replied.

From then on, we always signed our love letters with "Y.T.T," symbolizing the promise we had made to each other: to stay together, forever.

Lots of men would have run a mile, after being questioned like I did Richard, but he just said, "I respect you even more for knowing exactly what you want, sweetheart, and for just being you. I fully understand your reasons for asking me all your questions."

Besides the question list, I also had a "character check" list. I wrote down 50 characteristics on a piece of paper with two columns next to each characteristic. We both had a copy.

In the first column, each of us had to write the value you would give yourself and in the second column, the value you would give the other person.

The values were between 0 and 10 (0 being you wouldn't say that characteristic applies and 10 meaning that characteristic definitely applies).

The aim of this "game" was to see if we shared a lot of the same characteristics, as well as how well we knew each other at this stage of our relationship.

A few characteristics that were listed included anxious, competitive, confident, disciplined, efficient, faithful, funny, gentle, honest, helpful, independent, introvert, loving, materialistic, optimistic, reliable, shy, stubborn, etc.

After we saw each other's results, we gave one example of why we put the number we did. It was great fun, and we learned a lot about each other that way.

That weekend changed the course of our lives. It was the best time we'd had together, and we laughed so much; we loved each other's humor. We decided then that we would stay together forever and that together we could overcome whatever problems we faced.

Neither of us had the slightest desire to change anything about the other. We accepted each other exactly as we were. We were utterly perfect for each other.

It takes a special man to love a woman who has been hurt and broken. A weak man cannot handle a strong woman. Richard gave grace and kindness where there had been none before.

I loved everything about Richard, and he loved everything about me. I had no doubts he would pursue his divorce without any hesitation or second thoughts.

One of us would have to move sooner or later, because we weren't satisfied with a long-distance relationship. We needed to live together. With complete confidence, I told Richard I would be happy to move to the UK to be with him. He had rescued me from misery and unhappiness. Whatever would happen in the future, I was forever thankful to him for giving me pure and honest love.

At the end of the Liongate visit, we swore to each other that whatever obstacles life threw at us, we would overcome them together. Richard returned home, and I went back to Keldonk with renewed hope that one of us would move soon.

An extract from a letter Richard wrote to me after the weekend spent together at the Liongate Hotel:

My wonderfully tender, dearest darling Christine,

I thank you deeply for the wonderful days in London, days that are embedded in my memory forever.

The more that I learn about you, the more I love you.
I feel so very proud and thankful that you even consider giving up your company and coming to England to be with me. I am sure that we would be very happy in the UK, and maybe one day we will end up there.

At the moment though, your company, of which I am so proud, is becoming a major success. I do not have the right to rob you of your moment of triumph.
I know in my innermost senses that we will get it together and that the future will hold all we desire.

Keep your spirit high,
Feel me with you all the time,
I adore and love you, my sweetheart

With all my deepest love, respect and devotion forever.
Yours forever in heart, body and mind.
Y.T.T.
Richard

An extract of my reply:

My dearest, sweet Richard,

The day we met, something inside me changed.
I don't quite understand it, but I know the change is because
of you.

It's such a good feeling that I hope will never end.
No one in my life has ever made me feel the way you do.
I have learned with you what real love is.
I would give up everything I have, if only I could be with
you every day.

I miss you so much that it hurts.
I love you deeply and always will,
I will always love you with all my heart, my heart belongs to
you.
Longing to see you again,
Y.T.T.
Christine

These were the happiest days of my life, beyond anything I could have conceived of as a young person. I had found my knight in shining armor and we would live happily ever after. I kept thinking it was all too good to be true and was fearful that my happiness would end soon.

Long Distances

"Achievement of your happiness is the only moral purpose of your life, and that happiness, not pain or mindless self-indulgence, is the proof of your moral integrity, since it is the proof and the result of your loyalty to the achievement of your values." – Ayn Rand

2016, St. Vincentius Hospital, Age 57

Mum was doing better. She was stable and responding exceptionally well to her medication and treatment.

I made a last-minute decision to attend the fundraising event that Saturday. I still had time to sort out my speech and learn it well. My brothers insisted that I go and that mum would be fine. I decided to stay with mum a few more hours and then prepare to head home, mildly exhausted after a few days' worth of emotional upheaval.

Richard, who had returned to mum's room, grabbed my hand and whispered: "I love you, sweetheart" in my ear. That moment, the nurse entered the room and we decided to sit down in a small waiting area, just outside mum's room. We started talking about the days after the Liongate weekend and memories came flooding back.

1988, Belgium, Age 29

Charming, sophisticated, non-judgmental, and funny—these are just some of the words I checked off my criteria list for Richard. He ticked all the boxes. The longer I knew him, the better things became between us.

He proved himself to be a true English gentleman, opening doors for me, giving me his jacket on a chilly evening, letting me walk in first when entering a room, always being punctual, paying for meals, just to name a few.

He was the star that shone above me, the path to a life I had always wanted. Good natured and trustworthy, he put me in the throes of an otherworldly passion. As a bonus, he had that dry English humor, which I absolutely loved. He loved my Belgian humor too.

I spent every other afternoon wrapped in the poetic words he faxed to me, longing to be with him again. Soon, faxing was not enough and we spent hours talking on the phone, almost every day.

Over the next six months, we took turns travelling to visit each other. We saw each other as much as we could, but a few obstacles, mainly money and time, prevented us from seeing each other often.

Travelling and booking hotels got expensive. Richard was earning good money but he had a mortgage, four children, and a wife to support, so not much was left at the end of the month. He was too proud to let me pay for any of his trips.

It wasn't easy for Richard: his wife was struggling with her mental health; she was on anti-depressants again and often in a psychiatric hospital.

Richard had to take care of the four children and juggle several jobs, such as: the household chores, getting the children ready for school, driving them to school and after school activities, make dinner, do the shopping, make carnival costumes and on top of that, make sure he spent enough quality time with them.

Obviously, the divorce and their mother's mental health struggles were hard on his children. Richard spent as much time as possible with his children during the weekends, doing all of the normal things families do to keep their lives as stable as possible.

I would bide my time muddling through business expansion to get to Friday, on the weekends Richard would visit. He couldn't leave work before 5 p.m.

At 5 p.m. he would start the two-hour car drive to Dover in Kent. By 8 p.m., after checking in, he was on the boat, sailing from Dover to Oostende, in Belgium.

Richard travelled as cheaply as possible; he took the 4-hour boat instead of the 90-minute boat. Once the process of checks at border control was completed, he still had to face the two-and-a-half-hour drive to Keldonk, arriving at 3 a.m. on Saturday morning.

Then, at 3 p.m. on Sunday, he would make the return trip, arriving home at 1 a.m. on Monday morning, getting very little sleep as he had to be at work again at 8 a.m. Monday morning.

He spent 10 hours travelling each way. Our love was so powerful that he would travel these 20 hours to be with me for 36, and every minute of it was worth it. There were often delays and problems, so the total travelling time could take as long as 25 hours.

Sometimes Richard came as a foot passenger instead of crossing with his car on the boat. This was cheaper, and then I drove to the port to pick him up. That way, we could spend more time together. We were in the car, but still, we were together for longer.

Of course, the same applied to me when I travelled from Belgium to the UK. The difference was that I didn't have a boss who could fire me; I could leave earlier on Friday to be in the UK with Richard and arrive at 5 p.m. when Richard finished work.

Often, I used to arrive back in my office Monday morning around 9 a.m. to start working immediately after my journey back from the UK. I usually travelled on the 90-minute boat, so my journey was a few hours shorter.

Our love never saw the limitations of distance, only the challenge to overcome it. I found another human being who believed in achieving the impossible.

We did so smoothly and equally, never complaining, but instead delighting in the hardship that resulted in the sweet fruits of our love on arrival. It was a whole new world with Richard in it.

"The world is yours, my love," he would tell me when we found each other again. He fought through financial problems, the guilt from leaving his kids behind, and pure fatigue to get to me, not only once as a grand gesture of love but consistently and resolutely. It was the kind of romance that you can't even dream up, because it seems so impossible.

Eventually, work demands grew, and more weekends had to be skipped. AM Computers was growing at a steady rate, and the pressure on me was high.

Richard also needed to spend more time with his children, who were very important to him; and because they were important to him, they were important to me. We decided to take short holidays together instead of travelling during weekends to give each other time to catch up with life.

Richard continued to write to me, and I to him. We poured our hearts out on paper, freeing the trapped feelings of love and delight that bonded us. Poetry flowed like wine at a dinner party when we thought of our love. I gave him promises, and he accepted them as truth. He made me assurances, and I knew that he would never break them.

A healing feeling had started to seize me somewhere in the depths of my chest. It felt good to love someone so much that it hurt.

Even the ache I felt for him was ecstasy because it was incredible to feel so alive with the absence of something too great to live without. My heart grew wiser and narrowed its focus, blind to every man but Richard. My past pain cowered in the shadows of these new feelings.

The Press

"Don't be afraid to give up the good to go for the great."
– John D. Rockefeller

1989, Belgium, Age 30

Soon, my business was so successful that I now had 16 staff members. I could pay off my loan and pay all my staff with ease, and I had a lot of money left over each month.

I instructed my sales staff to focus on large companies because they didn't purchase one, but 20, 30, or 100 computers at a time. We sold a lot of computers to the Top 500 companies.

After a while, the company was running itself, with my supervision. I understood the power of delegating. I had regular meetings with all staff members, but soon concluded that I had time to start up another business.

The computer world was my kingdom, and at 30, I was its queen in Duffel. My finger was always on the pulse of any new opportunity that might arise, and arise they did that year: a new company stepped on to the computer scene. Acer Computers wanted to expand into Europe, and I wanted to get into the wholesale market.

I called Acer's head office in Taiwan to set up a meeting. All I had to take with me was a successful track record, my wits, and a winning attitude. I could not lose; I would not allow it. Soon I was winging my way to Asia to meet with the Acer team. Richard travelled with me.

A few days later, and I had won the exclusive rights to sell the Acer brand in Belgium and Luxembourg. The deal with Acer Computers was that I would build the brand, and once I had reached a certain turnover, Acer would take over from me and establish themselves in Belgium.

I arrived back home in Belgium and got to work setting up my new business—AM Distribution: a wholesale/distribution company supplying goods to computer dealers.

Sales volumes would be higher and profits would be lower, but stability was guaranteed in this booming industry. By now, I knew the industry well and I had big plans. I rented a big office 500 meters away from my dealership. I wanted all the dealers in Belgium to stock Acer computers.

Sales started to flow in and I went to the bank for another loan, which was easy to get with my successful track record in business.

Only a few months after starting AM Distribution, I bought an industrial building with a big warehouse and lots of offices. I took on four sales people, a secretary and two computer engineers, as I knew the business was going to grow fast.

At the next major computer exhibition in Belgium, I put on a grand show attracting thousands to my stand. I took a big financial leap and invested in an enormous stand with casino tables, music, drinks, entertainment, presentations, etc. all with the aim of acquiring a lot of new customers.

I wanted all of Belgium to know about Acer! At the exhibition, I was rubbing shoulders with directors of the biggest companies in Belgium and Luxembourg. It was a grand success and everybody was talking about me in the computer industry.

Quite suddenly, I was in the press everywhere you looked. With millions in sales, I became known as a phenomenon in the computer industry—a woman who had outdone her male competitors.

My face and details about my company were all over the press in Belgium. I had reached several million in sales in a very short time. The following headlines were seen all over magazines and newspapers:

- Hard lady—soft solutions!

- A phenomenon in the computer business!

- This woman makes millions in sales!

- Being the managing director of a computer company: that's emancipation for you!

- Dynamic Lady is managing director of a computer company!

- The manager is a woman!

- This lady reached the top in a male world!

- Only 1% of girls reach the top!

Few women in Belgium had ever achieved what I did and none in the computer industry, which was a male-dominated field. The risk I took with the exhibition paid off and my income was increasing.

My lifestyle changed. I was achieving my goals one after the other, but I was never short of my next opportunity or my next obstacle.

Richard was so very proud of me. Despite the fact that he earned far less than I did, he never showed even the slightest bit of resentment or jealousy about it, unlike Harry.

I would often stare at him in wonder and ponder how anyone quite so perfect could exist in the world and love me at the same time.

Out of all the men out there, I'd found the most wonderful one. He made me feel extraordinary even on my most ordinary days.

Letter to Dad

"I look up to the stars and wonder what things would be like if you were still here." – Unknown

I constantly wished that my dad was still alive and could see me. He would be proud of me. I sometimes wished the nuns could see me too, so they would no longer say I was useless. It was my dad who truly haunted me.

He never knew me as a successful person. It grieved me that he died thinking of me as a failure and I suffered bouts of crushing guilt over his strange, wordless visit to my home. He had made the large gesture of coming to my house and I had failed to respond. He reached out and I stood there in silence. That is the single biggest regret of my life, my second being leaving home without thinking about my mum.

He had been a harsh, violent man but no one is entirely bad. I searched my memory in quiet moments at night, seeking his good side. He had taught me useful things. He taught us all the value of hard work and that has helped me to succeed in business.

Every business victory came with a slap of guilt and regret that my dad could not see it and that I had never thanked him for all he taught me.

I hated myself for hating my dad when I was young, but now, seemingly, I was unable to abandon him in my mind. It was too late to tell my dad I loved him, too late to show him that I was a decent daughter. The only comfort is thinking that maybe now he *can* see me and what I've accomplished.

I felt a tremendous sense of forgiveness. I had to forgive the nuns, the bullies, my ex-husband and my dad. In my mind, I did, and I felt a big weight lifted off my shoulders. I knew a lack of forgiveness would influence my life in a negative way.

Forgiveness didn't mean that I was forgetting, nor did it mean that I was okay with what people did to me. It just meant I let go of the anger or guilt towards the people who'd hurt me. I didn't want to be a bitter person for the rest of my life. It's only the weak that can never forgive.

I had to forgive my dad to heal from my troubled childhood. If I clung to past pain, I could never move forward. Likewise, I realized that I had to forgive myself as well. I figured that because I was torn apart with guilt, maybe I was forgiven.

I was young and in a very painful situation when he came to my house. I'd been preoccupied with the fear that Harry would stumble in drunk at any minute. I'd done the best I could at the time, and maybe that was also the case for my dad during my childhood.

As I aged, I came to believe that my dad was perhaps not the monster I once thought he was, just a human being with bad parenting practices, doing the best he could to teach us all something about life. I believe he did his best in his own way.

Although dad had a lot of money, he never gave any of us luxuries. I desperately wanted a car to drive to my job at a super market during the holidays, but instead I had to bike it, rain or shine. He always used to say if we wanted luxuries, we had to work for them. This was something I would pass on to my children, if I would be lucky enough to have any.

He did many things that were simply wrong and unacceptable, but why did he do them? Did he believe he was doing the right thing to help us succeed in life? Was that how he was raised? Or, was he just overwhelmed with the pressures of the competitive diamond business and having five young children and a wife who seemed to have trouble coping?

At the time, I felt he sent me to boarding school because he didn't want me around, but he sent all of us to the very best boarding schools in the country.

Did he do it because he believed it was best for us? Because he could see how our mother was struggling with five of us? Or simply, so he could brag about where his children were being educated? It cost a fortune to send us to such expensive schools.

He must have cared for me, for all of us, to make such an investment. He could have put us in much less expensive schools and enjoyed his own life more.

It was always during times of great sadness and great joy that my dad was still most important to me. With the passing of time, his guilt visits are less frequent but when they do arrive, they are painful.

In evening school, I had taken some psychology courses in an attempt to understand the relationship between my dad and me, and why he behaved as he did. I will never know his real motives and beliefs. It is easier for me to cope thinking there was a reason for his ways, rather than living with the idea that I was dumped and never wanted.

A few years after my dad's death, I wrote him a letter. I wrote it out of love and pain, at a time when my success seemed to have no limitations.

The title of the letter: *"Can you hear me, Dad?"*

It read:

My dearest dad,

What more do I need to do to win your love?
Even in death you seem unsatisfied, taunting me with unresolved guilt.

I am sorry for the daughter I was to you. I have let her go. I realize now that though your ways were wrong, your advice was right, but I was too young to distinguish one from the other. Though you were a misguided teacher, I wish I had a chance to speak to you now and let you know that I understand.

I have always followed my own way of living, against your direction but each time I paid a price for it!
I should have followed your advice. Please forgive me.

What more do I need to do to win your love?
Please forgive me the disappointments of my youth. I wish I could tell you, dad, that I love you. I wish I had done things differently. I wish I could turn back time and make things right.

All I have are my memories, and they have cursed me with guilt. I understand you, dad. I know that your advice came from a good place. I am so sorry that I was deaf to you because of your struggles. A thousand thanks for the values you imparted. You may have scarred me, but I believe your intentions were good.

I am so sorry that you have only ever known me as a rebellious, good-for-nothing and unhappy daughter.

Have I done enough for you to love me?
I only relax after I've worked hard.
I never sleep in late.
I work hard.
I hardly ever watch TV.
I don't hang around with the wrong people.
I analyze the core of the problem.
I am trying really hard to make something of my life.
I am doing useful things instead of "hanging around," as you always hated that.
This is what you wanted, isn't it?

Now I understand why you always repeated that I would understand it all when I was older. You were right; I do understand it all now. I do get what you tried to tell me all those years. That's why I am now following your advice, and I am succeeding.

When I see you again, you will be proud of the woman I have become. You will see my life, my love, and my achievements, and you will know that you did well.

Please may I be your daughter again, dad.
Can you hear me, dad?
I hope you can.
Please forgive me. I am so sorry.
I love you

Your daughter,
Christine

Holidays

"The moment that judgement stops through acceptance of what it is, you are free of the mind. You have made room for love, for joy, for peace." – Eckhart Tolle

The 1989 Cruise and the San Francisco Trip, Age 30

Every year Apple gave their high-achieving dealers a special bonus if a certain sales target was achieved. This year the bonus in Belgium was a seven-day Caribbean cruise and the bonus in the UK was a five-day trip to San Francisco! Richard and I both wanted that bonus, and all year round, we worked hard for it. Because Richard was the manager of an Apple Dealership in the UK and I owned a dealership in Belgium, we competed to win those coveted targets. The winners were allowed to take a partner.

When we finally heard we had both reached the targets and won the holidays, we were excited beyond words. Our hard work had paid off! We had spent less time together in our efforts to win, but now we'd be rewarded with luxurious holidays together.

The Caribbean cruise in March 1989 was pure joy and happiness for seven days, absolute paradise. The other passengers on the cruise were all Apple prize winners from all over the world. Richard and I got the feeling that they were not very friendly to us. He felt one of the main reasons for this was because I was the only woman who achieved the target in a male dominated industry.

While they didn't actually "do" anything to make me feel uncomfortable, I felt an undercurrent through their conversations that they were just not happy to have me there. After all, I was a threat to them – taking the top seller's trophy.

I paid no attention to their unfriendliness, I had Richard as company and we were together for seven days, treasuring every second of each other's company.

We enjoyed moonlit strolls along the beach, romantic candle-lit dinners, cuddling up and relaxing under a palm tree, holding hands everywhere we went. The most important thing, however, was the feeling of togetherness and love.

Soon after the cruise, we flew to San Francisco. It was nothing but bliss and delightful memories from when we went there for the first time. Richard was his usual charming, caring self and made every moment of our trip something special.

When we talked about business he said: "Money comes and goes but my love for you will stay forever." I will always remember that as there is so much truth in that.

Everywhere we went he held my hand, a security that I grew to love about him. Then on the last day, Richard decided that a lavish restaurant visit was in order.

He took me to a popular romantic restaurant in town that was known for serving fine dishes of exquisite flavor and texture. I sat at the table, the white linen cascading over the sides like a white waterfall. Silver utensils and china plates with gold leaf shone on the surface. It was the last day of our amazing holiday together. Every day had been better than the last. After the romantic meal, we went back to the hotel and I was resting on the bed.

"I love you, sweetheart," Richard said to me.

"I love you too, darling," I responded.

"I've loved you from the moment your hand touched mine at the sales floor back home, the very first time I saw you." he continued.

I looked down and saw Richard on one knee beside the bed. He reached into his jacket pocket and pulled out a small box, and opened it.

"Christine, I want to spend the rest of my life making you happy. Will you marry me?" The words floated through my brain like wisps of smoke, and I sat suspended in shock for a few moments.

Then a rush of emotion overtook me. I knew that I wanted to marry Richard. I loved him more than words could express. I cast around my mind for reasons to doubt myself and found none. I looked into my heart and found only love for him there.

I said yes. We agreed that a date would be set once his divorce was final.

An extract of Richard's letter after I accepted his proposal:

Your acceptance of my proposal of marriage has made me the happiest person in the world. I promise to always try to please you and make you happy; your happiness and love are of prime importance to me. I will be a totally faithful husband, giving my utmost to you emotionally and physically until I die.

I have an undying, totally consuming and passionate love for one person in this world now, you. No matter what happens to us both in the future, this love will, against all odds, survive and blossom from its initial seeding to a strong and binding vine of life.

I do not believe that it is possible to love you more deeply than I do, but each time I see you and hold you in my arms the depth and breadth of my affection grows and grows. My heart is filled to a bursting point with my love and passion, and it hurts so much to be separated from you.

I am confident that the separation we are experiencing will cement our love and make us able to more readily cope with the situations that life does impose on us humans over the coming years. It will provide us with a bedrock of unbreakable devotion that no one will be able to destroy. Once we are together permanently, we will never be separated again!

We have managed to build a love under very difficult circumstances, and if we can do that, we can certainly cope with the pressures of life together.

I will always know that life is good because of you
And I will always be there for you,
And I will be the best husband I can be.
Have faith in us, and we will live a contented and better life
that will make the rest of the world envious.

Until I feel your breath and face again,
I remain your devoted admirer,
With all my deepest love and affection,
I love you more than anyone could.

You are my love, my life.
I dedicate my heart and soul to you.
No one in the world knows my inadequacies like you.
In your hands are my pride, my sorrows, my future, my everything.

My heart belongs to you,
My body belongs to you,
My mind belongs to you,
I am yours, with all my heartfelt love and devotion,
Y.T.T.
Richard

A poem from me after the proposal:

For once in my life
I trust someone implicitly.
I feel like it's okay to let that someone in
To let them see me emotionally and physically
I have given myself to you and
I've told you things I've never told a soul.
You are the one person who could see me

Trembling and being as fearful as an injured bird;
I trust you with my secrets and
You can trust me with yours.
This sharing...this special sharing...
Is the nicest dimension my life has ever known!
Your goals have become our goals,
We will dream dreams and make them reality,

Now that I know you, I love you so much;
I will always be hungry for your tender touch.
You are the most wonderful thing that happened in my life,
I can't tell you how proud I will be when I will be your wife.
I will adore you...day in, day out, every future year,
And I will always whisper, "I love you," in your ear.
I will do everything that I can
to make you a very happy man.

One day I will find the words to tell you
How much I love you,
How much I adore you,
How much I admire you,
How much I worship you,
How much I respect you.
I will always love you for the rest of my days,
because you are the love of my life.
Yours forever,
Y.T.T.
Christine

After the visit to San Francisco and our engagement, we faced some obstacles. Richard was still in the process of getting divorced and accepting me would not be easy for his children. We knew it would be hard but we were meant for each other.

We decided to close the gap that kept us apart. "I am going to move to Keldonk to live with you," he told me one day. "I won't let you close your companies when they are doing so well, and I will not let you sacrifice your success for me."

I took his hand.

"All right but if being away from your children is too much, we will uproot and move to the UK instead."

Richard explained to his four children that he would be moving to Belgium. I met his children briefly during one of my visits to the UK and they all seemed to be well behaved and very friendly.

Richard and I had previously discussed the house he had lived in with his wife and children. The house was in their joint names and Richard was still paying the mortgage so to stop those payments that house would have to be sold, once the divorce was final. Usually the profit of the sale is to be split between two partners but Richard agreed that his wife would be allowed to keep all the money to care for the four children.

I agreed to this because I did not want to appear to be the stereotypical horrible stepmother. I could have insisted that Richard demanded half of the sale of the house but I didn't. Richard wanted to adequately compensate and maintain his children and wife; therefore, he had to leave everything behind. I fully understood this.

So, when Richard finally made the move to Belgium in July 1989, he came without any savings or possessions of any kind and started looking for a job immediately.

I wrote a letter to Richard's children telling them that it would never be my intention to become "a second mum" or "replacement mum," but that I would always respect their wishes and take care of them as best I could.

I told them I would always welcome them if they wanted to visit us or talk to me about anything. I also told them I would take very good care of their dad, as he was very special to me and I would live the rest of my life to make him a happy man.

Everything fell into place like the pieces clicking together in a grand clock. As it turns out, Kane was looking for a sales manager to set up branches worldwide in the diamond business. He thought Richard was suitable for the position. This was lucky, as Richard could not speak Flemish, so finding a job for him would be challenging.

A week later, Richard and Kane had a meeting and he started working for my brother. He would be working from Kane's office in Antwerp but most of the time he would be travelling all over the world. It was agreed that he would earn a basic salary and commission on whatever he sold. Richard was a brilliant sales person, excellent at meeting targets, so he was motivated to sell. A large part of his pay checks, however, was spent paying alimony and child support.

We decided not to buy a house yet. My mum allowed us to rent a small semi-detached house in the center of town in Keldonk that she had inherited from my dad. All my brothers had also lived in that house just after they got married.

We paid very little rent, but the place was small, with just two tiny bedrooms and barely any living space. It did not matter. With the savings we made in rent or mortgage payments, I was able to invest more money into the companies.

Now that we were finally living together, it was as if we had moved into the Hilton Hotel. Finally, after years of being together, we no longer had to travel hours on end to see each other!

In August of 1989, Richard's children were all on school holiday. The diamond business in Belgium shuts down during this month, so Richard had free time. I was able to leave my businesses behind under the capable hands of managers and staff. We took his four children on holiday to Marbella so that I could get to know them better.

On the first day of the holiday, I could feel my nerves tingling as if a small feather was tickling me, but I was determined to conceal my nerves. I am sure the children were nervous too. Entering their lives as a stepmom was not easy for anyone.

I wanted to leave a positive impression and I wanted us to get on really well, as I knew it was important for Richard.

After the first day, the nervousness soon disappeared for all six of us and it turned out to be extremely enjoyable. We went for walks, played mini golf, sunbathed, went swimming and had a lot of meals together.

We talked a lot, about everything and nothing. We all had a wonderful time and it is my most memorable holiday I had with all of them.

Richard continued to learn Flemish and make his way in the diamond trade, which was brand new to him.

One year flew by, and in August of 1990, we went to Disney World in Florida and had a magical time. Richard's daughter Clara didn't come with us. Mateo jumped up and down with delight as he watched the light procession, and Richard cried, overcome at seeing his young son so very happy.

Richard and I travelled the world together, working and succeeding—planning a life together, while waiting for the moment he was officially divorced.

When I could, I went with him on his business trips; he worked during the day, and during the evenings, we went sightseeing and enjoyed the world's big cities together.

Later that year, we went away for a weekend to Wales, in the UK, with Richard's children. Clara joined us this time. Richard was extremely pleased about that, as he knew Clara had also accepted the situation and started to see that nothing was going to change. Richard was glad that now all his 4 children accepted the changes.

We lived together but still didn't see each other every day, as Richard was travelling a lot for his job. Each time Richard travelled abroad, he sent me flowers, a poem or a card. I received flowers from Indonesia, Hong Kong, New York and Arizona—from everywhere in the world. I kept each and every message that came with every bunch of flowers.

Whenever we were apart, I missed him, but when he came back, it was a feeling of incredible relief and love. Richard missed his children and that was clear in his writing.

Here is poem Richard wrote around Christmas time:

At this special time of the year,
I thank you, Christine, for your love so clear.
For over 36 months you have been in my life,

And soon I hope to make you my wife.

You are to me a most radiant star,
Once admired only from afar.
My soul and deepest devotion
To you I dedicate with intense emotion.
I treasure all the days we have been together,
And I pray that they can go on forever.

Though my problems may sometimes get me low,
There is one thing that you must definitely know,
My love for you will stay forever true and pure,
And through all dark days will endure,
But my ever-present tearing fear,
Is of my losing you, my wealth so clear,
As you too have the burden of problems to carry,
Which may make you think again before you marry
An English man whose heart is heavy and torn,
With mind distraught and outlook forlorn.

You are my true love, now and eternally,
I love you, my treasure, my Christine.
Y.T.T.
Richard

Then one day Richard was late for dinner. In all the time I had known him, he'd never been late for anything. I immediately knew something was wrong. By 10 p.m. I had still not heard from him. I was preparing to go out to look for him when he arrived home by taxi at 11 p.m.

"I was driving behind a lorry on the way home, and a large piece of metal jostled free and fell in the road on top of my car," he told me as my stomach lurched and twisted into a sailor's knot.

"It hit my car, missing me by inches. When I swerved, car after car behind me started slamming into me. There were five cars involved. I only just finished talking to the police about what happened. I phoned you but couldn't get through. The police told me the phone lines were down because of storm damage but I'm okay, my love, I'm okay."

I burst into tears and wrapped my arms around his neck.

Here's the poem Richard wrote to me after the accident:

Once again I am reminded that life is but a floating moment,
Here today and gone tomorrow,
leaving behind only tears and sorrow.
In a few seconds today I walked the edge between life and death, This time life has won,
I pray that we will have many years yet,
Before the sad farewell that we face arrives,
But when it does, remember this:
I have been proud and honored to know and love you, more deeply than anyone else could.
Remember me only with happiness, for I will be waiting for you and only then will life be complete.
I love you,
Y.T.T.
Richard

I almost lost him that night—to a piece of metal. I shudder at the thought of what I almost lost. It reminded me how precious every second of our lives were and how every moment with him was a gift. I could not wait to marry him, but we couldn't set a date, as his divorce wasn't yet final.

The Unexpected Miracle

"Our deepest wounds surround our greatest gifts." – Ken Page

1991, Belgium, Age 32

Richard and I settled into our new life together in Keldonk, and it was good. He saw his children regularly, taking them on holidays and seeing them on weekends.

Mum attended English lessons in an attempt to be able to communicate better with Richard but it was simply too difficult for her and she stopped going.

While we tried to forge a life for ourselves in the small village, one afternoon I received a disturbing phone call from my brother Oliver.

"I've been arrested for robbery and sentenced to two years in prison. I didn't commit the crime, but they said I did," he told me.

As I listened, I heard the sounds of officials behind him. He had been hiding his arrest for some time, and now that his sentence had been passed down, he was in a state of disbelief and panic.

"When was your court date?" I asked him, baffled by the sudden news.

"This morning. They're putting me on a train to a prison; I just wanted you to know." Oliver had been accused of robbing another diamond dealer and making off with cash and diamonds worth millions of Belgian francs. He, too, was hanging around with the wrong kind of people, who were getting him into trouble.

No one would believe that he did not do it. Perhaps that was because Oliver had run into some hard luck in his life.

He had to spend a lot of money paying off the diamonds that were stolen from him during a robbery in his house. He lost his business, his reputation—and now he had lost his freedom.

I wished that there were something, anything, I could do to help him. He was found guilty and that was that: two years in a prison with a thousand criminals shaping his future. To keep his spirits high, I visited him regularly and wrote letters to him. I still have all the letters he wrote to me.

That is how I came to be close with my oldest brother— whilst he was in prison. I encouraged him, visited him, sent him positive news, and lifted his spirits when I could. During that hard time, he also had problems in his marriage. I felt terrible for him.

Months after Oliver was taken to prison, we received word that Richard's divorce was official. Ecstatic, Richard and I set a date for our wedding—December 22—and preparations for the day began immediately. I had waited so long for the chance to marry him that it was like stepping into a perfect fantasy world.

This time I would do it right; I was marrying the man of my dreams, so I wanted it to be the wedding of my dreams as well. I wasn't even happy on my wedding day with Harry.

This time, everything was different. I had the chance to make sure that this would be the best wedding any of my friends had ever attended!

My local priest refused to marry us because I was already married once in church. We had the ceremony in a church in Antwerp instead, with a more modern priest. I arranged a luxury bus to transport everyone there and back to Keldonk for the reception. There was rice and a chimney sweep, the latter being an English tradition. It was a full day and night of celebrations with magicians, a DJ, a live band and lots of balloons.

In the center of the hall was a Belgian and an English flag near a grand Christmas tree, and the walls were lined with buffet tables of the most delectable kind. We had a live band play and my secretary's choir sang a few songs as well.

Richard's children were all present with their partners. Some of Richard's UK friends attended too and his old band, a pleasant surprise, came along too.

All in all, it was a lavish affair, with doves and romance and everything I had ever wanted. Richard and I exchanged our vows, and our rings were engraved with: "Y.T.T."

There were 350 people at our wedding, and it was one of the happiest days of my life. Richard even presented his speech in Flemish. Richard and I, neither of us good dancers, had taken dance lessons to be able to dance the first dance. We pulled it off!

As I was a businesswoman, I used to do business deals all the time. On the morning of my wedding day, I was on the phone doing business.

Richard didn't mind at all. He knew me, and I could be *me* at all times. Richard just said, "That's my Christine." There are photographs in my wedding album with me in my wedding dress on the phone doing business deals.

Instead of getting presents, we received envelopes with money in them from our guests, a Belgian tradition. Thanks to many wealthy colleagues and people in the diamond trade, we recovered all the costs for our dream wedding.

The day I said, "I do," I allowed Richard's love to rush in and overtake me, as I knew that I would never be alone again.

The last guest left at 5.30 a.m. After the celebration, many of our friends and family said that it was the best wedding they had ever attended. That filled my heart with joy.

Something else happened on my wedding day that changed my life *forever*—a gift that I received quite unexpectedly.

Richard and I collapsed, exhausted, that night, buzzing from the high of finally being husband and wife. We fell asleep together, wrapped in each other's arms.

That morning my eyes fluttered open and a cool breeze drifted through the bedroom window. The air smelled like cinnamon and scented oils from the night before. It was 11 a.m.

It took several seconds for me to realize what had happened—or rather what had not happened. We laid in perfect relaxation and contentment. Richard asleep next to me...and no wetness. Both of my hands shot down under the covers, but it was as dry as a desert down there.

"What the?" I said aloud, my heart rate rising. "Richard? Pssst. Richard!" I loudly whispered to him.

"Okay..." He swung his legs off the side of the bed as he thought I had wet the bed. He had stripped the bed for me each day he was home, taking the sheets to the washing machine.

"Hey, no, that's what I'm trying to tell you. I didn't wet the bed! I didn't wet it!" I exclaimed. I could not believe it! I woke up in a dry bed!

I was overwhelmed with happiness, overjoyed. It was an exceptional, blissful moment.

Richard's eyes properly opened now.

"What do you mean?" he asked, still looking tired from the celebrations of the day before. I threw the covers open, and the delightful scent of clean linen danced in the air. "You didn't wet the bed?" he asked, just as surprised as I was.

"No, I didn't!" I said, as surprised as Richard looked.

"That's...that's great, sweetheart!" he cooed, giving me a strong hug. "I am so happy for you! That is absolutely wonderful!"

It was an unexpected gift from the heavens. For the first time, since I was 5, so the first time in twenty seven years, I did not have to bother about wet sheets or the embarrassment of wetting my bed. It was an otherworldly delight of the highest order! Richard held me close and I started crying tears of pure happiness. It was the start of a new life together, one brimming with happiness and support, care and love.

I never wet the bed again after my wedding day. Not once!

After all the different methods and remedies that had failed, just like that, I stopped bedwetting, the day I married Richard!

Unbelievable! Mind-boggling!

A miracle is something that cannot be explained by natural or scientific laws, so the fact that I stopped wetting the bed was not only an unexpected gift, but an unexpected miracle!

It was, after all these years, the knowledge that I would always be safe and secure, loved and wanted, fully accepted for the person I was, that proved finally to be the remedy to the condition that had plagued me all those years. I no longer felt outcast or embarrassed to be the person I was. I was finally complete.

Each time I think about that night, I still can't quite believe that my bedwetting days were over, forever.

Planning

"All those clichés, those things you hear about having a baby and motherhood—all of them are true. And all of them are the most beautiful things you will ever experience." – Penelope Cruz

1992, Belgium, Age 33

After our honeymoon tour through Vermont, Chicago, Montreal, Michigan and Boston, we settled into daily life together. The computer business was becoming more competitive, so I worked day and night to expand my companies and keep my profits up. Richard always made his targets and earned good money, but he still had to pay alimony for his wife and maintenance for his children.

Richard's youngest son, Martin, was not doing well in school. He moved to Belgium to live with us, as his mum was ill and consequently couldn't give him the attention and education he deserved. We paid for him to go to the International School of Antwerp, a private school where he settled in very well and he even joined the local football club.

By the following year, he had even earned an "Outstanding in Dutch" certificate. Martin improved in his academic achievements and graduated from university in later life.

I could no longer travel with Richard very often, on his business trips, now that Martin lived with us. I was working long hours but I also spent as much time as I could with Martin, doing my utmost to give him love and a good education, making him feel comfortable in his new home.

It was not long after we married that we planned to have kids. I was 33 already, and even though Richard was 44 and already had four of his own, he was happy to have more children with me.

I had always dreamed of having a large family of my own to lavish them with love– but there was a problem. Richard had a vasectomy many years ago. Realizing that he no longer loved his wife, he decided to get it done to prevent any future pregnancies. We made an appointment in Belgium to see a doctor about having the procedure reversed.

In most cases this is impossible, but the surgeon in the UK, who operated on Richard was a personal friend and an old client of his with a brilliant reputation in the field.

"We have assessed the vasectomy, and there is an excellent chance we have reversed it successfully," the grey-haired surgeon said to us as we sat in his office, after Richard had the procedure done.

"The surgeon who performed the vasectomy procedure was very precise with his actions. The only thing left to do now is to test Richard's sperm, in a few weeks, to see if all is in good working order."

Richard and I visited the urologist a few weeks later to check out his sperm count and shape and to take note of any abnormalities, and we learned everything was in perfect working order. The operation had worked! We were delighted and in high spirits. We knew children might be possible; I put a plan in motion.

"Richard," I said to him that day, "you know I've always wanted a big family, but what I want most of all is twins. As you know, I've been dreaming about them for many years and I really want to try to fall pregnant with my identical twin girls. This is the moment where I will start working on making my dream come true."

Lesser men would have discouraged me. They would have laughed at the idea that I could work to make twins a reality. I knew better and so did Richard.

He knew me well and he knew if I said I would do something, I would! Of course, I didn't have all this completely under my control, as nature would decide, but nevertheless I set about the monumental task of researching how to fall pregnant with twin girls.

There were no twins in my family, therefore chances of having twins were very small. Still, I wanted to make my dream come true and I was going to make it happen.

As I waded through book after book, I began to compile my findings—I dedicated myself to trying every method that might work. Deep in my heart, I felt my twin girls calling me and I was not going to take any chances.

None of the methods I unearthed were clinically proven, so I was flying blind on faith alone. The entire time I was buried in research, two lights hung crisply in my future. I knew that my girls were counting on me to put in the work.

You cannot leave these things to fate or they don't happen! I spoke to countless doctors, specialists and medical professionals on how to improve my chances and wrote everything I learned down, charting it out.

Richard supported me 100% and never once scoffed at the idea that I could make it happen for us. I became well educated on the risks and potential complications of carrying twins and created a schedule of my most fertile days. I checked my cervical mucus and tracked my body temperature—both impacting my chances. I carefully counted my most fertile days.

I've read that you can increase your chances of conceiving a girl by having intercourse a few days before ovulation and then cease until a few days after ovulation, so that's what we did.

The more times you have sex, the higher the chances you will get pregnant. So, we had sex. We had lots and lots of it, as much as humanly possible.

We had sex in specific positions that I had heard worked best to become pregnant. Missionary position, doggy style, rock'n roller, the tilt, the dolphin and the zen pause are all sexual positions that are effective for conception.

Once we had sex, I placed a pillow under my hips and lay still for 30 minutes to let gravity do the work; to help the sperm swim to the eggs. This helps to maximize the chances of becoming pregnant *and* to maximize the chances of having twins.

I put Richard and me on a "twins diet" packed with nutrient-dense foods. We were eating foods that were thought to increase our chances of having girls.

It only took two months of planning and effort for all the pieces of my plan to fall into place. Richard and I both focused on it, determined to have not only twins, but twin daughters.

Finally, on a Saturday morning in early May of 1992, I started having the signs that my dream was coming true. I was already two weeks overdue for my period, but that morning was different. My breasts were tender in a way that I had never felt before. I told Richard that I thought I was pregnant just based on the way that they felt.

He went to the pharmacy and brought home a pregnancy test. The results: POSITIVE! We both started crying right away. The vasectomy reversal had actually worked. I tried to remain neutral—or at least cautious—because it was very early and things could always go wrong. The surgeon warned us that Richard's sperm might not be able to produce a normal, healthy baby; especially this soon after the reversal, but either way, we were overjoyed to be pregnant.

The moment I found out I was pregnant was the moment I stopped smoking. I knew that smoking could cause health problems for my babies.

Somehow, I just knew I was going to have twins. I was frequently sick and threw up often, but I didn't even care; I was pregnant and that was all that really mattered to me.

Then one morning I had bad cramps and feared the worst—a miscarriage. Richard was away on business, so I called the midwife and went to see her at the clinic. Nervous and feeling mildly ill from the pregnancy, I sat anxiously as she performed an ultrasound, holding my breath for the news.

"Uh huh, yes, I see what's going here...you said you've been having bad cramps? You mustn't worry about them. Cramping is completely normal when you are pregnant." She smirked from ear to ear.

"Especially with twins, when the womb expands quickly."

"What?" I said in disbelief. "Twins? Really?" That was just so amazing and wonderful! I couldn't believe what I heard. I was ecstatic! That was a wondrous moment in my life!

That was the first confirmation that I was pregnant with twins. Tears rolled down my face as joy poured out of me. I hugged the midwife several times to thank her for the good news.

As soon as I possibly could, I called Richard, who was in Canada. I told him what the midwife said. "Everything is okay. The pain I have is perfectly normal as the womb expands." I heard Richard breathing a sigh of relief.

I left a short pause, before I continued loudly "Especially when you are having twins!"

"No way! Really? We are having twins?"

"Yes! We're having TWINS!" I confirmed. "I knew we could do it! Thank you so much for believing we could!"

Richard couldn't believe it and started crying. He knew how important this was for me, but it was equally important for him.

I will never forget that feeling. It was better than winning first place in a swimming competition. Better than coming first in a triathlon. Better than being the most well-known female seller in the computer industry in Belgium.

I was floating now on a cloud of happiness that completely overtook me. Never in my most desperate dreams did I ever think I would find a life so blessed and so full of magic and miracles.

Richard was over the moon and suggested I fly to Canada so we could celebrate. I immediately booked a flight for the next day. I cried all the way in the car to the airport and I cried for hours during the flight. I just couldn't stop crying. This time tears of joy!

I stayed in Canada for a few days and I remember extremely well being sick over Niagara Falls. For the rest of my life, I will associate Niagara Falls with being sick.

In the space of a year, I had achieved the life I always wanted. I was married to the love of my life in December and I was pregnant with my twins a few months later.

I went for another ultrasound in July 1992 to make sure that everything was developing normally with the pregnancy. I would also find out during this ultrasound if the twins were both girls, both boys, or one of each.

I knew that it wouldn't matter to me, but all of my life I had dreamed of those identical twin baby girls, so deep down, I was still hoping for them. After all, I did everything I possibly could do to ensure that I was pregnant with twin girls.

The ultrasound showed that everything was progressing normally first and foremost, and then came that moment I had been waiting for: the babies were in fact both little girls. I was going to have the twin daughters of my dreams!

I was floating on cloud nine and raptured in laughter. I felt I was swimming in love. I just couldn't believe it! I didn't know yet if they would be identical girls, as I had to wait until after the birth for the placenta investigation.

Around this time, Richard's ex-wife moved in with another man therefore he was able to stop the alimony payments.

We went on holiday to Dallas for 2 weeks, with all of Richard's children and their partners, even though I was six months pregnant with twins.

In October 1992, my blood pressure was high; I had gained 44 kilos (about six stones) in weight and was feeling ill all the time. Richard was looking for a new job now that we were about to have twins, as he wanted to be home more after the birth.

The diamond industry was dangerous, and people were regularly shot and killed near his offices in Antwerp for their diamonds and cash.

Seven months into my pregnancy, I was instructed by my midwife to stay in bed, so I could not work—which was driving me mad.

Deals did not close themselves! We placed a bed in our lounge so I could make phone calls whilst in bed.

At approximately eight months into my pregnancy, I was taken to hospital so that they could keep a closer eye on my pregnancy, as my blood pressure was sky high, well over the acceptable limit. I called Richard, who was at work, and told him to come immediately.

Once a room was allocated to me in hospital, Suzy, a very friendly midwife came to see me and retrieved a stethoscope out of her bag.

"Is everything going to be alright?"

"I don't know," replied Suzy. "You said you would like to have a natural birth but there is a higher risk of complications if you stay with that thought."

I could feel my whole body changing and reacting. My whole being was preparing for what would come next. Sweat coated my forehead. The midwife's face contorted into one of concern.

"Is something wrong?"

She sat back and sighed.

"Seems we've run into a problem."

"What problem?"

"One of your babies is not growing at all." She bit her lip. "One baby is getting all the food. That is a very big concern. On top of that, your blood pressure is extremely high and that is an equally big concern."

"Oh no!" A bead of sweat ran down the side of my face. It took all of my concentration to keep even the faintest form of composure.

"W-well what does that mean, are both babies going to be okay?"

"Honestly, I don't know. For now, we'll just have to monitor and see what happens."

Another hour passed. Suzy kept a diligent watch; a monitor was connected to my stomach to constantly listen to my babies' heartbeats.

Another device soon appeared on my arms to measure my blood pressure every 10 minutes. The nurse walked in and out of my room every few minutes to check. The last time she checked she had a very concerning look on her face and said: "I'm afraid both babies are now in distress. I will go and get the doctor."

The doctor came rushing in and shouted to everyone in the room:

"Prepare for a caesarean. NOW!" Another doctor rushed into the room and looked at the results on the monitors. He immediately took my bed, started rolling it into the hallway and I was taken to the operating room.

On our way, I caught a glimpse of Richard, but we couldn't speak to each since the doctors rushed my bed off.

He shouted as he ran behind the bed.

"It's going to be OK, Christine." There were possible complications we were told, so Richard wasn't allowed to come into the operating room. Whilst I was crying and hoping for the best, I waved him goodbye and heard him shouting "I love you. It's going to be okay."

I shouted back, "I love you too."

In a matter of minutes, I was ready for the caesarean and Suzy asked me: "What will the first baby be called? And, the second one?"

I replied, "The first baby is Amelia and the second is Samantha."

After a few minutes, the first baby was born. Suzy wrapped Amelia in a blanket and immediately took her away, without giving her to me. I knew that was a concern. Ten minutes later, Samantha appeared into this world but she didn't cry. A situation every mother fears. A chill trickled down my spine.

"What's wrong? Is something wrong?"

No response.

"Nurse?" I called again.

Then I heard Samantha crying. She was also immediately taken out of the room, without me having the chance to say hello to my newborn daughters.

It was deeply upsetting not being able to hold my babies and I thought, for a few seconds, that perhaps I had failed again by not delivering healthy babies. I pushed positive thoughts to the front of my mind and had to wait for news from the nurse, which soon came.

Amelia was 2.5 kg and Samantha 1.5 kg. I was still doped up on the anesthetic and had to sign papers because one of the babies' lungs was underdeveloped. Both babies needed immediate intensive care.

Amelia was rushed by ambulance to another hospital for treatment, while Samantha was taken to the baby intensive care unit because she was so small and fragile.

I was exhausted and needed sleep, but my gynecologist told me, "They're going to be fine and they are going to grow up as two beautiful girls." I trusted that. She was the best gynecologist in our area, so I had concluded after my investigations before I even became pregnant.

I was allowed to hold Samantha the same day but couldn't hold Amelia until 10 days later, when I was allowed to leave the hospital.

The next day, Richard went to the laboratory to pick up the results. He was holding a medical report, and I felt his warm hand grip mine.

"The placenta investigations came back…" he started to say. This was it. I would find out for once and for all if my girls were identical twins, like my dreams had predicted.

"You were right!" he said, more tears welling up in his eyes. "They are identical. I can't believe it! Your dream has come true!"

My breath caught in my throat and I started crying again too. Such joy cannot be communicated in words alone; it simply is beyond descriptive power. We hugged each other and kissed, I knew that everything was going to be as it should be.

For three months, every three hours, Richard drove my breast milk to Amelia in the other hospital 45 minutes away. He was my hero. Kane allowed him to take time off work.

Samantha came home first, when she was three months old. Both babies were home by the time they were six months old. Finally, we were all together and I could hold them and breastfeed them both at the same time.

I remember that these babies were what I dreamed of when I was at my lowest and most unhappy. I kept thinking of those beautiful babies and how I would shower them with love every single day, the way that I wished I could have been loved.

Now I did not have to dream about it because I had love and I had my babies. What more could a person want or need?

Martin was besotted with his new born sisters and so were all Richard's children, who came to visit us, to see and hold them.

I found a full time nanny and went back to work some months later. Then we settled into the incredible life we had carved out for ourselves, raising our family and growing our careers.

I had been researching, both by speaking to professors and through reading about bilingual education. Every bit of advice suggested that the earlier you start, the easier it is, so starting from birth, I spoke Flemish to the girls and Richard spoke English. By the time the girls were six years old, they were fluent in both.

Every single day, I told my girls that I loved them. Nobody ever told me they loved me when I was young, so I wanted to make sure my girls would never experience that horrible feeling.

From The Foundations Up

"The foundation stones for a balanced success are honesty, character, integrity, faith, love and loyalty." – Zig Ziglar

1993 - 1999, Belgium, Age 34 - 40

We had been talking about whether we should stay in Belgium or move to the UK. We were both worried about the dangers of the diamond trade, and Richard hadn't found any job leads outside the diamond industry.

Changes hit my business. Acer Head Office contacted me to say they were interested in taking over Acer distribution in Belgium and Luxembourg themselves.

I had reached the agreed turnover, as per the agreement with Acer, which stated that Acer could take over. We negotiated the pay out to me, and Acer paid me the agreed amount of money. That was the end of AM Distribution.

Richard missed his children, all six of them, and couldn't see them as often as he wanted because he travelled a lot for his job. After having lived in Belgium for 4 years, he could feel that slowly his 3 older children had grown apart from him. Some of them said they would come and live with us should we decide to move to the UK.

Plus, AM Computers' sales were steadily declining because of the rise in competition. Richard was in a dangerous job that was becoming an increasing concern for us as a family and he missed his music. He tried to join a band in Belgium, but being unable to speak the local language, it was tough.

Richard was very happy about spending more time with his family; it became the main influencing factor in moving to the UK.

It would also be nicer, for both of us, if we could see each other more often and be together all the time, every day, without any travelling involved.

The final decision to move to the UK was made when diamonds were stolen from Kane's office. Kane accused Richard of stealing the diamonds from him. He had no problem dragging Richard's name through the mud.

The police investigated Richard and found that there was no way he could have taken the diamonds. The real "thief" was never caught, but Kane had shown his true colors. Richard never spoke to Kane again after this day.

In July 1993, we made a major decision and we moved to the UK. We found a six-bedroom house in Kent, the south of England, with a few acres of land. We didn't use our savings to buy a property, as we didn't know how well we would be, financially. With our assets, we were able to secure a mortgage.

We wanted to live in the south of England so it would be possible for me to visit my mum on a regular basis without having to travel too far. New motorways had been built, shortening the journey in comparison to the duration it took us when Richard and I first met.

Mum was happy as a widow and we had become quite close, so it was very difficult for me to leave her on her own in another country. We talked about her moving to the UK with me but the fact that she didn't speak English was of course a major problem, so it wouldn't be possible for her to make new friends in the UK. Furthermore, she had many friends and was constantly travelling with them and meeting them at restaurants, taverns and evenings out. She said she would come and visit me often with her friends, and so she did.

Mum always liked Richard very much and was delighted for him that he could move back to his own country. It was very clear that she had no intentions of trying to find anyone for herself.

She was very happy living alone, so she told me, and never wanted another man. She always said she had enough misery for a lifetime with one husband.

In photographs taken the last few years, she looked very different than in photos taken when my dad was alive. It wasn't that she had aged dramatically; it was that now she smiled. I don't think I've ever seen a single photo of her smiling, whilst she was with dad.

Richard and I couldn't be happier, as we both had been desperately waiting for the day when we could be together *every day*.

Two of Richard's children, Nina, 23 and Mateo, 17 also came to live with us in the UK for a while, expanding our family to seven.

Moving to the UK gave Richard and me the opportunity to excel in every facet of life. We could build stronger foundations for life, love and business. As parents, we showered our girls and Richard's children with attention, love, and guidance—all the things I never had growing up. In business, we needed to make some important decisions.

Neither of us had any income when we first moved but we had enough savings to survive for a while. I knew I was going to start up a new business but didn't know the UK market very well, so I needed to investigate more.

I had learned over the past years how expensive flashy cars are, after having had a few. The maintenance prices, the repair bills and petrol bills cost an arm and a leg. Each time a bill came, I got terribly annoyed with it and decided I wouldn't waste any more money on overpriced cars. Instead, we bought a standard 7-seater as we needed a big car.

We decided that one of us would get a job to guarantee a monthly income. I applied for a few and immediately found a position with Eurotunnel. The Eurotunnel wasn't open yet, but they were building it.

My gift for languages proved to be useful yet again in this position, as I had to speak with the French Eurotunnel managers all the time. I could make my own decisions, which I liked.

I didn't mind working for another company for a while, as that gave me time to think about what I wanted to do for my own business.

I worked for Eurotunnel just for a few months as I soon found other ways to make money.

To earn extra money, I taught Dutch to English people through the local council.

I also worked for a marketing research company in the evenings, cold calling customers, as they wanted somebody who could speak fluent Dutch. I applied for this job after having seen it advertised for several weeks so I demanded double the normal salary, as I knew they couldn't find the right person for the position. They agreed. I was used to cold calling, and the rule of 10 kicked in again. I did pretty well in this job.

I did translations from English to Dutch, and vice versa, and managed to get a contract for London Borough Council.

I started my first UK company running training courses. I hired a hotel room and I ran four different classes: How to Sell Yourself to the Top, How Buyers Like to Be Sold To, Captivate Your Customers, and How to Interview and Hire People.

In spite of juggling multiple jobs, I made it a point to make time to spend with my daughters and Martin. Nina and Mateo where not home very often, as they were mostly out visiting their friends.

I had a full-time nanny during weekdays, but I always organized my day to be home from work as early as possible to give my girls a bath, read them a story, play games and tuck them into bed. Once my girls and Martin were asleep, I started working again. That's just how I was and still am: working hard, spotting business opportunities, getting in money from different sources, as I've never believed in putting all my eggs in one basket. I was getting income from several sources but I was earning a lot less than I was used to.

With all the expenses we had; a family of seven and a mortgage, our savings were quickly dwindling.

Richard started a company himself, doing cholesterol testing, which was the "in thing" at that time. He also launched another company, providing telephone on-hold messaging.

As my girls were born premature, I rented a baby respiration monitor to detect their breathing patterns, to help prevent cot death. I couldn't find a good baby respiration monitor to rent in the UK, so I discovered there was a *big* gap in the market.

I created a second business and set myself the huge task of manufacturing a monitor. It was not easy to get the product approved to sell in the UK market, as several certificates were required by law. It was a fierce battle and Richard helped me a lot. After a while, the product was launched: the CR95 Respiration Monitor.

Almost all hospitals with a baby care unit in the UK bought my monitor. The monitor was sold by several organizations, institutions and dealers; and the best thing was that I had worldwide rights to sell the monitor. After a few years, I sold the company. The monitor is now on the market under a different brand name.

I started my third company supplying promotional, personalized products to the Top 500 companies. We initially rented offices and a small warehouse a few miles away from where we lived. However, we both wanted to see our children more, so we underwent renovations to enable us to both work from home.

When I moved to the UK, I had many adjustments to make. One thing I missed a lot was Belgian food. I particularly missed Belgian chocolates and sweets. I preferred them so much more to what I found in the UK and I was sure others would too.

In Belgium, the tradition is that you give your children little hollow chocolate figures at Christmas. Although living in the UK, I kept some Belgian traditions.

I couldn't find any hollow figures to give to Amelia and Samantha; once they reached the age that I allowed them to eat chocolate. That meant one thing to me: a gap in the market I could successfully fill.

I knew I would need a lot of money for stock, so I decided to get a bank loan. I did market research and prepared a business plan.

The bank manager said I would never reach the sales figures I predicted, but he believed in me and he liked what I had achieved in business in the past.

My new company, ChoCoSa (Chocolates, Confectionery, Sales), was born in June 1997. I had learned that wholesale was a more rewarding business than retail, primarily because once you landed a customer, you would have repeat business from them.

Once again, my language skills became very useful as I could speak to European suppliers in their native language.

I started selling hollow figures made with Belgian chocolate but I expanded the company quickly and started to import goods from all over Europe, not just chocolates but also confectionery and sugar free products. Today, I am one of the largest confectionery importers/wholesalers/distributors in the UK. I proved the bank manager wrong and achieved seven times more sales than predicted in my business plan.

We worked very hard, and as a family, we took regular holidays, building memories that would last a lifetime.

I managed to juggle raising my daughters and Martin, who still lived with us, with becoming a successful businesswoman in the UK, proving once again that I was neither useless nor worthless. Nina and Mateo no longer lived with us. Over time, Richard's oldest four children moved away.

I saw mum on average once a month and mostly she would come and visit me in the UK with her friends.

I travelled to Belgium for a weekend to attend a wedding. Janine, the pub owner, was at the wedding too. She told me that Harry was found dead, face down in a ditch. Nobody had ever found out what happened to him. She further informed me that a few years after our divorce, Harry had moved in with a girl from a wealthy family; he set fire to the girl's house.

Life had its highs and lows, as no expanse of time comes without lessons and hardships. We were a close family, as true and as solid as families could be.

Caught up in the joy of raising my girls, I left it too late to conceive more children…and unfortunately then discovered I could not. I waited to have more children because I wanted to be sure that I gave them all my attention and love when they were very small.

I wanted to space my children out instead of having a baby every year as my mother had. She was unable to cope with so many children so close together, and I didn't want to make the same mistake. My dream was to have 10 children but it was not meant to be.

After five miscarriages in two years, which was extremely difficult to cope with, I took it as a sign from the heavens that I should stop trying. No doctor could explain my recurrent miscarriages. I had to accept I couldn't have more children and felt blessed to have my twin daughters.

For the following years, until they left home to attend university, educating my girls and spending time with them was priority, building forever lasting memories with them.

Fast Forward

"The bad news is time flies. The good news is you're the pilot." – Michael Altshuler

2000 - 2015, UK, Age 41 – 56

The next 15 years flew by, filled with laughter, love, work, my girls moving out and sadly some medical problems. Life was, and always will be, like a rollercoaster: ups and downs, twists and turns.

At 41, I had symptoms of menopause. The doctor said it was all in my head and he offered antidepressants, which I refused to take. I loved my life; it was menopause I wasn't happy about. I was surely not depressed.

I had the most horrendous time for many years: crying for no reason, fear of people, insomnia, insecurity, low self-esteem, hot flushes, night sweats, anxiety and fatigue.

Finally, I was diagnosed with early menopause and I was told it might have caused my miscarriages. Richard, the sweet man he is, walked the menopause route with me and was always there for me.

In 2001, on our tenth wedding anniversary, Richard gave me an envelope, and the voucher in the envelope read: "This voucher entitles you to receive breakfast in bed for the rest of your life!" To this day, Richard brings me breakfast in bed *every single day*.

I consistently forget our wedding anniversary. It was one of the best days of my life, but I'm always busy with work. Richard never minds and just jokes about it. He never forgets however.

My girls had their normal rebellious teen years like most teens do, but because of my experience, I kept them from making the same terrible mistakes that I did.

They came out the other end of those years stronger, and while I could not keep them from life, I did manage to guide them in a healthy direction.

Love and security, I knew from experience, are of utmost importance for children, which Richard and I provided for them.

I wanted to make sure that they realized that life does not always go as planned, setbacks can be overcome, fear can be faced and failures can be forgotten simply by trying again.

I was a strict parent but I was also very focused on their needs. I was consistent and stuck to routines. I always told them I loved them when I kissed them goodnight. They always said they loved me too—until their 13th birthday.

I cried that night when they did not respond when I told them I loved them, but Richard, as always, was the voice of reason. He'd raised four teenagers already and reassured me it was normal. I was afraid they didn't love me, but he knew it was simply a phase and their way of asserting their new teenager status.

Parenting teenagers, when your own teen years were a disaster, is not always easy. I was so afraid of my girls being lured into the type of life I had as a teen—drinking and sleeping around.

I now realize I behaved the way I did, when I was young, because I was searching for love and my girls *were* loved so it wasn't the same situation but still, I was afraid they would end up on the wrong path.

I refused to let them go to parties, which caused a lot of upset. Richard always backed me up; we were a united front to the girls. My early menopause did not help the situation, and of course, teenage girls have their share of hormones too.

I found myself getting too strict with them. The more they pushed for new freedoms, the tighter I clung to them in fear of what mistakes they might make.

I worried, though, that I was starting to make the same mistakes as my dad. He'd been right about the people I was mixing with, but he had failed to explain it to me, and I just thought he was cruel.

It stung deeply when my daughters shouted at me. I couldn't bear to see them estranged from me as I'd been from my dad.

I did some deep soul-searching and found the strength to break the cycle. It was, so I found out later, a generational cycle of abuse. I finally learned from my uncle that my dad's father used to drink, shout at him, and beat him, so my dad did the same to me and my brothers.

Lots of people bring their children up the same way they were raised, but I could not do that. I *had* to change things. I became determined that neither my upbringing nor the menopause were going to prevent me from being the best mother I could be.

So, the next time my girls asked me if they could go to a party or a school disco, I said yes. They were over the moon. I was very scared though, scared that the girls would hang out with the wrong people, but I had a plan.

Richard agreed to go as a parent volunteer to help supervise the disco. The girls didn't mind as they adored their daddy, plus they had nothing to hide.

Over the next few months, things around the house changed completely. If I told my girls they were not allowed to do something, I always gave them a reason. That's what my dad never did. I am proud to have broken my family's cycle of abuse.

Richard and I were doing great but I knew music was once a big part of his life. I could feel that he missed it; he kept telling me stories about the past, when he was a full-time musician.

I asked Richard if he would like to play music again and form a band. "I have lost one wife over music," he replied, "and I am certainly not losing you over it."

A big problem in his previous marriage was that his wife didn't like him going out to play with his band and that caused a lot of arguments.

She asked him countless times to stop being a musician but Richard continued with his music, as he needed the extra money to pay for all the expenses. His first wife never understood this. I understood that he loved music; I wanted him to enjoy it.

He'd done so much to ensure my happiness over the years; I wanted to make him happy and wholeheartedly supported his desire to play again whenever possible.

By pure coincidence, through Richard's daughter Clara, Richard met up with Boden, a former band member and a friend he hadn't see for more than 15 years. Shortly after, Richard and Boden were meeting regularly with all of the other former band members. They still get together regularly today to write and play music.

I could see how happy Richard was with his music, and I encouraged him to start up his own band. Richard bought his dream drum kit: a limited edition Gretch. I was surprised to learn that the price for his drum kit was a deposit for a small house! It was well worth it for the joy it brought him.

In 2005, when I was 46 and Richard was 57, I was earning enough money, so I told Richard he didn't have to work any longer. He was now officially "a kept man" and a musician.

As he believed in old-fashioned principles, he struggled with the idea of me being the sole provider but I insisted he focus on his music. He still helps me in my businesses.

We built a large music studio in the back of our garden, fully soundproofed and filled with all the equipment he needed.

Richard started his new band and wanted to fulfil one of his dreams: to be the manager of his own nine-piece band. Before long, he recruited all members of his new band and started performing again. He still travels all over the country to perform and loves it.

I have become a workaholic but I love it. When you love what you do, it doesn't feel like work. I love seeing results.

I had a few successful companies running smoothly with little work on my part, as I had staff and that meant I had free time.

It was no surprise to anyone who knew me when I announced I was setting up an Internet marketing company. I knew absolutely nothing about it but I *did* know it was a very expanding market.

It had a slow start, but I had the time and determination to invest in it. I didn't want to spend a lot of money learning all about it. I worked hard for my money and I hated spending it.

Every business that I have initiated over the years has been with minimum personal start-up costs in order to keep it viable. My new Internet Marketing followed the same pattern.

It was hard work and a lot to absorb. I was on the verge of giving up but then, after a year, I made my first sale online. It was a defining moment that made me realize the potential and effectiveness of making money online. I developed several websites that created automated and recurring income. I became an "Autopilot Income" fan.

I also achieved recognition as a bestselling author and wrote five books, all Internet marketing related. I love writing books and helping others to achieve business success! I am now a respected Internet marketer. People appreciate my honesty as there are thousands of Internet marketers on the web who sell "get rich quick" scams, whilst I admit that hard work is needed to become a successful Internet marketer.

I stumbled upon digital publishing and outsourcing on my road to Internet marketing success. I graduated to the world of self-publishing and have self-published more than 600 informative niche books (written by outsourcers), in printed format and eBook format, with worldwide distribution. I also teach others to publish their books.

When Amelia and Samantha left home to attend university, I was like most mums: sad to see them go and I struggled to control my tears. However, I realized that once little birds grow feathers and are able to spread their wings, they fly away.

It had been an absolute pleasure educating them, giving them values in life and seeing that they had absorbed all the things I taught them. I wrote them a letter and a poem, a separate letter to each, slightly adjusted.

Here is an extract:

To my wonderful daughter,
You truly are the most amazing daughter any mum could wish for. I can't believe that my dream came true and you were both born.
A greater love from a mum towards her children, I believe, does not exist. I love you deeply, with all my heart and soul. I know it is your dream to have identical twin daughters-better start the production line as soon as you are ready!

The best day of my life was when you arrived on this earth,
I even fulfilled my dream with a multiple birth.
I've tried to teach you what's right and wrong,
I've also told you that you always have to be strong,
because life will throw things at you that are not nice,
and unfortunately you can't just throw the dice
to make difficult decisions that matter
and nobody will give you the solution on a silver platter.

I've tried to warn you about the dangers surrounding you wherever you are,
as you already know, some people are simply just horrible and bizarre.
I've tried to tell you to believe what you see, not what you hear,
guess you're now old enough to know that, my dear, go forward without fear.
I've tried to make you realize that you can't always believe what people say,
just check it out in your own intellectual way.
I've tried to inform you that sometimes you have to accept things out of your control,
In that case, move on and just keep fighting for your goal.
I've tried to show you to make the best out of a bad situation,
just decide things based on your higher education.
I've tried to make you see that happiness and health are more important than money,

although often you need money to be happy, honey.

I've tried to tell you not to trust anyone,
but keep to your track and do what must be done.
I've advised you to eat a mixture of the five groups of food,
it will do your mind and body good.
I can only hope all my lessons and advice will travel with
you,
wherever you are and whatever you will do.
Never forget I will always support you whatever decisions
you make,
even if it turns out to be a mistake.
If you ever need any help or advice,
come to me, don't even think twice.
Although you will be miles away,
you can contact me any time of the day.
I am so proud of you for who you are and what you have
become so far, you are my star.

May you meet love, happiness, health and lastly money,
I will miss you my honey!
All in all, I've tried to give you a flying start,
because I love you with all my heart.
Whatever life brings,
always see the bright side of things.
Good luck my dear daughter,
Your biggest supporter, EVER
With a mountain of love, forever and ever.
Mum

Something began to change in me. We've all done it: walk in a room to get something and once you are in the room, you forget why you were there. I did it many times—so many times that I started to worry about it. I knew something was wrong. I was embarrassed to meet new people knowing I simply couldn't remember their names. When I had guests over, I would ask them if they wanted tea or coffee.

By the time I was in the kitchen, I forgot and I had to ask them a second time. I was so worried that I asked the doctor for an Alzheimer's test, which I had in 2011. I was told that I clearly had cognitive deficits, shown by the memory tests and scored well in all the other tests. Nothing to worry about, and it certainly wasn't Alzheimer's.

Still, I knew the symptoms I had were not normal. Something was wrong somewhere and I wanted to see a specialist. After having seen several specialists in the field, I learned the root cause, as one London specialist, Dr. Murton, explained.

He started the conversation by asking:

"Did you have a bad childhood?"

"I did indeed."

"Tell me more about it."

After having told him what I went through, he continued:

"Chronic stress in your childhood is very likely the cause of the memory problems you are experiencing."

I asked, with a puzzled look on my face:

"I don't understand, please explain in detail." He expatiated so I would grasp it fully.

"When we have a stressful situation to deal with, the stress hormone, cortisol, is released to help us manage the stress. Cortisol helps humans deal with everyday problems and to stay alert during a bad situation. Everyone carries ongoing stress throughout life, but too much of it, especially as a child, can be harmful in adult life. It is difficult for children to handle extreme and long-lasting stress without the support and care of a loving adult, often resulting in lifelong consequences."

Dr. Murton paused and looked at me, as if he was expecting me to ask a question.

"OK, I get that but how does that explain my memory problems?"

He continued explaining: "When stress starts in early childhood and is intense and long in duration, the level of cortisol is out of balance and exceeds normal ranges. When cortisol levels are too high for long periods, permanent and long-term damage can alter the normal functioning and development of some parts of the brain. Irreparable, incurable damage has been done to your hippocampus, the area in your brain that deals with short-term memory. This is because you had an unnatural amount of stress for many years of your life. *Only* your short term memory is affected by this"

"Oh No! That's not good news! Will my short term memory get better?"

He looked at me and I could tell from the expression on his face that he wasn't going to give me good news.

"I am afraid that your short term memory is definitely not going to get better. You will have to find ways to deal with it."

I was shocked and sat in silence for a few seconds and asked:

"Does this mean that other parts of my brain will be affected too, in the future?"

"There is a possibility for that but I am hopeful that this will not happen. Usually the short-term memory suffers the most in these sorts of situations."

He added, to conclude: "Another possibility is that with all the beatings and knocks to your head you've endured; you have suffered brain damage in the hippocampus."

I left Dr. Murton's office feeling sad but in a way I was relieved. I couldn't do anything about it, but I stopped worrying about having Alzheimer's. I've had much worse to cope with in the past than this diagnosis. I tried to accept things and move on.

I don't let my short-term memory problem affect my everyday business or personal life, as I am never more than two meters away from sticky notes and I carry them with me everywhere I go. The doctor told me that as soon as something is written down and you look at the note, the message moves from your short term memory part of your brain to a different part.

The same year I was diagnosed with Cervical Spondylosis (an incurable condition) in my neck. This was my "punishment" for working too long on my computer without any breaks.

I always thought an office was a safe environment. Now I know it can be detrimental to your health. Everything in my office was replaced with ergonomic equipment and I also installed break software on my computer so now every hour, my keyboard is blocked and I am forced away from my computer for 10 minutes.

My neck and my businesses are doing fine now because I'm looking after both. One of the biggest lessons I've learned in life is that I do not have to tolerate being miserable. I have the power to fix it.

For the next few years, life took its normal course. I was getting used to my girls no longer living with us. This meant I had more time to work.

I often wonder if I work most of the time because, in the back of my mind, my past is still present and I have to prove, especially to my dad, that I am not a useless person. When I talk about this with Richard, he assures me that is not so.

I believe he is right. I work because I love working. I have never been a person to slouch on the couch evening after evening and watch one TV program after the other. Work is my hobby, I love it. Just like Richard will play music as long as he can; I will work as long as I can.

The Business of Life

"Life isn't about finding yourself. Life is about creating yourself." – George Bernard Shaw

2016, Fundraising event in London, Age 57

I received news that my mother was up and about and eating on her own. She was rapidly recovering from the infections that had threatened her life. The doctor said she would be able to leave the hospital soon. Today was the fundraising event. Tomorrow I would travel back to Belgium to see mum.

The event would begin shortly, and then I would have to stand on stage and deliver my speech. The five-star hotel room where Richard and I stayed smelled like laundry detergent and little mint chocolates were placed on the pillows.

The room was decorated in shades of green and white. The wooden desk where I was sitting was white, an ornamental mirror was propped up against the wall so that I could see myself working.

Back in 1986, 30 years ago, I had made a list of the things that I wanted to achieve. One of them was speaking on a stage in front of people without fear and without nerves, and at this point, that was the last thing on my list to do. I have read studies that said that some of the most stressful things a person can go through are moving house, divorce and public speaking.

For many years of my life, I had been told that I was not worthwhile and that I was useless. I had decided that I was going to change not only my own perception but that of the people around me, and that meant that I was going to face this fear head on and defeat it once and for all. If I do something, I do it well.

I was always too afraid to stand in the presence of an unfamiliar audience, at their mercy.

Then, a while ago, Richard broached the subject one evening over dinner.

"You talk about public speaking like it's a life goal."

"It is, I guess," I said to him, recalling the feeling of fear that bubbled in my stomach when I thought of the challenge. "Scary though, especially with my low voice. I sound like a man."

"Scary? I've never known anything to scare you," he replied. "It sounds like a challenge to me. You should work on it. Prove to yourself that you have it in you. Your gorgeous voice will be an instant hit. You are a natural. I know it!"

After we had that conversation, I decided that my life would not be complete until I had developed the confidence to stand in front of a strange crowd and speak to them.

I followed the courses of two very well-known people in the field: Joanna Martin and Andy Harrington. Each course was four days long and quite expensive, but very valuable. During one of these courses, we were separated into groups of 10, with each person giving a three-minute speech in front of their group. After the speech, each of the other group members would offer advice and critique the performance. I mentioned to the members of my group that I did not like my speaking voice because it was too low. I did not mention anything about my past to anyone as I hardly ever do.

After my speech, the comments that I received included:

"Your voice is authoritative."

"Your voice is perfect for speaking on stage."

"Your voice is very sexy."

"You would be a brilliant speaker."

"You sound very dominant when you speak."

Afterwards, one woman from my group approached me. She told me that she had worked with abused children for over 25 years. Then she asked if I had a lot of stress when I was young, explaining that women who have had a lot of stress tend to develop lower speaking voices. It was just yet another surprise consequence of my past.

One of the instructors agreed with Richard. I was a natural.

"You have the presence and the perfect speaking voice; now you need the message," my instructor told me.

The comments from my group members and my instructor fueled my determination to pursue this. I had told my children over the years that they should face their fears no matter what, now it was time for me to practice what I preached.

I had spent quite some time searching for the right thing to speak about. It was a huge moment in my life! I used to break out in a sweat just thinking about it. I decided to speak at an Internet marketing event about self-publishing, a familiar topic for me. I found an event where I could speak and because I am a respected author in the Internet marketing field, the event organizers accepted me as a speaker.

I put together a speech with slides. I practiced it repeatedly, probably 100 times, at least. I wanted it to be perfect. I sold an expensive publishing course from stage. In broad terms, I spoke about some of my past failures and my violent marriage. I convinced the audience that just like me, they can achieve things in life they never thought possible.

After that, I spoke on stage many times, and each time I was the top selling speaker at every event, but more importantly, I was able to show people that you can change your life, no matter what you have been through. People would often burst into tears during my speeches and I almost always received a standing ovation at the end. People would come up to me after my speech to thank me for sharing my story and to tell me how inspired they were. That moment was when I decided to write my life story. I didn't realize until then that my life story was an inspiration to others.

Today's fundraising event was for the "Happy Child" charity, which sponsors shelters for abused and homeless children. Because of my upbringing, their cause was very special to me. I had experienced the cruelty of being without help of any kind.

The fundraiser would prompt important business folk to donate money to build more shelters in the UK. It was a worthy cause, and I wanted to contribute to its success.

If I managed to deliver a good speech, they would have no problem achieving their donation target, which meant fewer lost and confused children on the streets. I had never delivered a speech of this kind before. I looked at myself in the mirror in the hotel room and recognized an older version of my face. The same determination still flashed in my eyes.

My appearance has changed drastically over the last few years. I wear glasses most of the time when I am not sitting on the computer. I've put on a lot of weight and I am constantly yo-yo dieting. My hair is slowly going grey, but I cover it up with a blondish-brown highlights.

"I will deliver a powerful speech today and help the foundation achieve its donation goals," I told myself.

I rose from the pastel green chair and exited the bedroom. In the lounge part of our suite was Richard, already dressed and reading the newspaper.

"Ready for it?" he asked me, those same kind eyes resting on my face. Richard was in his sixties now but as lovely and kind as ever. In that moment, I thought of my life as a successful businesswoman, determined and strong, never allowing opportunities to pass me by.

I have a reputation of being a Rottweiler—because when I want something, I won't let go, and I will fight until I have it. Underneath it all, there is insecure Christine; although now, I have the armor of good decisions to protect me. Such a vast difference and it all began with saying "enough" after my coma.

"Absolutely ready," I told him, returning the smile and I added, "I love you so much darling. Thanks for your love and support. When I count my blessings, I count you twice!"

Together, hand in hand, we made our way out of the hotel room, down the long hotel corridor, into the elevator, and down to the room where I would be speaking. There were a lot of people milling around across the diamond-patterned hotel carpet.

They wore name tags and were dressed in their business best.

"Hi, mum!" Amelia called to me, hurrying over to us with her sister Samantha. We hugged hello and made our way into the large venue.

"We're sitting over here on the left, right up front, so you should be able to see us from the stage," she said to me, gesturing to the seats out in front.

"Good luck, mum." Samantha threw a kiss.

We wove our way around the seated crowd to friends I spotted in the front row.

"We just thought it would be nice to support you," one said.

"Good to have you all here," I smiled. "We'll go to dinner afterwards." Bustling off to the organizers, I was led back stage and took a seat on an old metal chair.

I controlled my breathing as the conference began and introductions were made. There must have been 700 people crammed into the hall, each of them with their focus on where I would be standing in a few short minutes.

Voices sounded out over the loud speaker as I concentrated on going over the note cards in my hand. All too soon, I heard my introduction.

"And now, an address by Christine Clayfield, one of our most esteemed members and the keynote speaker for today. Christine will be speaking about the business of life, delivering some important lessons she has learned on her journey.

I walked onto the stage, blinded by the lights aimed directly at my face. I was calm and steady...determined to stand tall and take charge.

"Good morning, colleagues, friends and family. When Hannah and her team asked me to speak here today, I agreed, not having the slightest clue what to say to you all but I had time to create a speech that would hopefully inspire and stimulate you all to be greater in your own lives. Then...the day before I was going to write my speech, I got a phone call. My mother had fallen terribly ill and I had to drop everything to be by her side in Belgium. Doctors

prepared us for the worst. We were told...she was going to die. Say your final goodbyes..."

The crowd stirred, listening raptly to my every word.
"...I didn't say my goodbyes. Instead, I sat by her side keeping her company until she woke up, against all odds. A ninety-year-old woman with dementia woke from her coma—and she recognized me. It was a miracle. And that's what I want to talk to you about today. Creating miracles in your life.

I have been in situations where I could see the end falling over me like a curtain that closes. I have travelled many roads, some very difficult and steep ones but nobody can see it.

Nobody can see the roads I have travelled. Nobody knows how difficult it has been because I have taken my struggles with pride and I don't allow my past to affect the image that I project to the world today. My past does not define me but has given me the strength I have today.

It is my intention to help others and to make them understand that they do not need to be defined by bad experiences and negative feelings, no matter how bad everything seems to be.

You can't look into a bright future if your eyes are still filled with tears from the past. My past made me better, not bitter. I have learned that you never know the power of yourself until someone hurts you badly. You can't change your past but you can choose your destiny so nobody can see your past.

You might know me as a successful businesswoman, the owner of several businesses, with a loving husband, four stepchildren and twin daughters. My girls—yes, they are seated over there."

I pointed to Amelia and Samantha, who smiled.

"But I was not always that person. In fact, like many people here, I came from an abusive childhood.

By the time I was a teenager, I was so confused because of my home strife that I made all the wrong choices. When you are born into a state of fear, or loneliness, or constant contention, happiness is a foreign emotion. Because of that, you never fully realize what it is or how to get it. By the time I was an adult, I was in a very abusive relationship with my first husband. I found myself beaten into a coma just eleven months after marrying him.

When I woke in the hospital room, I understood that I had two choices ahead of me. I could either do what I had always done and return to my life of misery or I could start over again.

It would have been easy after everything I had gone through to become an alcoholic, or a drug addict, or to end up a statistic of domestic abuse or to live on the streets. According to the statistics, I shouldn't be standing here, now.

But I chose the other path, and with every step I took further away from the life I had, the more I realized what happiness really means. It is not something that happens to you or something you can find in the people around you. Happiness does not hide—it is bold and bright! You can pursue it, but that is like chasing the Loch Ness monster!

I have learned that real happiness is not found; it is created. Let me explain. For the first 26 years of my life, I lived in misery and agony—why? Because I allowed life to happen to me. I was so beaten down that I accepted any circumstances I was presented with. My heart was full of fear and despair. All I could create were the products of my own heart.

But like in business, life is about creation. I like to call it "the business of life." The day I started running my life like a business was the day everything changed for me. I started actively creating my future—and suddenly I was the thing happening to other people. I always made sure that wherever I went, victory and positivity were most important.

I put myself in situations that made me happy. I made plans, I set goals and one by one I started to achieve them. I began to choose what happened to me and I started making happiness a regular part of my day. My confidence grew. Everything around me changed. I didn't look back but instead, I looked at the beauty of the future. Suddenly my heart was filled with determination and courage, and these helped me build my businesses and gain the success I now enjoy.

I have learned what is truly important and how precious life and our loved ones truly are. It's not what is in your pocket that matters but what's in your heart. I am by no means perfect but I have become a good person, I stand for traditional values and I love with all my heart.

Yes, in business, I learned how to make a lot of money—but I was happy and loved while doing it. How you feel right now is the reality of your life! In business, it is easy to blame other people when you fail. The greatest entrepreneurs know that failure is just a stepping-stone on the road to success, and I believe this is true in life as well. I could have blamed my past or the people who made my life miserable and never achieved anything in life. I could have sat in a corner and cried. Instead, I started to create.

I am proud to say that I created my life. And I did it by working hard, achieving my goals and believing that I had the capacity to lead an extraordinary life despite my horrible childhood and my violent first husband. The self-doubt that plagued me ultimately made me triumph. I am not sad when I look back on my life, even if my past was full of pain, but I look back and smile because my past made me who I am today.

In my own life, I have experienced many miracles. The first was when I had the courage to have my no-good husband thrown out of the hospital after nearly beating me to death..."

The crowd erupted into cheers and support for a brief moment, and I felt an overwhelming sense of community in those seconds.

"Thank you, thank you. It was difficult. The second was meeting my darling husband, who somehow managed to tick every single box on the unrealistically long list of questions that I asked him before we started dating..."

The crowd broke out into a few jovial giggles, and I saw Richard smiling at me from his seat.

"My husband is not often with me when I speak on stage; therefore, I don't often have the opportunity to thank him in public. Please, would you give my husband Richard a round of applause for being the best husband in the world? Richard, please, could you stand up?"

The audience all stood up and gave Richard a deafening applause as he stood up grinning and gave a small wave.

"And the third was managing to have identical twin girls, even though so many people told me it was impossible to achieve that dream—there they are again, yes," I said to the clapping crowd, who tapered off.

"I experienced several more miracles over the years in business and reached a level of success few people dare to believe is possible. My whole life really has been a miracle. And that is why I am speaking to you today. I decided to

make that decision all those years ago and change my fate but so many children may never get that opportunity.

It is our responsibility as adults, as parents and as a business community to help those who live in fear and isolation as children. Kids are too young to realize that the situations they are in can change for the better when they are older. They suffer because they feel alone. It is our responsibility to let them know that they are not alone. That alternatives exist.

We need to be the miracles for them, until they can begin to create the happiness that will help them thrive in their personal lives and in business when they grow up.

Happiness is not handed out; it is a choice, a decision. I choose to be at peace with myself, I choose to be happy. I accept what I cannot change. Happiness is a way of travelling, not a destination. It starts with those of us who have already achieved our goals. So now I want to urge you all to create the next generation of happy leaders by being the miracle they need today.
Thank you."

As my voice faded into the stage light, clapping broke out— and cheering; it rose like a crested wave crashing over me and I was soaked in happiness. One by one the members of the crowd stood. As I watched their faces, I knew that no one would ever laugh at me again. My confidence was my truth and my nerves vanished into the storm of the standing ovation.

Where once I had been bullied into a life I never wanted, I stood tall on that stage secure in the knowledge that the life I had was one of my own perfect design.

A Big Loss and a Major Gain

"Don't be dismayed at goodbyes. A farewell is necessary before you can meet again. And meeting again, after moments or lifetime, is certain for those who are friends."
– Richard Bach

2016, UK, Age 57

Mum used to have a very active social life after dad died. She used to go out every day to taverns, shows, theatres and on holidays. She had about 20 friends she hung out with. However, since mum was diagnosed with dementia, all her friends simply disappeared. None of her friends ever came around again, even just to say hello.

I remember one incident very well. Every Tuesday and Thursday afternoon, mum used to go and play cards, which she was very good at. That day mum entered the hall and sat at her usual table, awaiting the arrival of her usual play buddies. Instead of going to sit at mum's table, they left mum on her own and sat at a different table. Mum was so shocked that she stood up, cried and said: "If that is what they think, I am never coming here again." She never did, she refused to go again.

Her friends told me afterwards that mum simply could no longer play cards and they didn't want to play with her any more. Those friends had been her friends for over 30 years and overnight they ended their friendship, just like that. It was horrible for mum, especially since she didn't understand why because of her dementia. This just shows that most friends are not real friends when you need them.

I read once that dementia patients don't remember what you said to them but they do remember how you made them feel.

When we bumped into some of her friends a few days after the card game incident, mum never said a word to them. I guess she must have remembered how they made her feel.

As mum got worse, my brothers kept trying to convince me that a care-home was best for her. The main reason for this, in my opinion, was that they wouldn't have to worry about her anymore. We agreed that each one of us would look after mum for a few hours each weekend, to give her full-time carer a break. I created a rota for every weekend so once every five weeks one of us would look after mum.

The challenges with my siblings were difficult, they all seemed to be too busy with their own lives and none of them even considered looking after mum full time.

On a few occasions, they had already told me that mum was getting so bad that they couldn't take her anywhere with them. I responded by saying that if I could take mum everywhere I went, so could they. Looking after mum once every five weeks was already too much to ask! My brothers, except for Roger, didn't seem to care about mum at all, or at least that is the impression they gave.

After the dementia diagnosis, I traveled to Belgium every month, either because mum was admitted to hospital for recurrent infections, or just to spend time with her. When mum was ill, I sometimes traveled to Belgium 3 times per month.

I took her on weekends to some of the places she loved, went to concerts with her and I booked a holiday in her favorite Belgian coastal town. I created lifetime memories and it gave me utter joy to see mum happy, as she was always smiling on our outings.

It would just break my heart to take mum to an elderly home. There are too many horror stories about abuse; and besides, mum always said that she preferred not to go into an elderly home. So, I respected her wishes. I wanted to preserve her dignity.

Mum moved to England to live with us so I could take care of her. I wanted to keep her in her own environment for as long as possible, which is why I didn't bring her over sooner.

The moment mum asked me: "When am I going home?" whilst sitting in her lounge chair, is the moment I decided to bring her over.

When she moved to the UK, mum was slipping into her last stages of dementia. She had been suffering from difficulty speaking, partial epilepsy, hallucinations, incontinence, recurrent infections and cataracts in both eyes. It was absolutely devastating to see her deteriorate so quickly and there was nothing anyone could do. To watch your mum, the way you know her, disappear and change into someone you don't recognize, is painful.

Nobody could predict how long mum would live with me, as it could be three weeks, three months or three years. Richard didn't mind at all that mum lived with us for a while. I gave mum more attention than I gave Richard and he understood.

I couldn't be "me" when I looked after mum, as I couldn't work at my usual pace; but my love for mum took over my desire for success. I soon learned that looking after a dementia patient is a 24/7 responsibility and a full-time job. I had put my own life on hold and turned it upside down to care for mum. Mum might not have been the perfect mum for me when I was young, but she is who she is and I love her dearly.

I've learned the hard way that you cannot change people and you have to accept them for who they are. That's what love is all about, in my opinion. I felt happy when I could make mum happy. I treasured every moment with her, as I realized that before long, she wouldn't be able to do or say anything at all.

Looking after mum helped me to understand the true meaning of caring, not just loving. I wanted her to know that she was loved and I made sure to tell her and show her that.

One thing that was particularly nice to watch was when mum played with her dolls. I bought her a few dolls and she talked and sang to them and bombarded them with kisses, as she thought the dolls were real babies. I imagined that those babies were me and my brothers—bombarding us with kisses too.

Unfortunately, she could never fully express her love for us, as we were all in boarding school from a very young age. It must have been very painful for mum to see us go.

Then, in October 2016, mum had a large stroke. The consequences of the stroke were that she could no longer walk independently, and she couldn't color in her coloring books anymore, something she loved to do.

She could no longer sing along to nursery rhymes, something we had been doing a lot over the last few months. She was no longer able to put together a four-piece puzzle; although she used to be superfast at doing 5000-piece puzzles. It was heart breaking to watch, but all I could do was look after her as best as I could.

The doctors warned me that another stroke was extremely likely and it would probably be bigger next time. I feared the worst and asked the doctor if I could transport mum back to Belgium so she could die peacefully at home.

The doctor told me that they couldn't give permission to transport mum to another country. I informed my brothers and told them that, if they wanted to see mum alive, they would have to come to England. Nobody rushed over. Roger was planning to come, but still took his time.

Very soon after that, mum started to have trouble eating and drinking, and she also couldn't swallow her medication. The moment arrived when I had to crush her medication into mashed food.

Two weeks after the first stroke, mum had another stroke, a bigger one this time. She never regained consciousness. The doctor put mum on "end of life" medications and five days later, mum died peacefully, in my home, at the age of 91.

Richard, Amelia, Samantha, Roger, Dylan (my cousin who, together with mum, came to visit me often in the UK) and myself were in the room with her.

The moment mum died, I was holding her hand and my other hand lay on her chest. I felt her very last breath and heartbeat. An extremely bleak moment that I will never forget. I burst into tears, mum was gone.

Roger was scheduled to arrive on Thursday and mum had her second stroke on Wednesday, so Roger never saw mum "alive" again. My other three brothers never did come over to see mum, something I will *never* understand.

Looking after mum during the last stages of her dementia is the most precious and fulfilling thing that I have ever done in my life.

Mum's body was transported to Belgium and her funeral was held there. The tradition there is that before the funeral, there is a "viewing" day, announced in the local paper.

This means that mum was put in a coffin, at the funeral director's premises and people could come and see mum to say their goodbyes before the coffin was closed forever. Mum was buried with her favorite doll.

On the viewing day, I experienced a shock in the form of a very pleasant surprise. The viewing time was from 3 p.m. to 6 p.m., and promptly at 3, the first person who walked into the room was my friend Maddie. I simply couldn't believe my eyes.

I certainly didn't expect to see her. We smiled when we saw each other, followed by a very emotional hug, which resulted in both of us crying. Maddie said to me, "I am here to support you and I will stay here as long as you are here."

A few minutes later, the second person who walked in was Annie, again, to my pleasant surprise! To them as well, since neither of them knew the other was coming. We too smiled when we saw each other and after a heart-warming hug, we both starting crying.

It wasn't the right moment or place to speak to Maddie and Annie about the past, so we didn't. They came to support me through tough times, which I was grateful for.

During the funeral church service, it really hit me like a ton of bricks: my mum was gone. I cried buckets of tears. I loved her so very much. I now understand what people mean when they say "my heart hurts" because my heart actually did hurt.

Around 250 people attended mum's funeral.

At the reception afterwards, there was literally a queue of people wanting to speak to me, so I could only briefly speak to Maddie and Annie. We exchanged emails and promised each other to stay in touch.

I just couldn't believe how many people wanted to talk to me at the reception. People told me they admired me for being so selfless and moving mum to the UK to look after her.

For me, it was the most normal thing to do and I just couldn't have done it any other way. Everyone kept saying that most people wouldn't have done what I did.

While this made me feel good, it made me feel even better knowing that the vast majority of people who attended the funeral were seeing me for who I am today. They have always known me as the rebel, the good-for-nothing-crazy-about-boys-girl and the drunk of the village.

Now, people knew that I had changed and that I had become a good and caring person. Not that I was not a good and caring person when I was young but I never got the chance to show it.

This meant that when I talked to people, I no longer felt as if they were assuming the worst of me and looked down on me. I was able to confidently carry on a conversation with aunts, uncles and people from Keldonk without feeling awkward or uncomfortable.

Back in the UK, after the funeral, I emailed Maddie asking when we could meet up. I couldn't wait to travel to Belgium again, just to go and see her and find out what happened to her after we lost contact. Within a month, I travelled to Belgium and we met up.

I read this quote once: "*You meet people who forget you. You forget people you meet. Sometimes you meet those people you can't forget. Those are your friends.*" —*Author Unknown.*

I have never forgotten Maddie.

Maddie told me that her mum died of dementia too and that she looked after her until she died, although her mum was taken into a home.

She told me she used to phone me countless times when I was still living at home but my dad always said I wasn't home or I wasn't allowed to talk to her.

Her dad burned everything she had when she ran away from home: clothes, memories, school stuff and my letters to her. Literally, everything was destroyed. She didn't speak to her dad for many years but decided to make up a few years ago. Now she makes sure her dad, who is in his eighties, is happy and she visits him practically every day. He still lives in the same house, next to my childhood home.

Maddie lives with the same boyfriend she was with when she ran away from home. She worked and lived in pubs too but made a better future for herself by finding a very good job. When that job ended unexpectedly, she went through some very bad times but struggled her way through it. She never married and couldn't have any children due to medical reasons.

I am so happy I found my best friend and after all the talks we had, it feels as though there was no time lost. My big loss, my mum's passing, gave me a big gain: reuniting with an old friend.

A big comfort for me whilst getting over mum's death was knowing that I did everything I could for her when she needed me.

"Behind the tears of our sadness, hides the smile of nice and precious memories" is a thought that keeps me going and now, every time I think about mum, instead of a tear, a smile appears on my face.

Present Day

Today, in 2017, I am 58 years old and I have achieved my mission: to be so busy loving my life that I have no time for hate, regrets, negativity, worry or fear.

I still work long hours because I chose to do so. I am not a big spender. I've been there, done that. I've had the big flash cars, the expensive designer clothes and lavish jewelry. I have the money to buy fancy clothes but hardly ever do, only for special occasions. Between not having much interest in making time to shop and not wanting to waste time choosing outfits, I typically end up wearing jeans and a black cotton polo shirt every day.

I know how hard I had to work to be where I am today therefore I hate wasting money on luxury items. I now realize that you do not need material things to be happy. They don't last but memories last forever. I don't collect things, instead, I collect moments, happy moments.

You can't buy love or friendship, however much money you have. Money comes and goes but love lasts forever, as Richard said.

I am totally at peace with myself. I am deeply embarrassed about the things I used to do when I was young, but after the coma, I became a better person. I am a kind, gentle and warm-hearted person. If others are in trouble, I will help them. I am very tough in business but not in my personal life. I am soft and strong at the same time, a combination few people master, says Richard.

When we are adults, we look at things from a completely different perspective. When I went through hell, never did I think that hell would make me a better person in the end.

My achievements

While I'm proud of what I've achieved in my life, I have been humbled by my experiences; so, it isn't easy for me to share my achievements with others for fear of being perceived as boasting, as that's not how I am.

I've merely told you in this book what happened to me, the good and the bad. The only reason why I am listing some of my achievements is because I hope you can learn from my story that, whatever your past, with hard work and determination, you can achieve almost anything.

I donate monthly to the RSPCC, the Royal Society for the Prevention of Cruelty to Children.

I have achieved more than the average woman: through sheer hard work and dedication I am in the top income earners in the UK.

I don't do anything household related, not even the cooking or grocery shopping, as I have household staff to do those jobs. Pure bliss!

I have bought a few houses to rent out as an investment and I paid cash for them. My stepchildren have set themselves up in ways of their own choosing and all have a place to live. My girls will have to get their own mortgages so they can appreciate the value of hard work and financial management. Only when they have experienced financial struggles, I believe, can they learn to appreciate the value of money in later life.

I was not born an entrepreneur but became one with hard work. I've worked very hard for everything that I have. I worked so hard that I now have a choice never to work again. All my businesses require minimal effort from me and are either run by my staff or create income on autopilot through the power of Internet marketing.

Although I no longer *have* to work, I am constantly setting up new streams of income. Richard says I will never stop working, as that's just the way I am.

I take great satisfaction in my achievements, especially the willpower that led to my girls' birth. None of my business achievements can outshine that level of belief and determination.

Maddie

I have travelled to Belgium a few times to see Maddie. We email each other very regularly and I scan photos of our youth and hundreds of the letters she wrote me and email them to her—I keep everything!

It is amazing how many similarities there are between us: the things we like and dislike, as well as our life views. We both went through very bad times after we left our homes and even the partners we chose to spend the rest of our lives with have a lot of similarities.

She knows me like nobody else does as we used to tell each other "everything" when we were young. Sometimes, when I meet new people, I am a bit scared they might judge me, should they know what I've been up to in the past. With Maddie, it's different, as she knows that no matter what I did in the past, I was never a bad person.

We have a jolly good time each time we meet up. Maddie and I sometimes meet up with Annie when I am in Belgium.

My brothers

I don't see my brothers very often—mainly because we live in different countries, but also because we have never been a very close family. We have different opinions on many aspects of life, but one thing will always unite us: our dad and our upbringing.

Each of us found a different way to cope with our past. Whatever my brothers say or do, I will always think: "They had some tough times when they were young, just like I did."

When I travel to Belgium to visit Maddie, I invite all my brothers for a drink in a local tavern. Usually, most of them do try to make time to meet up, except Kane.

There is a lot of squabbling going on between my brothers and me regarding mum's will and a few small properties that she owned. Court cases, judges, solicitors, lawyers, fines, fees, contradictions, arguments, heated discussions, and assigning guilt—it all borders on the unbelievable.

I could write a separate book about it so best not go into details about all that. I can give away two things though.

Firstly: the ones, who have done the least for mum, whilst she was alive, now want the most, especially Kane.

Secondly: Oliver, Kane and Lucas want to pretend that mum's will doesn't exist, as doing so is to their advantage. Ignoring mum's will, to me, is inconceivable but I have three brothers against me.

All of my brothers, except Roger, followed our father into the diamond business but they seemed to be plagued with wrong decisions, lack of business acumen and bad luck. They have all left the diamond industry behind them.

We all fared the same in our marriages too—bad decisions and worse luck. All five of us had been divorced. It isn't a surprise considering the abuse we had suffered in our childhoods. We grew up hearing we were stupid, so of course we made stupid choices as adults.

Yes, I do believe my dad had good qualities and loved us, but his behavior toward us and the example he set for us did not set us up for future happiness and security.

Oliver settled back in with his wife, after their separation. Kane and Roger have had several girlfriends over the years but never re-married. Lucas re-married.

Kane and Lucas both had heart attacks a few years ago but survived. When I visited Kane in hospital, I handed him a get-well card and wrote on it that I was always happy to help, if he ever needed help. He cried after he read the card, but he also made it very clear during my visit that he didn't want me there as he hardly spoke to me.

Richard's Children

Nina, Mateo and Martin graduated with university degrees and Clara graduated with a diploma in beauty therapy. They are all married and are all employed or self-employed.

Richard has nine grandchildren. He would have loved to have spent more time with his children and grandchildren over the years but the distance combined with everyone's busy lives made it impossible. We see them sporadically, but not as much as we would like to.

Amelia and Samantha meet up regularly with their siblings and they have a good relationship.

Amelia and Samantha

My girls, wonderful, beautiful and intellectual women in their 20s, have graduated. Both received distinctions in their Master's degrees. I am a very proud mum.

They have moved out of our house and are now financially independent. I have never spoiled my children and have always paid them a basic weekly fee to cover the necessities to live.

I could have bought them all the latest gadgets or designer clothes and handbags, but I tell them all the time that if they want luxury in life, they will have to work for it, just like I did.

I made one exception: I bought them a brand-new car to save them the humiliation I had to go through when I had my old banger.

My girls are happy; they have the unfathomable bond that twins possess. They are extremely good friends, confidants and although they are separated by distance, they try to see each other as much as possible.

Seeing my girls grow up as sophisticated women who want to make something of their lives puts a smile on my face all the time. Now it is up to them to make their mark on the world. I gave them roots to know where home is and wings to fly away and practice what I taught them. It's up to them how high they will fly.

Richard

Richard's gentle touch, reassuring smile, endless devotion and sweet love have been a source of strength throughout the years. Every single day I feel loved and I am forever grateful for Richard, just for being Richard.

Some people say: "It is difficult to find one good friend in your life." I can say, unequivocally, that I have found mine!

I love Richard exactly how he is, and he loves me exactly how I am. We are best friends. Wherever we are, we hold each other's hands. We are one. I found someone who goes out of his way to make it obvious that he wants to be with me.

He has made me laugh, seen me cry, made me proud, seen me fail, cheered me up and he made me believe in my dreams.

He loves me unconditionally. I need him like I need air to breathe. I adore him and I tell myself every day how blessed I am to have him in my life. He is my soul mate, my best friend, my everything. I will love him unconditionally until my last breath.

I can never thank him enough for making my life so blissful and wonderful. I met him 31 years ago and last year was our 25th wedding anniversary. Richard is always on my side and always will be.

If somebody says something negative about me, I get flashbacks and start to think I am useless again. Every time, Richard comes to the rescue and instantly makes me feel better again.

Richard will be 70 years old next year and we go on weekends and holidays as much as we can. He will enjoy his music and play drums as long as he is physically able. He performs all over the UK with this band.

He still gets together with the band members he was with 56 years ago, either for a meal or to write/play music. He thoroughly enjoys relaxing in his studio, listening to music whilst puffing on his cigar.

His 3 favorite sayings lately are, "I am getting too old to worry about stupid things," "Onwards and Upwards" and "I love you."

He is like a child during the holidays, and he loves Christmas. Every year around Christmas we play the song "When you wish upon a star" and every time he hears that song he cries, being the sensitive man he is. He often cries with sentimental songs about love and life.

Richard and my girls are all I need to be happy. Even if I didn't have a penny, I would still be happy simply by having them around me.

They fill my life with more joy than I ever thought possible. I am filled with the kind of admiration for them that will never fade.

I love my life because not only is my life as in my dreams but it is better than in my dreams!

Afterword

Writing this book has been a rollercoaster ride for me, although most of the time it has been a real pleasure. I have been walking around the house with a big smile on my face from reading Richard's love letters and poems again and thinking back to how we met.

First, I want to thank some people.

Thank you to Richard for accepting me for who I am, for telling me I was not useless but very special. You told me I could achieve anything. You believed in me. I am forever grateful. There are no words that can express my gratitude for your dedication and love. You are the best, most understanding husband in the entire world. Thank you for letting me be me. I love you with all my heart, Y.T.T.

Thank you to my daughters for listening to my advice and growing up to be respected, sophisticated, loving individuals. It is a delight to see you want to make something of your lives. Dream dreams. Don't let anyone limit your dreams. Follow your dreams. Believe in yourself and don't give up. Make sure you stand up for yourselves, and don't let *anybody ever* put you down. Should you be unhappy with something in the future, *you* need to make the change. Don't follow the crowd; jump out of the fish bowl if you ever end up in one. I love you more than words can express.

Thank you to my stepchildren for accepting my children and me into your lives. I love you all.

In a weird way, I am grateful to the nuns, the bullies, my dad and my first husband for being nasty and cruel to me. Without all those things happening to me, I wouldn't be where I am now.

Second, the past is always present.

Previous experiences will influence your life forever. In my case, I live with some things every day as a direct consequence of my past. None of these things bother me and I don't dwell on them.

In life, you have to accept things that are out of your control. Everything listed below is totally out of my control and none of these make me less of a happy person.

Here are the things I suffer from, on a daily basis, as a direct result of having had too much stress as a child and in my early adult life.

I do not list these everyday issues out of self-pity or for sympathy. These are just facts and all I want to say is that it is sometimes not easy to forget the past if you are confronted with it indirectly, daily.

Mental:

I have irreparable short-term memory problems. When I have to do something, I write it down immediately; otherwise, two seconds later, it will be wiped from my memory forever.

Given a choice, I will never sit in a room where I can't see who is behind me. I need to feel safe and see what's coming at me. In a restaurant, I always choose a table so I can oversee what is going on and nobody can creep up on me. In my office, I sit with my back against a wall. These choices I make are a direct result of bad memories when Harry used to attack me from behind and hit me with his full fist in my back.

I have trouble falling asleep, as my wake-sleep cycle or my body's internal clock is not functioning as it should. This cycle is influenced by hormones, and due to my childhood stress, combined with my early menopause, my hormones are not functioning correctly. I am currently taking a natural hormone supplement, which is working very well.

I need to be the best I can be, in all that I do, out of fear that people will laugh at me. I always want to deliver a great job, not a mediocre one.

I've learned that there are people who accept you for who you are, Richard being one of them. The nuns, my dad and Harry wanted to change me. They wanted me to be somebody I am not. I have applied this in my girls' education: they can be what they are and don't have to become what I want them to become. This also applies to Richard: he can be who he is; never have I attempted to change anything about him, nor has he ever tried to change anything about me. If you can't be yourself, you can't be happy. If you can't be yourself, who are you supposed to be anyway?

I treat other people as I wish to be treated myself. I know what suffering means and I don't wish any suffering upon anybody.

I am known as tough and blunt and indeed, I am. I had enough obstacles placed in my way in the past. However, deep down inside me is the shy and not so confident side of me that only Richard knows.

Physical:

I have a deep, low voice. People on the phone often call me "sir." This low voice is apparently due to too much stress as a child. I had some voice-training lessons, in an attempt to speak in a higher voice, but with little results. I've got the feeling, the older I get, the lower my voice becomes.

I have Restless Legs Syndrome. One specialist believes that this might be because my legs have been wet during the night or have been on damp sheets, due to my bedwetting, for a large part of my life.

I can only wear cotton clothing. I have to sleep in 100% cotton sheets. If I touch any other material other than cotton, I get allergic reactions: my face goes red, my body becomes itchy and I start sweating. A doctor told me this is because hormones are associated with allergies, and because my stress hormones have been totally imbalanced, I now suffer from this material allergy.

My temperature control is damaged to the extreme, because of incurable damage done to my hypothalamus - the part of the brain that deals with temperature control. It is located in the same area of the brain as the hippocampus, the part that deals with short-term memory! When I get too warm, I suffer for hours: my ears go red and start burning. I can easily get warm, but if I get too hot, I can't cool off. I walk around in a T-shirt when everybody else wears a thick jumper. All day long, wherever I am, I am scared I will get too hot. People around me are affected too e.g. Richard and my girls, as they are constantly too cold around the house.

So the question is…*do I mind having these problems?*

No, not at all! Everybody has problems to cope and deal with; these are just *my* problems. I'm certainly not comparing my story to anyone else's; I am sure others have suffered far worse situations and I feel for those people and their families.

Everything I have been through was worth the journey: a journey to love and happiness.

A message to everyone who knows me: I don't mind talking about any issues of my past life. Sometimes people don't know how to handle things, they are afraid to start talking about it, or they think I would rather not talk about it. That is *not* the case. I am over my past, and I am happy to talk about it. So ask me any questions!

Valuable Messages

Third, I wrote this book to share several valuable messages.

I transformed my life and I want to spell out valuable messages here. If I can change one person's life who will read this book, I will have achieved my goal. I have shared my life experiences and hope to make a difference in someone else's life.

I did not write this book merely to answer questions about my life, but to encourage you, the reader, to ask questions about your own life. Please don't put this book down and say, "The end" but pick it up when it is time for you to make a new start.

1. You must change things.

The first 26 years of my life were misery and agony. I should have said, "Enough is enough," much sooner, but I didn't have the strength. My message to you is this: if you are not happy *now*, get out *now*. Don't wait for things to get worse.

If you are in a job you hate, get out! I am confident there is a better job for you somewhere else. All you need to do is look for it.

Yes, there is a world of happiness out there. Don't be unhappy. Have the courage to change things.

No one is going to knock on your front door with a new life presented on a silver platter. *You* need to make things happen for yourself, get the drive to overcome obstacles and become a winner.

A winner will always find ways to achieve things and to make things happen. As John Wooden said: "Things always turn out best for the people who make the best of the way things turn out."

Look at the bright side of life and the world won't look like such a dark place anymore. Whatever you are going through, the hurt is not irreparable. *You* can make changes to your life.

Find the strength and the courage within you and implement changes to your life. You can't change the past, but you *can* change the future. The choice is yours. If I can do it, so can you!

We all have a story but no matter what happens, we can always find a way to overcome it. You have no responsibility whatsoever for what happened to you when you were a child but you do have complete responsibility for how you handle it and what you do about it.

Take control of your life and take full responsibility for the things that happen to you that you can control. Don't procrastinate. Push yourself.

Accept your past without regrets. Tough times don't have to define you, they can refine you. You never know how strong you are until strong is the only choice you have!

2. Don't play the blame game.

Lots of people blame bad economy or other external factors for not being successful. Others blame their past for who they are today. I don't play the "blame game" and blame the people who made my life hell to use them as an excuse for not making my life a success. I advise you to do the same.

Put your past behind you and start working on a better future. Don't blame anybody but yourself if you have not achieved anything in your life!

Just because the past didn't turn out like you wanted it to, doesn't mean your future can't be better than you have ever imagined. Don't play the victim, be the go-getter instead; there is always a way out.

You have to decide to let go of the past and move forward. Bryant McGill once wrote: "If you look at today through the eyes of the past, you can never see what the future may bring."

Forgive the people who have harmed you. I believe this is of utmost importance to be able to forget the past and not blame others for your situation.

The responsibility of what you do with your life and who you are is yours. *Now* is the only time that matters so stop wasting time by dwelling in the past.

There is a secret superpower if you have had a bad past: the determination to make a better future. You can go through life blaming the circumstances surrounding you or you can fight back, create great things, leave a mark on the world and write your own life story. Your scars tell your story. They show you that you are a survivor and have strength.

You must look at the scars of your past and remember they can make you a better person. Don't let your scars control your future by blaming them for who you are today.

3. Believe in yourself.

If you want to achieve something, you need to believe in your goals and believe in yourself. Others can encourage you, but no one can give you belief in yourself. Decide to believe in yourself and then seek out others who support you.

Don't surround yourself with people who don't believe in your goal, as they will drag you down. Some people will do anything to bring you down and will do even more to keep you down. You need to eliminate anyone who disrespects you, puts you down, uses you or lies to you. There are fallible people all around us; the moment they start intruding into your life, you need to know when to throw them out of your life. The quality of your life will be determined by the quality of the people in your life.

Negativity destroys your chances before you even start, but thinking positive and believing in yourself and your dreams, gives power to your dreams. You have the power to overcome everything life throws at you. A made-up mind is a very powerful tool to have. No situation, circumstance or person should define who you are or who you want to become.

The only limits you have are the ones that you accept. If you believe in yourself, anything is possible. Albert Einstein once said, "Everybody is a genius but if you judge a fish by its ability to climb a tree, it will live its whole life believing that it is stupid."

4. Work hard.

Anyone can get to excellence with grit, hard work and determination. Success is dependent on effort. Nothing worth having is easy to get.

I have created businesses that give me income without me having to be there. You can do the same, if you are willing to work hard.

If you work hard for a few years of your life like most people won't, you can spend the rest of your life like most people can't.

5. Nothing is impossible.

Don't ever say something is impossible if you haven't tried it. The word "impossible" has the word "possible" in it!

The most rewarding things in life are the hardest to accomplish. It might take time. You might need to set smaller goals along the way, such as learning new skills or saving money a little at a time. If you lack knowledge, self-educate: read, read, read. Independent learning can produce brilliant results but also requires great commitment. Focus and execute. Focus on your focus. If you work hard, you can do it! If I can do it, so can you!

I believe that the weaknesses we attempt to suppress in our character can become our strengths. No matter how difficult your past has been, you can always begin again. If you've made mistakes in the past, you just need to find the force in your faults.

6. Be strong in bad times.

When you are feeling at your weakest, you have to be your strongest. Sometimes you don't know your own strength until you are faced with your greatest weakness.

Don't be guided by fear of the unknown. Fear has two meanings: forget everything and run, or face everything and rise. The choice is yours.

Fear paralyses and weakens you. If you let it, it will grow worse every day until there's nothing positive left in you.

Put fear and pain aside and instead, rise and shine! Use pain to earn success that defines you. That first step to freedom leads to happiness and happiness has always been in you; it's up to you to release it. Napoleon Bonaparte said, "Courage isn't having the strength to go on; it is going on when you don't have strength."

The strongest people are those who won battles we know nothing about, not the ones that show visible strength. Without my struggles, I wouldn't have stumbled across my strengths. When you go through tough times and you don't surrender, that is strength.

Experiences that break you and tear you apart can build you into a better person, if you allow it to happen. No matter how long and cold the winter, spring is sure to follow and remember that the stars can't shine without darkness. Learning to let go of the past is the key to future happiness.

I smile because when I was knocked down I got back up, and I smile because I have survived everything the world has thrown at me. You can do the same.

Try to find something positive in every negative situation. If you look at everything with a negative mind, you will only see obstacles but looking with a positive mind will create opportunities. Your thoughts will become your actions.

Focus on the positive and ignore the negative. Anything in between is the wrong choice. Positive thinking, at *all* times will make a big difference in your life. Think positive not because everything is good but because you can see positive in everything.

7. Make a list.

Lists keep you focused. Make lists for what you want to get done each day, week and month, but also make a list of your life goals.

I made my list of things I wanted to achieve and put them in a purple frame. Thirty-two years later, I have achieved everything on my list that was within my control. When are you going to make your list?

8. Visualize the future.

When I was 26, I started to hang pictures of things I wanted to achieve around me: a happy family, twin girls, a big house, money to go on holidays, etc. These pictures were a constant reminder to me. They gave me purpose and kept me focused on what I wanted to achieve in life.

I suggest you hang some pictures in your room too! Your mind is extremely powerful and the pictures will create an image in your mind of what your future life can look like. Subconsciously, you will focus on achieving those things. Visualizing your goals and dreams is pivotal in reaching them.

9. Make your dream a reality.

Whatever you dream about, whatever it is you want to achieve, you can make it a reality! Dreams do come true. *You* have to put in the work though. Step by step, keep going.

The reason most people don't reach their goals is because they don't define them. You need to believe that your goals and dreams are achievable.

Never let small minds or negative people convince you that your dreams are too big. I am living in a dream marriage but it's not a dream! I had my dream identical twin girls but it's not a dream! Dream dreams and trust in your dreams!

Take a pen and write down your dream. Perhaps a nice house, a new car, a big kitchen; whatever you dream about. By writing it down, you make it a goal. Now make a plan to achieve that goal. Make a contract with yourself and sign it. Without a plan you will *never* achieve your dream.

You must dream, act and plan for your dreams to come true. Push everybody away that is standing in the way of your dreams and keep chasing your dreams.

Dreams don't work unless you take action. To make a dream come true is not easy. It takes determination and hard work. Some people want it to happen, while others make it happen. Make sure you are in the latter group of people.

10. Don't ever give up.

Whatever you are trying to achieve, remember what Sir Winston Churchill said, "Never give up. Never give up! Never give up! Never, never, never-never-never-never!"

I fought hard to achieve my goals. Make sure you never give up your fights. Rock bottom became the solid foundation on which I rebuilt my life. It wasn't easy but I never gave up. Sure, I made some mistakes but I've learned from them.

Failure allowed me to find things I wouldn't have otherwise discovered. With a strong will and even stronger belief, you can achieve great things, whatever your past. Winners are not people who never fail but people who never quit.

When life gives you a hundred reasons to break down and cry, show life that you have 101 reasons to smile and laugh. Stay strong.

11. Love is just a word until somebody gives it meaning.

Success in business, sports, or the arts is a wonderful feeling, but there is no better feeling in the world than love. You can't love someone, unless you love yourself.

If you are in a relationship and you constantly argue or your views differ on everything, perhaps it is not a right fit. Cut your losses and move on! Your dream partner is out there...somewhere.

Richard is the sweetest man on this planet. Since the day I met him, my whole life changed. He still brings me breakfast in bed every day.

On all issues in life, we share the same opinion, whether it is business, pleasure, education or money. He truly loves me and I feel the same about him. We have never argued about anything. He has been, and still is, my rock, my greatest support.

Love is everything; without love, everything is nothing. Find the one who will leave footprints on your heart and you will never ever be the same again. That person will bring out the best in you and make you forget all the bad things in your past.

Nothing in life is more important than to be with the one you love. The love we hold within our hearts is far more important than the money we hold in our bank account.

12. Become an achiever.

When you want to achieve something, strive until you achieve it. Don't accept "no" for an answer. Since the coma, it has always been a goal of mine to become an achiever in whatever I do.

You, too, can make things happen. You, too, can become an achiever! To achieve great things, you must ignore the people who put you down and you must surround yourself with people who believe in you. Often, the people who criticize your life are the same ones who don't know the price you paid to get where you are today. Your critic's words will fade but you won't.

If you surround yourself with the right people, with people who believe in you, things will change. I used to think I wasn't good enough. I no longer wasted my time with that kind of negative energy and it made me an achiever.

Most people won't care about how difficult your life was or still is. *You* are the author of your life's story and only *you* can start creating the story you want to read. Don't live in the past, don't fear change and don't put yourself down, instead: become an achiever.

I hope good fortune and love will find you and shower you in abundance.

Zig Ziglar once said:

"If you can dream it, you can achieve it."

Start dreaming! It is Your Sky. Your Limit!

Final Thoughts

Misery has been a large part of my journey but it has also shown me what is precious in life: love. The best things in life are not things! You are richer than you think if you have love, friends, a roof over your head and food on the table. If you lose all your money but still have love; you are still rich.

I am now a happy person, a good human being, surrounded by love—and you can be too, whatever you've been through in the past. I count my blessings instead of my years of misery.

When I look back on my life, I see mistakes, heartache and pain. When I look in the mirror now, I see lessons learned, strength and value in myself. I regret that I didn't value myself earlier.

The scars that mark my mind and body are with me forever but the passage of time and my new life have made them fade into the background. My scars are a reminder of my struggles, battles and victories. They show pain and suffering but more importantly, they show my will to survive.

All of us have scars. I hope that mine, by writing this book, will give strength to other people who are suffering and are not happy with their lives.

If only the nuns, the bullies, my dad and Harry could see me now… Now I have control over my life instead of others having control over me.

The pain and misery I went through made me into the woman I am today. I've rebuilt my life, coming back stronger than ever. The lessons I have learned throughout my life have served me well. I have become a strong woman.

Anybody who thinks they can take me down after all I've been through can give it their best shot. They will not succeed. You cannot break me; I will always rise above any obstacles.

Review request

Thank you for reading my story. If you enjoyed reading this book, please don't forget to give it a review on Amazon or on the retailers' site you purchased it so that others can benefit from your reading experience. Even just a two-word "Liked it" review helps so much. Thanks for your support!

BONUS: My life in pictures

I have created a picture page showing some of the events in my life I have photographs for:
www.nofourthriver.com/pictures. Only people who have read my book know about this page! I hope you enjoy it.

Sign up to be notified

I've enjoyed writing this book and I am planning to write more books. You can sign up on
www.christineclayfield.com/mynovel to be notified when I will release a new book. This is NOT a newsletter signup. You won't be bombarded with emails. Your information will never be shared with any third party.

Websites and social media

www.christineclayfield.com
www.nofourthriver.com

www.facebook.com/christineclayfield
www.twitter.com/clayfieldchris
www.linkedin.com/in/christineclayfield
www.instagram.com/christineclayfield